I0817206

Upholstery School

First published in Great Britain in 2025
by Kyle Books, an imprint of
Octopus Publishing Group Ltd
Carmelite House
50 Victoria Embankment
London EC4Y 0DZ
www.octopusbooks.co.uk
www.octopusbooksusa.com

An Hachette UK Company
www.hachette.co.uk

The authorized representative in the EEA is Hachette Ireland, 8 Castlecourt Centre, Dublin 15, D15 XTP3, Ireland (email: info@hbgi.ie)

Distributed in the US by Hachette Book Group
1290 Avenue of the Americas, 4th and 5th Floors, New York, NY 10104

Distributed in Canada by Canadian Manda Group, 664 Annette Street, Toronto, Ontario, Canada M6S 2C8

ISBN 9781804191682

A CIP catalogue record for this book is available from the British Library.

Printed and bound in China.

10 9 8 7 6 5 4 3 2 1

Publisher **Joanna Copestick**
Art Director **Yasia Williams**
Designer **Helen Bratby**
Senior Editor **Leanne Bryan**
Copy Editor **Natalia Price-Cabrera**
Proofreader **Katie Hardwicke**
Photographer **Sarah Weal**
Illustrator **Claire Huntley**
Deputy Picture Manager **Jennifer Veall**
Production Manager **Allison Gonsalves**

Additional picture credits
Alamy Stock Photo: Neil Baylis 10b, Andreas von Einsiedel 11; Bridgeman Images: National Trust Photographic Library/Andreas von Einsiedel 10a; Interior Archive: Butter Wakefield Garden Design and Simon Brown 133; iStock: clu 8b, Duncan1890 8a; living4media: Are Media 123; Shutterstock: Paolo Gallo Modena/imageBroker 9.

Heidi Francis styled the images on pages 165, 168 and 207.

SONNAZ NOORANVARY
Upholstery School
Practical projects for updating furniture and furnishings in your home
PHOTOGRAPHY BY SARAH WEAL
K

Contents

3. SOFT FURNISHINGS

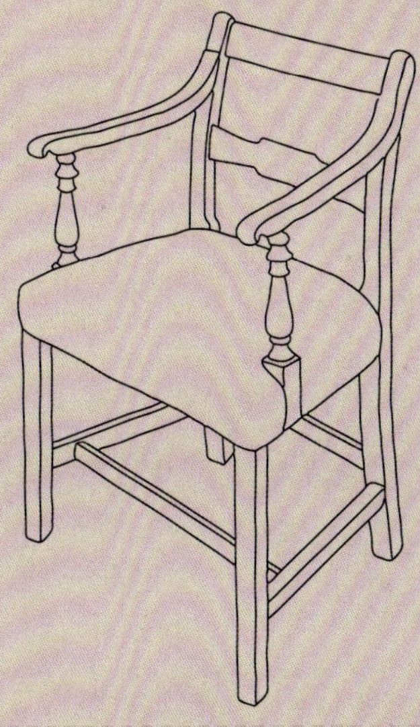

Why I wrote this book

Home is what you make it. I want to inspire you to transform your home into the sanctuary you have always dreamed of. I want to empower you with the confidence to tackle simple upholstery projects that breathe new life into your existing furniture, and then add unique soft furnishings as the cherry on top. Your home reflects who you are, and by injecting personality into a space through upholstery and soft furnishings, you can bring everything together to make the space uniquely yours.

As a professional upholsterer, I am dedicated to fulfilling my clients' vision for their living spaces. Day in and day out, I witness the profound impact that transforming a house into a real home can have on the human psyche. Your home can be an extension of who you are, creating a specific feeling in every room depending on what aspect of your personality you want to project.

We all deserve a home we feel proud of. I am passionate about sharing my knowledge of creating furniture and furnishings through clear, easy-to-understand instructions. There's nothing quite like looking at something you have upholstered or sewn and thinking 'I made that'. It's one of the best feelings and one that I want you to experience, too.

Throughout my childhood, I always felt proud that my Mum created rich interiors that told a story because she had designed and made them herself. So it's no surprise that, growing up, I was also drawn to drawing and making things, setting me on a path that brings us to the present day.

From the moment I first stepped into a workshop, I've been sustained by the fulfilment I get from looking at something I have created and thinking 'I did that'. It is truly one of the best feelings, so I have written this book first and foremost to share my enduring love of making with you.

As a professional upholsterer, if sharing this book with you also means I can help preserve some of the time-honoured skills and knowledge that are at risk of being lost (along with so many other heritage crafts), then all the better.

Ultimately, I hope this book will inspire and equip you with the confidence to tackle simple upholstery projects, and provide you with the means to breathe new life and style into your existing furniture and homes. After all, we all deserve to have a home we feel proud of.

A short history of upholstered furniture

There is evidence that furniture was upholstered dating back to ancient cultures. Over 3,000 years ago, the ancient Egyptians sat on simple mats and cushions on the floors of their homes, as did many people across the Middle East. To improve the comfort of seating, the Greeks and Romans used wooden frames filled with materials such as hay and feathers to create padded furniture. While this was a significant leap forwards, these homes were still relatively primitive compared to the comforts that we enjoy today.

The Silk Road, which linked Europe with the Middle East and Asia, greatly aided the exchange of cultural influences and creative techniques between regions, introducing new and unfamiliar materials. This exchange in exotic woods, fine fabrics, tools and techniques enriched furniture styles over time, leading to refinements in design and improvements in comfort. The cultural fusion along these global trade routes resulted in increasingly varied and sophisticated approaches to home furnishings, often adopted by the wealthy elites of the European courts.

During the Middle Ages, interiors reflected the status, wealth and sophistication of the family. Affluent homes showcased intricately carved wooden furniture upholstered with fine silks. Tapestries adorned the walls, designed to minimize draughts as well as add decoration, while handwoven rugs from far-flung places covered the floors.

From the 15th to the 18th centuries, the interiors of the Renaissance and baroque periods were characterized by grandeur and opulence, with a profound emphasis on individual artistic expression. During the Renaissance, inspired by a revival of classical ideals, interiors featured harmonious proportions with symmetrical arrangements. Walls were adorned with ornate panelling, elaborate frescoes and delicate tapestries. Furniture, carved from rich hardwoods like walnut and oak, boasted finely wrought details and intricate inlays. Luxurious fabrics, including velvet and brocade, heightened the sense of prestige. As the baroque style emerged in the 17th century, interiors grew ever more exuberant, defined by elaborate

I am fascinated by the fact that contemporary craftspeople are still recreating designs from the rococo era that influence the styling of people's homes today.

designs and bold colours, gilded mouldings, sculpted marble and ceiling frescoes. Artists, designers and skilled craftspeople from across Europe were integral to developing this ornate style.

The rococo influence evolved out of the baroque period in the 18th century. Extremely ornate, highly decorative and incredibly detailed, it is a style associated with the court of Louis XV of France. The colours of the rococo era were softer, with pastel shades introduced in wall decoration, window treatments and woven textiles used for upholstery. The rococo interior style is imbued with opulence, exclusivity and wealth, realizing the ambitions of the social elite.

From 1750 onwards, the Industrial Revolution transformed the production processes of furniture making, as well as design, architecture, fashion, food and more. In the 19th century, the Industrial Revolution propelled many industries forward, enabling experimentation with readily available materials without huge development costs, allowing products to be mass-produced and sold at attainable prices. Upholstery manufacturing advanced with the advent of springs and the invention of foam and other man-made fibres. For the average family, this meant greater variation in furniture design and upholstery. But it didn't stop at furnishings and fabrics; the effects of the Industrial Revolution rippled through just about every area of life, changing our world forever.

The English textile designer William Morris personifies the early years of 20th-century interiors, stripping back intricate shapes and ornate patterns to create simpler forms inspired by nature. It was a rebellion of sorts, moving away from elaborate, crowded Victorian interiors to an aesthetic of minimal designs in all aspects of the decorative arts. The Arts and Crafts Movement that Morris spearheaded at the end of the 19th century focused on craftsmanship and function combined with beauty. This approach was reflected in fabrics, woodwork, ceramics and metalwork. While the Arts and Crafts Movement valued the handmade, and thus not the mass-produced, it became a status symbol both for its cost and for what it stood for – a rebellion against the mechanization of the industrial age.

Later, in the 20th century, Modernism gave rise to a new style of art and design coupled with continued advancements in manufacturing processes. A new cohort of post-war designers experimented with form and mass production, bringing style, individuality and choice to home interiors in a way that had never been experienced before. Furniture companies like Ercol, G-plan and Habitat set new standards, making it possible for more people to save, purchase and express themselves in their homes. It was a period when the 'buy once, buy well' ethos was prevalent. 'Make do and mend' had become a way of life during the Second World War, and this mentality continued in the post-war years. Domestic sewing machines were soon put to good use by homemakers who began making their own curtains and cushions, and tackling simple upholstery projects. Haberdashers, or fabric shops, allowed easy access to a range of options, giving people the freedom to choose a rococo-style fabric and upholster a contemporary dining chair, creating a completely personalized aesthetic.

The mid-20th century also saw the rise of Scandinavian design, which emphasized functionality, simplicity and minimalism. Designers like Arne Jacobsen and Hans Wegner brought clean lines and organic shapes into home furnishings, influencing global design trends. Their work underscored the importance of combining beauty with practicality, which is a hallmark of modern interior design.

The influence of popular culture and media in the latter half of the 20th century further democratized design. Television shows, magazines and, later, online platforms, showcased a plethora of styles, making interior design accessible and appealing to a broader audience. Iconic pieces like the Eames lounge chair became symbols of this era, blending comfort with cutting-edge design.

The late 20th and early 21st centuries have seen a renewed interest in sustainable and eco-friendly design. The awareness of environmental impact has driven designers and manufacturers to create furniture

During the 20th century, quality products became more affordable thanks to the evolution of manufacturing and design processes. With great design being more widely accessible, individuals were empowered to make their own mark on their homes.

using recycled materials, sustainably sourced woods and low-impact manufacturing processes. This shift not only caters to a growing market of environmentally conscious consumers but also encourages innovation in materials and design.

The rise of passementerie during this time also deserves mention. This intricate art of creating elaborate trimmings and edgings, which includes tassels, braids and fringes, added a new dimension to interior design. Passementerie, often seen as the finishing touch, brought an extra layer of sophistication and detail to upholstered furniture and home decor. Once a symbol of wealth and luxury, it became accessible to a wider audience, allowing more people to add a touch of elegance to their homes.

Today, we have unprecedented freedom to create our own styling inspired by our personal tastes, preferences and backgrounds. DIY stores, antique shops and affordable home furnishing superstores have made upholstered furniture and soft furnishings accessible to many. The internet has spurred the rise of online classes and tutorials, enabling people to revamp, reupholster and discover their own interior style. With the continued development of fabrics and a growing appreciation for global design aesthetics, we live in a world where once elite and unattainable designs are now available to all. We can design, make, restore and reupholster to our heart's content, creating homes that truly reflect our individuality as human beings.

As technology continues to evolve, pushing the manufacture of materials and furniture towards a more sustainable route, who knows what our interiors will reflect in another 200 years. With advances in smart home technology, future interiors might seamlessly integrate comfort, style and functionality in ways we can only imagine today. The evolution of upholstery and interior design is a testament to human creativity and adaptability, promising an exciting future for our living spaces.

1.
Before you begin

Making your workspace work for you

Before you tackle any upholstery or sewing project, it is important to consider the space you have to work in. This is especially crucial if you do not have a dedicated 'making' room and are using a corner of a multi-purpose space or a limited area. Your workspace might need to be easily packed away when you are not sewing or making. Here are some key points to consider:

WORKSPACE Ensure that you have a clear area to work in, with at least 1 metre (3.3 feet) between you and any other furniture so you can work on a piece while it is on the ground. Keep the work area free of any trip hazards.

LIGHTING Choose a spot with plenty of natural light so you can see what you are working on. Avoid having a window directly in front of you, as it can cast shadows on your work. Ideally, position your workbench side-on to the window to maximize daylight from either side throughout the day. For artificial lighting, use daylight bulbs for better visibility and accurate colour representation of fabrics, trimmings and threads.

WORKBENCH I recommend a pair of upholstery trestle tables to work on. They differ from regular trestles in that they have raised edges to prevent furniture from sliding off while you work. If you are using a regular trestle table, ensure it has a large surface area, ideally wider than a standard roll of upholstery fabric (137cm/54 inches wide). For a temporary workbench that you can easily store when not in use, you can place a thick piece of plywood or MDF (at least 18mm/¹¹⁄₁₆ inch thick) on top of your trestles. The temporary surface should be a minimum of 130cm (51 inches) long by 122cm (48 inches) wide, however, consider where you will store this piece when not in use and adjust the measurements accordingly.

STEP If you need extra height to reach the piece of furniture you are working on while it is on the workbench, use a step to help you to reach over comfortably.

TOOLBOX A toolbox with plenty of compartments is essential for keeping your tools organized. Return tools to the same place each time to maintain tidiness.

NOTEPAD AND PENCIL Always have a notepad and pencil on hand, perhaps kept in your toolbox, for planning your projects.

DUSTSHEETS Use dust sheets, old throws, fabric remnants or bed sheets to protect the floor from debris when stripping furniture.

DUSTPAN AND BRUSH I always tidy my work area at the end of each day, sweeping up with a dustpan and brush. If necessary, I'll use a vacuum cleaner too, to ensure the area is clean and ready for the next session.

M.H.H.

Tools and materials

Upholstery and sewing tools haven't changed much over time, so whether you've inherited tools, bought them at a car boot sale or purchased new ones, they will all be functional. There's no need to rush out and buy a whole new set of tools right away – work with what you have, and gradually invest in your own tools as needed.

MEASURING TOOLS

I find it really helpful to have a few different rulers and measuring tools to choose from:

- **1 metre (1 yard) ruler** – I prefer a thick metal ruler for its weight, which helps keep the fabric in place when I'm marking against it.

❶ **Soft tape measure** – Ideal for measuring curves or oversized hessian or bottom cloths. When I started out, I used a longer ruler, but it would sometimes accidentally mark the wooden frame in unwanted places. Switching to a soft tape measure solved this issue. You could also use a retractable tape measure.

- **30cm (12 inch) ruler** – My preference is again for a metal ruler. Unlike wooden or plastic ones, a metal ruler has sufficient weight and the increments start from the very end, allowing for precise measurements.

- **Set square or roofing square** – I use both the larger and smaller metal roofing squares, which are totally flat, making them more practical for marking fabric compared to a carpenter's square. I also use plastic set squares for squaring up marry marks (see page 47); they are small, light and perfect for marking and cutting borders.

MARKING TOOLS

Always choose the appropriate marking tool for the fabric you're working with to ensure clean, precise marks that won't damage or permanently stain your materials. Ensure you test your choice of marking tool on a scrap of fabric before using it for real. And NEVER use a ballpoint pen. In fact, I ban all ballpoint pens from my workshop to avoid anyone accidentally using one – if you mark fabric with a ballpoint pen, 99.9 per cent of the time it can never be removed. Here are the essential marking tools for upholstery:

- **Pencil** – Use for general marking on the reverse (wrong) side of fabrics.

❷ **Tailor's chalk** – For fabrics with a heavy pile where pencil marks will not be visible. When marking the right side of the fabric, use chalk in a matching colour to reduce the risk of any visible marks, even after brushing them away.

- **Chinagraph pencil** – This versatile tool works on virtually any surface and comes in a wide range of colours.

- **Wax marker** – An alternative to tailor's chalk, but avoid using wax markers on the right side of the fabric as the marks will be visible and are difficult to remove.

ESSENTIAL CUTTING TOOLS

• **Foam saw (or sharp serrated bread knife)** – For cutting foam, an electric foam saw is ideal for the best finish. However, due to the high expense, you may want to consider alternative options like a larger serrated blade, such as an electric carving or bread knife. If you don't have either option available to you as a beginner, I recommend asking your foam supplier to cut the foam for you.

• **Jigsaw/hand saw** – Useful for cutting MDF or lengths of timber to make shapes and framework. Choose one based on the type of cut and precision you require.

❶ **Hand drill** – Essential for making precise holes in wooden frames and other materials. Also used for fixing screws into place.

• **Craft knife with a retractable blade** – Useful for cutting small or fiddly areas of foam. Always keep a sharp blade in the knife. The sharper the blade, the safer and more effective it is.

• **Upholstery scissors with 25cm (10 inch) blades** – These are one of my most widely used tools. Many upholsterers have their preferred brand and style, with 25cm (10 inch) scissors being one of the larger sizes available. I use a pair of 25cm (10 inch) scissors for general cutting and a modern pair of 25cm (10 inch) Kai 7250SL Professional Slim-Line Shears for cutting fabric and fine work. I LOVE these scissors and if I had to choose one thing to take to a desert island it would be a pair of these!

❷ **Scissors** – Sharp, durable scissors are crucial for cutting fabric, foam and other materials precisely. Invest in a good pair to ensure clean, accurate cuts – in fact, it's helpful to have a few pairs in varying sizes for different applications. You will find your preferences as you work. I find a small pair of scissors invaluable for reaching inaccessible places, cutting close to any finishing stitches and for shaping fabric.

These cutting tools will ensure that you can handle various materials and achieve precise results in your upholstery projects.

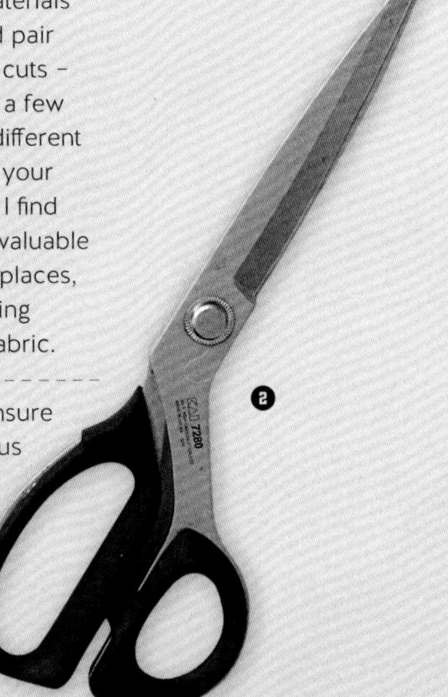

❷

ESSENTIAL HAND TOOLS

❸ Magnetic upholstery hammer (190g/7oz) – A traditional and widely used hammer, it has the ideal weight and handles beautifully. Originally used for securing traditional tacks in place, I use it for hitting down bulky webbing ends and for stripping out (see page 30) in tight areas where a mallet can't fit.

❹ Stud hammer with a nylon tip – This hammer is perfect for hammering in decorative dome-headed studs while protecting the surface of the stud. Well worth investing in for the perfect finish.

❺ Pin hammer – A lighter hammer with a smaller head, designed for pins as the name suggests. Its lighter weight makes it useful for tasks where a gentle touch is needed.

- **Claw hammer** – A versatile hammer primarily used in carpentry and joinery. It's heavier with a double-pronged claw, perfect for prying out heavy-duty nails or tacks that pliers can't remove.

- **Mallet** – Typically made of rubber or wood, a mallet is essential for getting tacks or staples out of woodwork in partnership with your preferred tack lifter or ripping chisel, and for setting tacks or staples into place gently. I prefer the rubber mallet for its weight.

❻ Bull-nose pliers – These have rounded jaws and are useful for gripping, bending and twisting, or pulling out fabric, tacks and staples when stripping out. They are particularly effective due to their rolling action, which is less repetitive on the wrists than that of combination pliers (see below).

❼ Combination pliers – The most common style of pliers, these come in many sizes and designs. They can pull out stubborn tacks or staples that resist the tack lifter.

- **Ripping chisel** – Used with a mallet to remove old tacks, staples or nails from furniture, this traditional tool has a wooden handle and a bevelled edge that slides under fasteners to lift them out carefully without damaging the surrounding fabric.

❽ Tack lifters and staple lifters – Modern tools for stripping out with precision and ease. A yellow, angled staple lifter with pronged, hardened ends is my go-to for most projects. Tack lifters are also available – they have spade-like ends to get under the tack head more easily.

❾ Bradawl – A multi-purpose tool that is perfect for marking and indenting wood to show where to drill a hole. It can also be used to regulate horsehair pads, and to hold fabric in place at tricky spots so you can staple it down without jeopardizing your fingers.

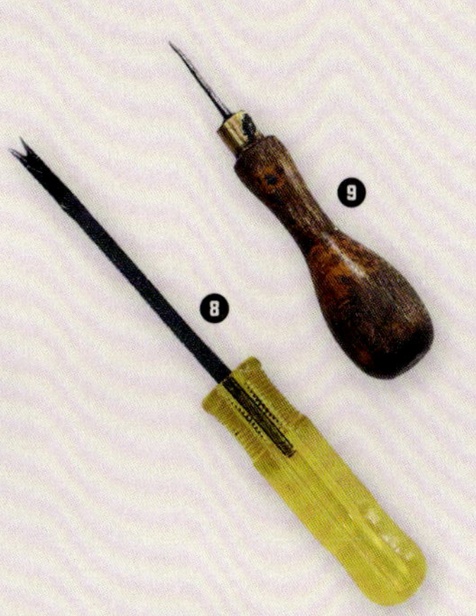

SEWING TOOLS

- **Sewing machine** – When starting out, a domestic sewing machine with the appropriate sewing feet will suffice. Your sewing machine should come with bobbins and needles. If it doesn't, you can find the correct ones by searching online for your machine model and purchase any additional or missing parts you need. It's a good idea to ensure you have everything in place before beginning a project. You'll need a standard straight stitch foot, a zip foot (which can sometimes double as a piping foot) and a separate piping foot.

- **Sewing needles** – Whether it be for slip stitching (if you prefer using a straight needle) or for any hand sewing, it's always worth having a good selection of sewing needles in various lengths and thicknesses. Try to avoid fine needles that are hard to thread due to their small eye as it can waste a lot of time.

❶ **Curved sewing needles (7.5cm/3 inch and 10cm/4 inch)** – Smaller curved needles are ideal for slip stitching and you may need different gauges (thicknesses) depending on the fabric. Larger needles are used for traditional stitching and for stitching in bridle ties (see page 34).

- **Single-pointed needles** – Available in sizes 25cm (10 inch), 30cm (12 inch) and smaller, these needles are used for buttoning.

- **Double-pointed needles** – Available in sizes 25cm (10 inch), 30cm (12 inch) and smaller, these have a point at each end, allowing you to sew through thick layers of padding with ease. They are used for hand-stitching traditional stitched edges, for second stuffing ties and more.

❷ **Upholstery skewers** – Skewers are useful for keeping fabric pinned in place if required before fixing. They come in different sizes.

- **Upholstery pins** – These are used to hold fabric in place before sewing or stapling. They come in various lengths and types.

❸ **Dressmaking pins** – Used to pin fabrics together. I prefer glass-headed pins as they tend to be of better quality. I use the Prym brand for their thicker gauge.

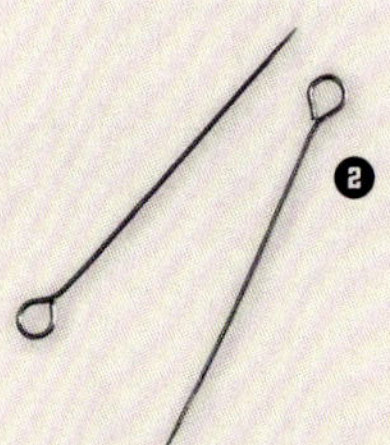

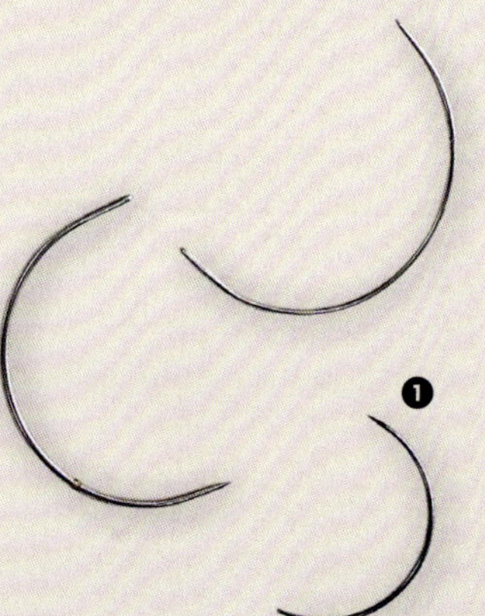

❹ Threads for machine sewing and hand sewing – Have a selection of cotton threads to match or complement the colour of your fabric when sewing, and a translucent, invisible thread for hand sewing braid to curtains.

❺ Twine – Also known as stitching twine or upholstery twine. A few millimetres thick, this is traditionally used for stitched pads (see page 195) to create the knots for blind stitching and the top edge. It is also used to create bridle ties (see page 34). Some upholsterers wax their twine using a block of beeswax, which helps them run smoothly through fabric.

❻ Buttoning twine – Nylon twine used for fixing buttons.

- **Barbour's twine** – Used for slip stitching thicker fabrics.

- **Stitch unpicker/seam ripper** – Essential for correcting sewing mistakes by removing stitches easily and quickly.

- **Steam iron** – Necessary for pressing fabric and seams for a professional finish.

These sewing tools will equip you for a range of upholstery projects, ensuring you have the right tools for precision and quality in your work.

MATERIALS

❶ **Cotton felt** – A traditional soft padding used as a top padded layer on traditional upholstery before the calico is applied.

❷ **Blue/black wool felt** – Used in the same way as cotton felt but gives a firmer finish.

❸ **Hessian** – Made from natural fibres (usually jute or sisal), there are a few different types of hessian for various applications. For beginners, I recommend 285g (10oz) and 340g (12oz) hessian. The 285g (10oz) hessian has a softer, looser weave. The heavier 340g (12oz) hessian, also known as scrim, has a tighter weave and is used mainly for stitched pads (see page 195).

❹ **Fire retardant (FR) calico** – A strong but inexpensive fabric, the calico layer always sits beneath the top fabric. For almost all traditional upholstery, the calico layer forms the final shape of the upholstery. It's crucial that this fabric is fire retardant (FR) to comply with safety regulations and ensure the furniture is safe for use.

❺ **Horsehair stuffing** – Horsehair comes in various qualities. For beginners, the horsehair available from standard suppliers is perfect. Although it is more expensive, horsehair provides a better finish and is easier to work with than black and ginger fibre.

• **Ginger fibre** – Ginger fibre is made from coconut coir and like horsehair, it is a traditional type of stuffing. Some upholsterers use ginger fibre as the initial layer because it provides a firmer base when stitched in, followed by horsehair as the top layer. Others prefer to use horsehair throughout. In this book, I recommend using horsehair for all layers.

• **Polyester wadding (55g/2oz and 115g/4oz)** – A man-made fibre that looks like white candyfloss and is used between the calico layer and the finishing layer of fabric to soften the top layer of the upholstery. This wadding is also used to wrap around foam. I use the 55g (2oz) more than the 115g (4oz).

❻ **Woolguard** – A naturally fire-retardant barrier layer that adds softness and a smooth surface for the fabric to sit on. Due to wool's naturally fire-protective qualities, Woolguard does not contain any added chemicals to make it fire resistant. This layer can often replace a polyester wadding layer.

• **Foam** – Available in a variety of types, foam can be cut to any size, shape or thickness. Foams are classified by grade based on their density (low, medium or high), firmness and overall quality. Different grades of foam are suited to different upholstery uses and foam density affects both comfort and durability. For most projects I recommend a medium-density, blue foam and use different thicknesses, ranging from 6mm (¼ inch) chip or scrim foam to 12.5cm (5 inches) deep, medium-density foam. Your upholstery supplier will be able to advise you which foam is best suited to your project.

❼ **Bottom cloth** – A synthetic cloth also known as Dipryl Base Cloth. Used to cover the underside of chairs, concealing the webbing and internal components and giving the base a neater appearance. You could also use 285g (10oz) hessian as a bottom cloth if you wanted to stick to natural materials. Alternatively, you could choose a finely woven cotton fabric if you prefer another option. This book primarily uses Dipryl and hessian.

• **Piping cord (6mm/¼ inch or 8mm/⅓ inch)** – Usually cotton, although paper and fibre versions are available. Cotton piping sits the best around curves and handles well. It's always best to buy pre-shrunk piping to prevent shrinking if the cover is washed.

❽ **Black-and-white webbing** – Known as 'English' herringbone webbing, this is used for seat areas where there will be significant weight and consistent pressure, as it is strong and durable.

• **Jute webbing** – Typically used for inside backs, if smaller and not sprung, and inside arms.

These materials will form the foundation of your upholstery projects, ensuring that you have everything you need to create durable and aesthetically pleasing pieces.

OTHER UPHOLSTERY TOOLS

❾ **Web stretcher** – Used to stretch and secure webbing under seats or cushions. The web stretcher ensures that the webbing is taut and properly aligned, providing a firm base for the upholstery. There are several types available, but my preference is the style with the dowel and a cut-out to loop the webbing into. It is the easiest to use to build good tension into the webs without strenuous effort.

• **Regulator (25cm/10 inch or 30cm/12 inch)** – A versatile tool with two distinct functions. The pointed end is inserted through the hessian fabric that secures fillings, like hair or coir fibres, to 'regulate' (manipulate) the stuffing into place, allowing you to redistribute and even out the padding. The flat end helps in placing and smoothing pleats on corners or deep buttoning, ensuring that the fabric lays neatly and aligns properly. I always keep mine in a separate compartment in my toolbox to avoid accidentally catching my hand on it. Some upholsterers keep theirs in a cardboard tube for safety. While regulators come in smaller sizes, I rarely use the small ones.

These additional tools will enhance your efficiency and precision in various upholstery tasks, helping to make your work easier and more effective.

FIXINGS

❶ Staple gun and staples – Staple guns can be powered by electricity or compressed air. If you don't have access to an air compressor, high-quality semi-commercial and commercial electric staple guns are available. Ideally, your staple gun should accommodate '72' series staples. Ensure you purchase the correct staples for your gun. I recommend having a selection of staples in 8mm (⅓ inch), 10mm (⅜ inch) and 12mm (½ inch) sizes to suit different layers and densities of upholstery.

❷ Dome-headed studs – Used as decorative 'nails' to hold leather and fabric in place. Available in different sizes, colours and finishes. The most popular size has a 10mm (⅜ inch) head width.

❸ Upholstery tacks/gimp pins – Traditional fixings used to secure webbing, hessian, calico and top fabric in place. Improved (IMP) tacks have larger heads than fine tacks. I recommend using the smallest tack length suitable for the job: 16mm (⅝ inch) IMP (improved) for webbing, 13mm (½ inch) IMP for hessian, 6mm (¼ inch) fine for calico and 6mm or 10mm (¼ or ⅜ inch) fine tacks for top fabric, depending on its thickness.

• **Coloured tacks/gimp pins** – Small, thin, long tacks that come in a variety of colours. Often used to final fix corners into place.

• **Back tacking strip** – This is a thick cardboard edging, usually 1cm (⅜ inch) wide and available on a roll. Fabric is folded over it to create a neat straight edge or seam on outside backs and arms.

• **Hot melt glue gun and glue sticks** – I only use a hot melt glue gun for applying braids and finishes. Avoid using watery fabric glues, as they may not provide the desired hold and finish.

These fixings are crucial for ensuring your upholstery projects are secure, durable and aesthetically pleasing.

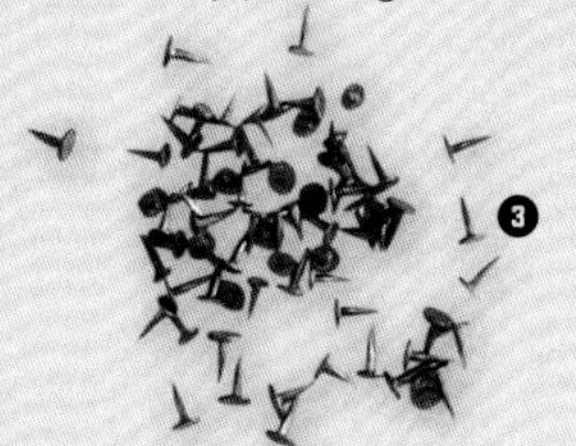

SPRAYS

- **Upholstery contact adhesive** – This spray is essential for bonding fabrics and other materials securely. Always ensure you use a vapour mask while spraying and work in a well-ventilated area to avoid inhaling harmful fumes.

- **Silicone spray** – Ideal for maintaining your tools and ensuring smooth operation. Silicone spray can be used on scissors and other cutting tools to keep them sharp and rust-free.

These sprays are vital for ensuring both the quality and efficiency of your upholstery work, helping you achieve professional results while maintaining safety and ease of use.

ESSENTIAL TOOLS FOR BEGINNERS

These tools form the foundation of a reliable upholstery toolkit, enabling you to tackle a range of projects with confidence.

- **Scissors** (see page 20)
- **Mallet** (see page 21)
- **Bull-nose pliers** (see page 21)
- **Tack lifter** (see page 21)
- **Double-pointed needle** (see page 22)
- **Upholstery pins** (see page 22)
- **Web stretcher** (see page 25)

❹ **Regulator** (see page 25)

Traditional or modern upholstery techniques?

Choosing between traditional and modern upholstery methods depends on various factors, and while there aren't strict rules, certain guiding principles can help you make an informed decision.

Age and value of the piece
If the piece is an antique or has significant historical value, either sentimentally or monetarily, it's usually best to use traditional upholstery techniques. Chairs that have always been upholstered traditionally often deserve to retain their original methods to preserve their authenticity and value. Reupholstering such pieces with modern materials like foams and synthetic fillings can diminish their historical and aesthetic worth. Therefore, for valuable antiques, sticking with traditional techniques is recommended.

Feasibility with modern furniture
Sometimes, using traditional techniques on modern furniture isn't physically possible. Modern and reproduction items often have 'tack-off' rails that are not deep enough to accommodate the multiple layers of fabric and tacks or staples required for traditional methods. Tack-off rails are the wooden areas on a chair that are next to the show wood section of the frame. These rails might only support minimal layers under the top fabric. In such cases, modern techniques are more suitable and practical.

Condition of the frame
Delicate, traditional decorative frames can pose a challenge. Over time, frames that have been traditionally upholstered can become frail and fragile. Even with restoration, using hammers to fix tacks into the frame can cause further damage. In these instances, a hybrid approach of using traditional fillings combined with staple fixings can help preserve the integrity of the frame while maintaining some of the traditional elements.

Suitability for modern designs
Modern furniture pieces are often designed with specific upholstery fillings and padding in mind. Large surface areas, such as those on upholstered coffee tables or headboards, are better suited to modern foam pads. Traditional fillings may not provide the same durability and support for everyday use in such applications. Thus, for modern designs, it is practical to stick with modern upholstery techniques to ensure longevity and functionality.

By considering these factors, you can make a more informed decision about which upholstery technique to use, ensuring that your project not only looks good but also stands the test of time.

Essential techniques

Stripping out

Stripping out refers to the process of removing all existing fabric, webbing and fixings from a piece of furniture to take it back to the frame, ready for reupholstering. This step is crucial as it allows you to understand how a chair is constructed and how the various layers interact with each other. However, it is arguably one of the tougher jobs in upholstery and also one of the dustiest. As a matter of course, I always wear a dust mask whenever I'm stripping the covers, webbing and fixings off any piece of furniture. You may also want to put on some protective eyewear as bits can sometimes fly up into your face.

Depending on what I am stripping out, I either use a tack lifter with a spade-like end for traditional tacks, or for staples I use a staple lifter with an angled, pronged end (see page 21). There is a traditional tool called a ripping chisel, but I find the modern tack lifters to be more effective.

STRIPPING OUT TACKS AND STAPLES

1. Strip out: Using the appropriate tack or staple lifter and a mallet, knock the fixings out of the frame by pushing the end of the tack lifter just under the head of the tack or staple. Hit the end of the lifter with the mallet to wedge the lifter under the fixing, then push down on the lifter to prise the fixing out of the wood. If it doesn't come all the way out, don't worry. Keep working along the row of fixings in the same way, then use bull-nose pliers or standard pliers to prise out any fixings left in the frame.

PRO TIP If you are stripping out tacks or staples next to show wood (any exposed wood frame or legs/arms of upholstered furniture that is intentionally left uncovered), adjust the angle at which you work so that you don't lever off the wood and mark it. If you cannot adjust the angle, place some leather or thick fabric behind the lifter to minimize marking.

2. Clean up the frame: Once you have stripped out as much as you need to, depending on how far you are going with the upholstery, brush and/or vacuum any dust or debris. Using your hands, check over the rails. You may find sharp spikes of wood that have been caused by the stripping out, or ends of fixings embedded in the wood, which you may catch your hands on when reupholstering. Use a magnetic hammer or pin hammer to hammer these down so they don't pose a threat. Lightly sand back any wood splinters to create a smooth surface.

PRO TIP I prefer to stand on a step so that I am slightly higher than the area I am stripping out to get a better angle. I also find that my shoulders and arms don't ache quite as much when I am a little higher!

When removing fabric and webbing, you can use scissors or a retractable blade. Be cautious with your cuts to avoid damaging the frame or other reusable materials. Some materials, such as horsehair stuffing, can often be reused. If you plan to reuse horsehair stuffing, make sure to clean it thoroughly by shaking out dust and debris, and then lightly steaming it to revive its loft and sanitize it (see page 48).

By following these steps and taking the necessary precautions, you can effectively strip out old upholstery, preparing your furniture piece for a fresh start with new materials and techniques.

Webbing

Whether on a seat base, a backrest or an inside arm section, webbing is the base layer of almost all upholstered frames, providing foundational support. You will most commonly see an evenly spaced lattice of webbing on seat bases and backrests. Sometimes, webbing is fanned out along the front rail of a seat, depending on the chair frame, and fixed to either the top or bottom of the rail, depending on whether there will be springs tied in (springing) on top of the webbing or if the upholstery is built straight on to the webbing. When there is springing on top of the webbing, the webbing strips must be close enough to enable three sides of the spring to be tied in and provide a secure area for the spring to rest on. On inside arm sections, the webbing will most often run from top to bottom, rather than be latticed. The key thing to bear in mind is that webbing is the foundation to building a firm base, which will enable the even distribution of weight across the area.

In this section, I refer to the terms *rail* and *back rail*. These terms are used to describe different parts of a chair frame.

FIXING WEBBING TO A SEAT BASE

PRO TIP For a seat base, you need to use black-and-white quality webbing that is stronger than jute webbing. Jute webbing is preferred for inside arm sections.

1. Mark the frame: Find and mark the centre point of the front, back and each side of the chair frame. Fixing the webbing strips from the centre outwards to the corners makes it easier to achieve an even webbing.

2. Secure the webbing: Secure the first length of central webbing to the centre of the back rail. Staple the webbing down in three places central to the wooden rail, once in the centre and then once on either side of the central staple.

PRO TIP Use staples that are long enough to achieve a secure fixing in the wood and ensure that the staple gun does not push the staples too hard, which could cut through the webbing. If you are using an air-powered staple gun, you can adjust the force by turning the pressure down. If you are using an electric staple gun, do not push the nose of the gun down too hard on to the webbing. Of course, you can also use traditional tacks and a hammer if preferred.

3. Fold and secure the webbing: Fold the end of the webbing over on to itself and staple twice more, in between the initial three fixings, keeping the staples central to the rail.

4. Insert the webbing: Using a web stretcher, with the cut-out facing upwards and towards the frame, loop the webbing down into the cut-out and then back up again, making sure to catch the dowel or peg through the loop underneath to stop it from pulling back through.

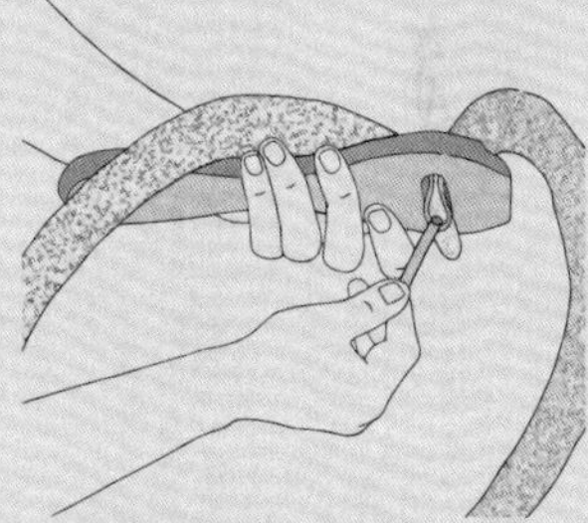

5. Stretch the webbing: Place the cut-out of the web stretcher on the bottom edge of the front rail at the centre mark while holding the handle and the length of webbing in your hand. Push the stretcher down to place tension on the webbing.

PRO TIP If you are webbing over any wood that will ultimately be on show, place some protective wadding or fabric in between the webbing and frame to preserve the wood.

6. Secure the other end: Secure the webbing with three staples placed over the width, again keeping the staples central to the rail. Cut the length of webbing to 2-3cm (¾–1¼ inches) beyond the frame. Fold the end of the webbing over on to itself and secure with a further two staples.

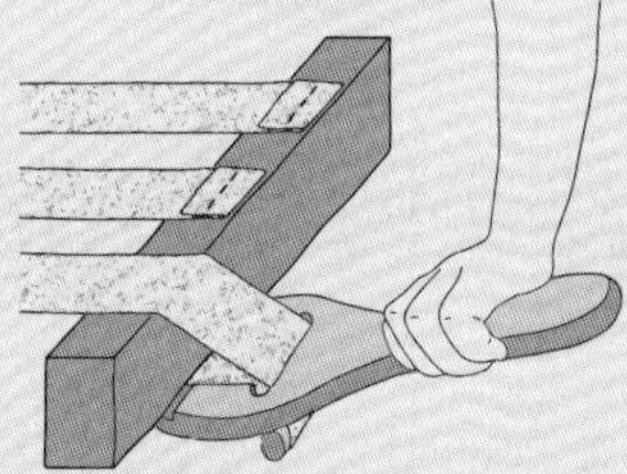

7. Add additional strips: Add another length of webbing on either side of the central webbing in the same way.

8. Weave the webbing: Turn the frame by 90 degrees so that one of the sides is now facing you. As before, add another central webbing strip, but weave it under and over the first set of webbing to make a lattice before fixing it to the rail. Do the same with the additional strips of webbing either side of the central webbing.

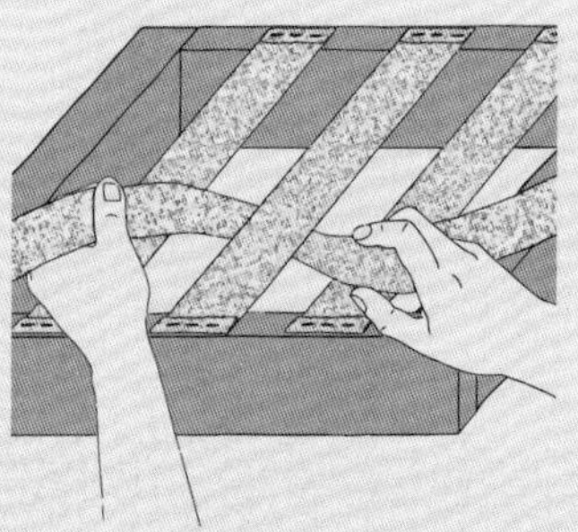

9. Repeat the process: Alternate between the front/back and sides, weaving the webbing strips to make a lattice until you have the required number of webbing strips.

TEMPORARY TACKING VS FINAL TACKING

These terms and techniques are used all the time by upholsterers. I use temporary tacking/stapling to get calico or fabric into position and/or to start building tension on to the piece I am working on. The difference between temporary and final tacking is, as the name suggests, that a temporary tack is impermanent and will eventually be replaced by a final tack. A temporary tack is not hammered all the way in so it is flat to the surface of the wood; instead it is hammered in only gently so it protrudes, meaning you can easily get a tack or staple lifter underneath it to take it out and replace it with a final fixing. A final tack is hammered all the way in, so it is flush to the surface of the wood. If you are creating temporary fixings using staples, tilt your gun to one side so that one side of the staple is fully in and the other side sticks up. This means you can access underneath it to lift it out easily with a staple lifter.

Stuffing

ADDING THE HESSIAN BASE LAYER

Applying a base layer of hessian over webbing provides a sturdy foundation for adding layers of stuffing. In the case of sprung furniture, the springs will rest directly on top of the webbing, with the hessian layer positioned above the springs.

1. Measure and cut: Measure the hessian, adding 5cm (2 inches) extra on all sides. Cut the hessian and position it over the webbing on the seat frame, ensuring the hessian weave runs parallel to the front edge of the frame.

2. Temporarily fix: Fold the excess hessian back on itself. Temporarily fix the hessian at the centre back of the frame. Pull it towards the front edge, maintaining tension, and temporarily fix it at the centre front rail, folding the excess. Repeat on both sides of the seat frame.

3. Permanently fix: Once satisfied with the tension, permanently fix the hessian around the seat base frame in 2cm (¾ inch) intervals using either upholstery tacks or staples.

CREATING BRIDLE TIES

Bridle ties are a specific type of process used in traditional upholstery to secure and hold horsehair stuffing in place. These ties are essential for helping to create the structure and support of the upholstered piece. They are typically made using strong, durable twine and involve a series of large stitches that hold the hair in place when stuffed underneath. Bridle ties are crucial for achieving the desired comfort, longevity and smooth finish found in high-quality, traditionally upholstered furniture.

1. Thread and stitch: Thread a needle with twine. Create a slip knot (see opposite) in one corner of the hessian, then create a 10cm (4 inch) loop, finished with a 1cm (⅜ inch) backstitch. Make sure each loop is large enough to fit your flat hand under for stuffing.

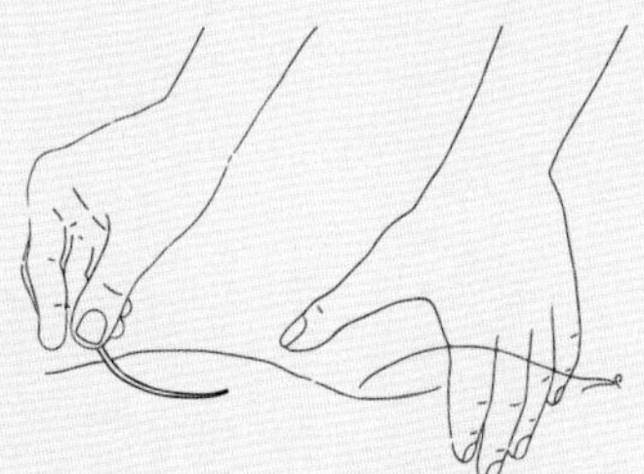

2. Create a grid: Work your way around the hessian layer making successive loops to create a square, grid-like pattern.

3. Tie off: Once you have enough bridle ties, tie off the end of the twine with a double slip knot (see opposite).

ADDING THE STUFFING

Add stuffing under the bridle ties, starting at the back of the frame and working towards the front.

1. Insert the stuffing: Gently lift each bridle tie and place a generous handful of stuffing material underneath, making sure that you smooth out any lumps.

2. Secure the stuffing: Once you are happy with the distribution, carefully tighten each tie loop to secure the stuffing. Work from the first bridle tie to the last.

3. Check the evenness: Ensure the stuffing is evenly distributed, correcting any hollow areas or large bumps using a regulator.

ADDING A COTTON FELT LAYER

Adding cotton felt creates a smooth layer on which to fit the calico.

1. Measure and cut: Measure and cut the cotton felt, adding 5cm (2 inches) extra on all sides.

2. Place the felt: Lay the cotton felt on top of the stuffing layer. Rest one hand on top of the felt layer to hold it in place and, with the other hand, work around the edges removing any excess felt.

3. Position the felt: Ensure the felt edge ends just on the edge of the wooden frame. This prevents the felt from being caught up when attaching the calico layer and avoids any lumpy edge finishes.

ATTACHING THE CALICO LAYER

This step in the upholstery process is crucial for shaping the piece. The calico provides the essential 'shape', while the top fabric simply sits on top of this. Take your time to fit the calico layer properly and be ready to adjust the stuffing and cotton felt underneath to achieve the desired shape.

1. Measure and cut: Measure and cut the calico, oversizing by 10cm (4 inches) on all sides.

2. Position the calico: Lay the calico over the cotton felt layer, ensuring that it sits squarely. Temporarily fix the centre of the back edge, then pull and smooth the calico towards the front, temporarily fixing the centre front edge. Repeat along each side edge.

3. Fix and adjust: Work outwards from each centre, temporarily fixing towards the corners, maintaining tension and smoothing wrinkles. Place additional fixings at 1cm (⅜ inch) intervals. Create neat corners and work around any back uprights (if applicable to the piece of furniture you are working on).

4. Final check: Inspect the overall finish, reworking any unsatisfactory areas. This is the final layer before you apply the top fabric so you want the shape to be perfect and for there to be no lumps or uneven edges. Replace temporary fixings with final fixings once satisfied.

5. Trim excess: Trim away all excess calico. The piece is now ready for the top fabric and bottom cloth.

HOW TO CREATE A SLIP KNOT

To tie a slip knot, start by creating a loop with the end of the twine or string, leaving a short tail. Hold the loop with your fingers and then take the tail end and pass it behind and through the loop. Pull the tail to tighten the knot. The slip knot will slide freely along the twine, making it adjustable. This type of knot is useful because it can be easily loosened or tightened as needed.

To create a double slip knot, simply wrap the tail end around the loop a couple of times before passing it through the loop to give you a tighter knot.

HOW TO SLIP STITCH

A slip stitch, also known as ladder stitch, is a hand-sewn stitch used to join two pieces of fabric together.

Cut a piece of thread about 50cm (20 inches) long, thread the needle and knot the ends together to create a double thread with a large knot that won't pull through the fabric. Working from right to left, bring the needle out through the folded edge on the first side. Guide the needle directly opposite into the folded edge. Bring the needle out from the fabric and take it back into the opposite folded edge, keeping the stitches hidden. Repeat along the seam, pulling the thread to close the gap.

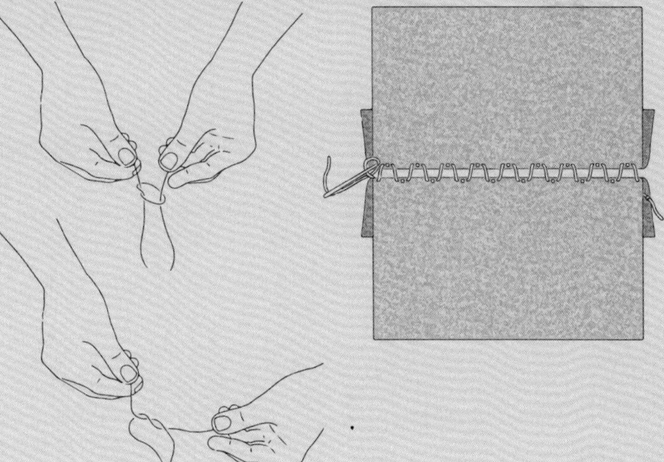

Box pleats

Box pleating is a commonly used technique for finishing the corners of upholstered pieces. A box pleat brings two folded edges of fabric together to create a rectangular, box-like shape. The fundamental principles of box pleating remain consistent across different pieces, though the depth and fabric may vary from item to item.

1. Staple the sides: Begin by stapling the fabric along the sides of the chair frame. The front and back sides will be pleated over these stapled sides.

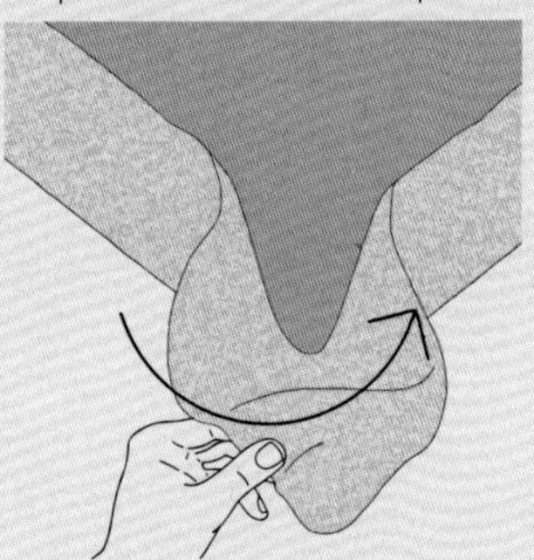

2. Build tension: With the frame resting on its side, smooth the fabric underneath and outwards to create tension up to the corner.

3. Position the fabric: Pull the fabric across the corner so that it wraps towards the front side. Place a temporary staple just above the wood near the corner on the front edge.

4. Test the pleat: You will have excess fabric flapping on the side. Before addressing this excess, test the box pleat by folding the loose fabric on the front under itself at the corner edge. Adjust the fold so that when the front edge is under tension, the fold ends 1–2mm (1/16 inch) from the edge of the wooden frame. This will give you an idea of how the box pleat should look.

5. Secure the excess fabric: Release the test fold and address the excess fabric on the side. Place a staple underneath close to the corner. Staple any gaps closed and trim away the excess (see Pro Tip, below). Smooth down any bulk.

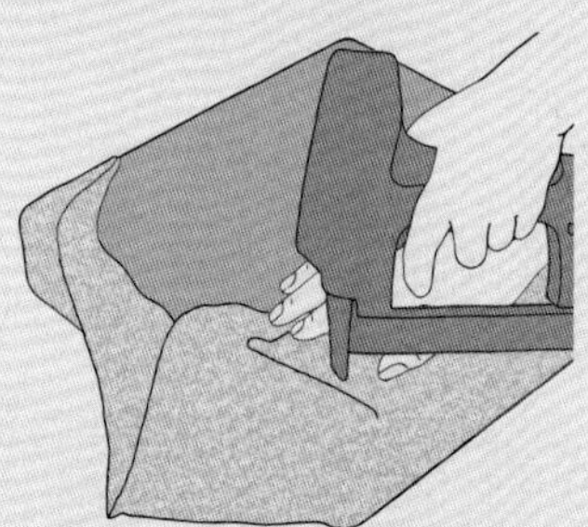

6. Refine the fold: Recreate the fold on the front side, now that the excess has been managed. If using a thick fabric, you may find excess fabric on the underside of the corner. Gently pull this excess under on to the bottom face of the frame. Take any loose fabric from the front corner where you had temporarily stapled and place a staple just on the inside edge to align with the row of staples securing the side. Trim away the excess up to this staple.

PRO TIP You may need to cut excess fabric from the inside of the front fold, especially if using a thicker fabric. Start by cutting out bulk up to the wood. Mark with chalk or pencil where to cut, and incrementally trim the bulk. Ensure the fold ends 1–2mm (1/16 inch) from the wooden corner edge, and taper the fold so it gets covered by the bottom cloth.

7. Make final adjustments: Reassess if any bulk needs to be removed. Hammer in the temporary staple or replace it with a permanent staple. If the bulk of the folded fabric is visible through the fold, cut out some of the fabric. Otherwise, staple the fold down on the underside of the frame. Fill any gaps along the front underneath with final staples.

8. Repeat and finish: Repeat the corner process for all four corners. You could use the pointed end of your regulator to manipulate the fold for a neater finish. Trim away all excess fabric as close to the staples as possible.

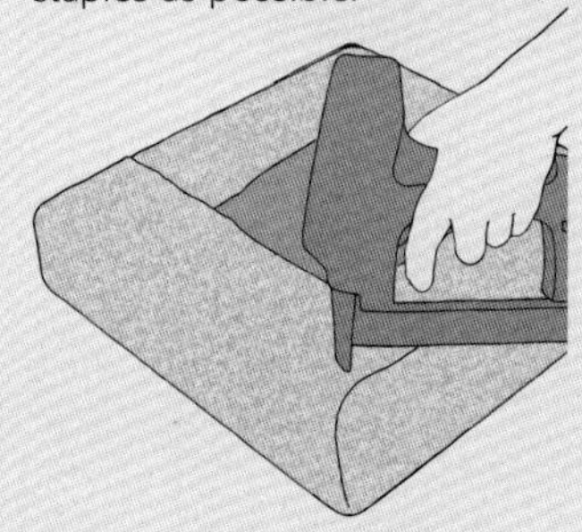

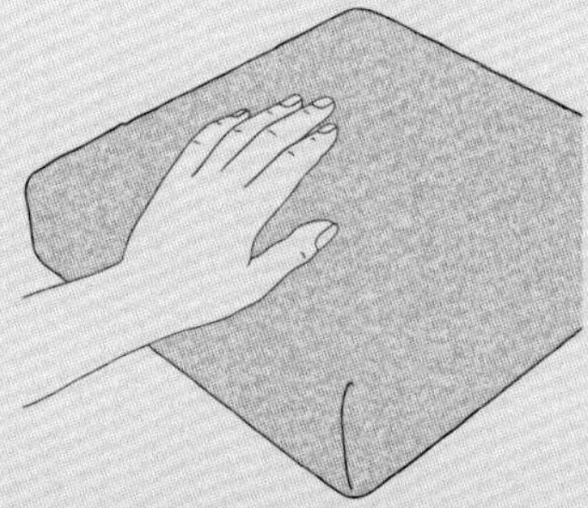

Piping

Piping is used as a finish along an edge, adding definition and decorative detail. You can choose to create self-piping, which uses the same fabric as the main top fabric, or you can opt for contrast piping, which uses a different fabric in order to make a statement.

CALCULATING FABRIC FOR PIPING

Ensure that you have enough fabric to make your piping. Piping works best when the fabric is cut on the bias (at a 45-degree angle). A general guideline for calculating the amount of fabric is to add an extra 1.5 metres (1.5 yards) of fabric to account for the piping, although the exact amount will depend on the size of your chosen project.

DETERMINING PIPING STRIP WIDTH

The width of your piping fabric will depend on the thickness of the piping cord you use. Here's how to determine the correct width:

1. Cut a piece of scrap fabric similar in weight to your main fabric.

2. Wrap the fabric around your piping cord then mark your desired seam allowance, measuring from the inside edge of the cord on the front and back.

3. Unfurl the fabric and measure the marked width: this will be the width of your piping strips.

MEASURING AND CUTTING PIPING

1. Using a soft tape measure, measure the length of piping that you need.

2. For small projects, you may be able to get a sufficient length of piping from a single 45-degree cut across the fabric width. For larger projects, join sections of fabric to cover the piping cord.

3. Using a metre ruler and an appropriate marking tool (see page 19), mark out your piping on the back of the fabric, then use fabric scissors to cut out the strips.

JOINING PIPING STRIPS

1. To join piping together, place two ends at right angles to one another, right sides facing.

2. Sew from the inside corner down to the bottom outside corner at an angle, creating a 45-degree seam.

3. Cut away the excess fabric leaving 1–1.5cm (⅜–⅝ inch) from the sewing line.

4. Open up the piping strip, and you'll have a seam that spreads the bulk across a wider surface area.

PRO TIPS FOR PIPING

- **Use the right tools:** A piping foot on your sewing machine ensures that the stitching is even and close to the piping cord.
- **Cut on the bias:** Cutting fabric on the bias provides flexibility, making it easier to wrap around curves and corners.
- **Be consistent with your seam allowance:** This will ensure that the piping is evenly stitched and lies flat against the main fabric.

By following these techniques, you can create professional-looking piping that will add a refined and decorative touch to all your upholstery projects.

French seams

A French seam is a finished edge where the raw edge is encased by another seam, providing a clean and professional look.

1. Start with the wrong sides together: Place the fabric pieces together with the wrong sides facing each other (the right sides should be facing out).

2. Pin the fabric: Pin the fabric pieces in place to prevent them from shifting while sewing.

3. Sew the first seam: Sew a straight seam along the edge with a 12mm (½ inch) seam allowance.

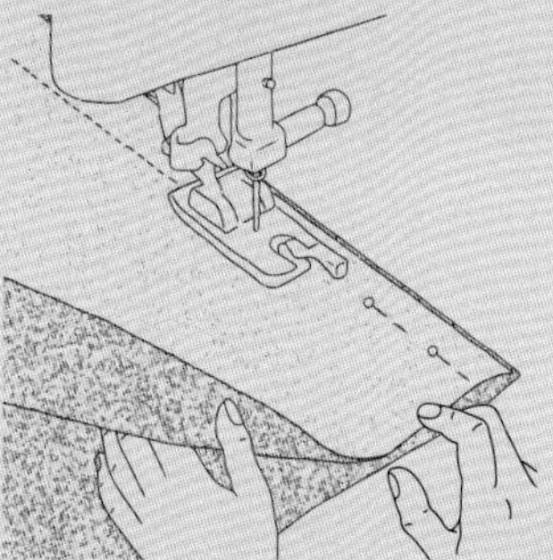

4. Trim the seam allowance: If the fabric does not fray, trim the seam allowance down to about 6mm (¼ inch) to reduce bulk. If the fabric frays, leave the allowance as is, resulting in a deeper French seam.

5. Press the seam: Using an iron, press the seam to one side from the back, then turn the fabric over and press it again from the front.

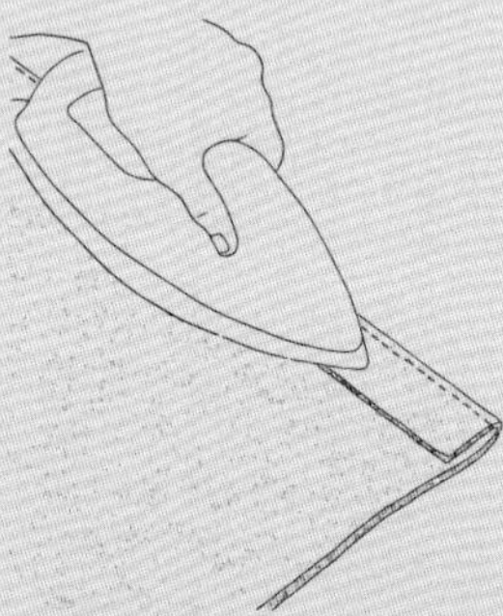

6. Fold and sew the second seam: Fold the two fabrics so that the right sides are now facing each other. Sew another straight seam along the edge, using a 12mm or 2cm (½ or ¾ inch) seam allowance, depending on whether you trimmed the bulk or not. This will encase the raw edges inside the seam.

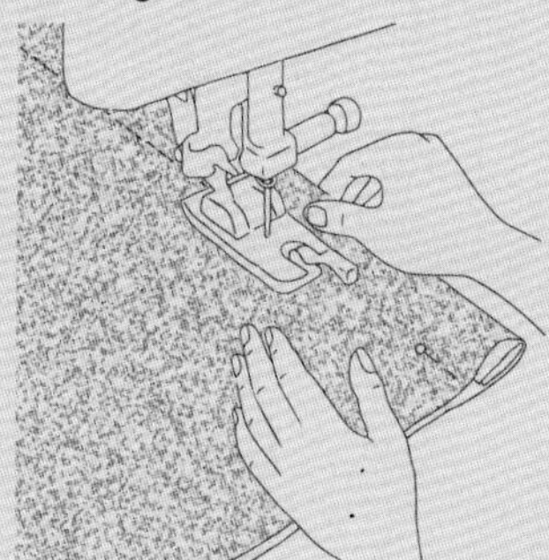

7. Finish the seam: Your French seam is now complete, with no raw edges visible.

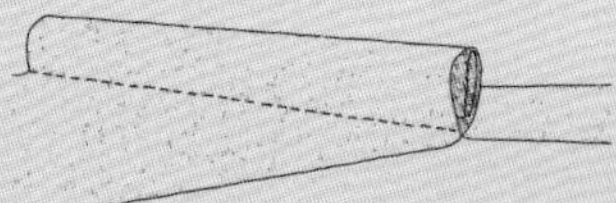

Fabric planning

When tackling any upholstery or soft furnishing project, planning your fabric and tools is crucial. Here are some of my pro tips for you to consider before starting your project.

Gather materials and tools
Ensure you have all the necessary materials, tools and sundries before you begin.

Set up your workspaces
Properly set up your workbench or trestles, and lay out all the tools so that you have them immediately to hand.

Triple-check fabric sizes
Triple-check the sizes of all fabric panels including layers, such as fire-retardant calico or Woolguard.

Calculate fabric amounts
Calculating the amount of fabric for your project depends on the type of upholstery. Take measurements with a soft tape measure and note them down to make a cutting list. For scatter or seat cushions, measure the length and width and multiply the length by two. For box cushions, measure the depth and length of one side and double this, then add it to your cushion total, allowing extra for the border and piping. Add an extra 5cm (2 inches) for seam allowances on cushions. For upholstered pieces, take the dimensions of all pieces, including any armrests or fabric covered rails, adding extra where fabric needs to be tensioned underneath the frame or tacked off. Round up your calculations and add an extra 10 per cent to allow for any mistakes. For patterned fabrics, allow extra to match the pattern repeat. Consult your fabric supplier as total meterage will depend on the width of your chosen fabric.

Create a cutting list
When you reach the fabric-cutting stage, draw up a detailed 'cutting list' that specifies the sizes of every panel of top fabric (or layers beneath) that you need.

Plan fabric usage
To ensure that you are using your fabric in the most economical way possible to minimize waste, pre-plan the layout of your pieces on the back of the fabric using chalk before cutting.

How to choose the right fabric

Choosing the right fabric for your project can be challenging. Here are some things to consider:

APPROPRIATE FABRIC FOR THE PROJECT

Usage and durability – Not all fabrics are suitable for upholstery. Check the fabric specifications to ensure that it is appropriate for your project, especially if the piece will experience heavy use. For example, dining chairs require really durable fabrics.

Martindale/rub test – The Martindale rub test measures fabric durability. Use the rub count to assess how well a fabric will withstand wear and tear. Avoid fabrics with low rub test results for high-use items.

Composition – When I choose a fabric I always check the composition. Natural fibres like cotton and linen are prone to stains and may be harder to clean. Fabrics with man-made fibres, such as polyester, are often easier to maintain and clean.

Size of project – To avoid having to join fabric panels together, consider choosing double-width fabrics for headboards, bedspreads and other very wide or long projects. Some standard-width fabrics also come in widths up to 3m (10ft).

PROJECT CONSIDERATIONS

Fabric suitability – Ensure the fabric suits the specific project (see page 44). For example, thick or heavily woven fabrics may not be ideal for lampshades. Consider the fabric's stretch and movement, as highly stretchy fabrics can be challenging to work with and may show tack lines. If you have pets that like to sit, sleep or climb on your furniture, consider avoiding fabrics with a heavy weave that could get caught on their claws. If you have young children, look for fabrics that can be easily wiped down and cleaned.

PATTERN

Pattern size and placement – Fabric patterns come in all shapes and sizes. If you are attracted to a larger pattern, check the size and shape will fit the piece you are planning to work on, as large patterns may not work well on small items. I do, however, love the drama of a large pattern when it fits well and is positioned in a way that makes it the feature! Small repeat patterns are versatile and work well on almost all projects. For matching items, consider using the same pattern in different colourways.

Stripes – Be mindful of how stripes will look on different sections of a chair. Ensure stripes are straight and aligned, especially on pieces like upholstered dining chairs. You may want to start off by only using a striped fabric on simple projects, such as drop-in seat bases for a dining chair.

THICKNESS

Sewing considerations – It's worth testing whether the fabric you want to use works with your sewing machine, especially if it's quite thick. Adding piping to a cushion increases the fabric layers, making it more challenging to sew. Conduct a test sample to ensure your sewing machine can handle the fabric.

DESIGN, STYLE AND COLOUR

Expressing your style – Whether you opt for a traditional design on a modern piece or vice versa, there are no hard rules. I would suggest that you consider the history and design of antique or collectible pieces, though. I believe that the home is a space where you can express your own interior design narrative – one that you find attractive, comfortable to live with and that expresses who you are.

Colour choices – Think about how you want to feel in the room where the piece will live. Choose colours that evoke the desired atmosphere, whether it's bright and energizing or calm and cosy. Consider how the fabric complements the existing interior. Always live with a fabric sample for a week so you can see it in different lights before making a final decision.

Reversible fabrics – These offer many creative options. For example, you could use the face of the fabric for the front and back of a cushion and the reverse for the cushion border. Reversible fabrics also provide a cheap and easy alternative to choosing a complementary fabric for a unique design, as you won't have to buy more fabric or spend hours searching for one that pairs well with the original.

Upholstery fabrics and their uses

Choosing the right fabric for your upholstery project is essential to achieving the desired look and durability. Heavier fabrics are more durable and suitable for upholstery, while lighter fabrics are better for drapery and decorative purposes. Always check the fabric weight to ensure it matches the needs of your project. Here's a guide to some common upholstery fabrics and their uses:

COTTON

Use: Ideal for slipcovers, cushions and light-use furniture.
Characteristics: Breathable, comfortable and available in various patterns and colours. However, it is prone to wrinkling and staining.

POLYESTER

Use: Suitable for heavy-use furniture, outdoor furniture and decorative pieces.
Characteristics: Durable, resistant to staining and fading, and easy to clean. Polyester is often blended with other fibres to improve durability and resistance.

FAUX LEATHER AND SUEDE

Use: Ideal for heavy-use furniture in households with pets and children.
Characteristics: Durable, easy to clean and available in a wide range of colours and textures. It offers the look of real leather or suede without the maintenance.

LINEN

Use: Suitable for decorative pieces and light-use furniture.
Characteristics: Strong, breathable and has a natural, elegant look. However, it is prone to wrinkling and can be difficult to clean.

VELVET

Use: Ideal for statement pieces and luxury furniture.
Characteristics: Soft, plush texture with a rich appearance. Available in various colours, but can show wear and attract dust.

WOOL

Use: Great for heavy-use furniture and cushions.
Characteristics: Durable, naturally resistant to stains and odours, and provides excellent insulation. However, it can be itchy and is rather challenging to clean.

CORDUROY

Use: Suitable for casual furniture and cushions.
Characteristics: Durable with a distinctive ribbed texture. Comfortable and cosy, but can attract lint and pet hair.

Finishes and trims

Passementerie is the art of making elaborate trimmings or edgings, encompassing 'point ornaments' such as rosettes and tassels, as well as 'linear ornaments' like trims. This includes chic leather piping, extravagant bullion fringing, adorable pom-poms, handwoven braid, jute cord, metallic plaits, faux-fur geometric borders and more. These details allow for endless creative possibilities and can add a unique and sophisticated touch to any upholstery project while elevating its appearance. Here are some common types of trims:

PIPING

Single and double: Adds a tailored look to cushions and upholstery. Single piping outlines edges, while double piping provides a more defined border.

BRAIDS AND CORDS

Use: Great for adding texture and detail to seams and edges.
Characteristics: Available in various thicknesses, colours and patterns.

GIMP

Use: Perfect for covering raw edges and adding decorative detail.
Characteristics: A flat, narrow trim that comes in various patterns and colours.

RIBBON

Use: Adds a delicate and decorative touch to upholstery.
Characteristics: Available in different widths, colours and patterns.

FRINGE

Chainette fringe: Super-fine fringe ideal for adding subtle texture.
Bullion fringe: Thicker, metallic fringe for a luxurious look.
Brush fringe: Multi-layered fringe that adds depth and interest.

POM-POMS AND BEADED FRINGING

Use: Add a playful or elegant touch to cushions and drapery.
Characteristics: Available in various sizes, colours and materials.

TASSEL FRINGE

Use: Perfect for adding a classic or bohemian touch to upholstery.
Characteristics: Comes in various lengths and colours.

FLAT BRAID

Use: Ideal for adding a simple, clean finish to edges.
Characteristics: Flat and available in various colours and patterns.

BUTTONS

Shank-back buttons: Used for tufting and decorative purposes.
Other buttons: Can be covered in fabric to match upholstery or used as accents.

By carefully selecting your fabrics and trims, you can ensure your upholstery project not only looks stunning but also meets the functional needs of your space.

Handling fabric

Once you have chosen and invested in the top fabric to complete your upholstery, this fabric requires careful handling, from marking out to cutting out, to ensure a professional finish.

SUITABLE WORKSPACE

Wide workbench – Make sure that you have a flat trestle, table or workbench that is wide enough to fit the width of the fabric and deep enough for you to work across (see page 16). Most upholstery or soft furnishings fabrics are up to 137cm (54 inches) wide.

Space requirements – You need to be able to lay out a pattern or cut out without moving the fabric; ensure that pattern templates don't overhang the edges. A large working space will make for more accurate marking and generally make your life easier (see page 16).

POSITIONING FABRIC

Orientation – Position the fabric with the selvedge (the woven edge of the fabric) running down the side. Check the orientation of the grain line when placing your pattern pieces before cutting out, so that the pile, pattern or weave is the correct way up. Fabrics with a nap, such as velvet, should be cut with the nap running down (parallel to the selvedge).

Weave – It is essential that the weave of the fabric is straight, both horizontally and vertically, before marking or cutting out to ensure that any pattern or visible weave runs true. You can adjust this by gently stroking the fabric into place and, if necessary, using a large set square and metre ruler to check.

Secure the fabric – Use weights or clamps to hold the fabric in place, especially if you have a particularly long piece on a roll.

MARKING OUT

Face down – Nine times out of ten I always mark on the back of fabric because if I make a mistake it doesn't show. Lay the fabric right side down and mark around your pattern template. Weigh the pattern down using a clean fabric weight, or tinned food cans also work well.

Transferring measurements – Transfer any measurements for panels or cushion pieces on to the back of the fabric using a set square, a metre ruler and tailor's chalk or a pencil. There is one major rule in my workshop – no ballpoint pens allowed! Ballpoint pen is almost impossible to remove from fabric.

Fabric economy – Ensure you use the fabric as efficiently as possible. If you are using a plain fabric, use as much of the fabric as possible by positioning the pattern pieces close to each other (see page 41).

CUTTING FABRIC

Fabric scissors – Use a large pair of fabric scissors that are sharp, and kept sharp. Some upholsterers use smaller scissors for finer fabrics, like silks.

Cutting direction – Cut away from you, never towards you, keeping your hand or arm away from the scissors' direction and holding the fabric down behind the scissors as far away as possible from where you are cutting.

MAKING PATTERNS

Patterning up – This is the process of creating patterns, or templates, from existing pieces of fabric or from measurements to cut new fabric pieces for upholstery.

Paper or calico pattern – On a piece of paper or scrap of calico, mark out the desired size and shape of the finished cover to fit your chair, bench, sofa or armchair. This acts as a test piece before you cut into your real fabric.

Foam guide – If you made a template for foam, you can use this as a guide for the fabric but don't forget to oversize the fabric by at least 2cm (¾ inch) all the way around.

Labelling – Label the pattern with 'front edge', 'back edge' and any other useful information.

Marry marks – These marks are strategically planned and drawn within the seam allowances at the edges of the fabric, either directly on to the fabric piece or incorporated into the pattern piece. When the fabric pieces are sewn together, matching these marks ensures that the fabric is aligned correctly.

Reusing – When reupholstering, try to remove the top fabric in one piece so that you can reuse it as a pattern for the new cover. If you are using an existing cushion cover as your template, only use it as an exact guide if it's a perfect fit. I always add my own design tweaks and preferred shapes into my patterns.

Sustainability tips

Fabric planning (see page 41) is key to reducing waste (and cost) wherever possible, but here are a few more of my tips for greater sustainability in upholstery:

SAVE FABRIC OFFCUTS

I keep a box full of fabric offcuts in my workspace, which I save for those moments when I need just a small panel. This works especially well for FR calico, which is used in almost every upholstery project.

REUSE LARGE PANELS

If you have stripped back a large headboard, consider reusing the large fabric panel for a smaller project. The fabric may require laundering, but it will likely retain its quality and integrity.

GET CREATIVE WITH OLD CLOTHES

Use old cotton shirts or denim jeans for upholstery or soft furnishings. Patching pieces of salvaged fabric is a really fun way of repurposing textiles.

REUSE HORSEHAIR STUFFING

Providing it hasn't disintegrated too much, the horsehair stuffing from old upholstery can be reused. It should be washed and dried thoroughly, which is best done in the warmer summer months. Place the horsehair stuffing in an old pillow case, wash it in the bath and then hang it out to dry. Once it's almost dry, spread it out to completely finish drying. Tease the horsehair to make it usable again by separating and fluffing strands to restore their volume and springiness.

USE SUSTAINABLE FABRICS

Opt for fabrics made from sustainable materials such as organic cotton, linen or recycled fibres. These fabrics have a lower environmental impact and are often produced under more ethical conditions than some synthetic alternatives.

CHOOSE ECO-FRIENDLY FILLINGS

Consider using eco-friendly fillings such as natural latex, coconut fibre or recycled foam for cushioning. These materials are more sustainable than man-made alternatives and can often be more durable, too.

AVOID HARMFUL CHEMICALS

Use water-based adhesives and finishes that are free from harmful chemicals. These are better for the environment and for your health.

BUY LOCAL

Whenever possible, buy materials from local suppliers. This reduces the carbon footprint associated with shipping and supports your local businesses.

OPT FOR ENERGY-EFFICIENT TOOLS

Use energy-efficient tools and machines to reduce your energy consumption. Turn off equipment when it is not in use and consider using hand tools where feasible.

RECYCLE AND DISPOSE RESPONSIBLY

Recycle any materials that can't be reused and dispose of upholstery waste responsibly. Many communities have recycling programmes for textiles, foam and other upholstery materials.

By incorporating these sustainability tips into your upholstery projects, you can help reduce waste, conserve resources and create beautiful, environmentally friendly furniture.

2.
Upholstered furniture

Box seat cushion / hand sewn closed with piping / no zip

A box cushion can be used on the existing seat of a wooden chair or bench, either indoors or outdoors, or as part of an upholstered armchair or sofa. There is a further variation that can be made for a chair with a wooden seat and no existing cushioning, which has ties to hold it in place and an optional piped finish (see page 56).

There are a couple of ways to make box cushions, but I find this method the most reliable way to achieve a neat finish. The following instructions are for foam padding. For a wooden chair or bench seat cushion, I suggest a minimum foam depth of 7.5cm (3 inches). For sofa or armchair cushions, use a minimum foam depth of 12.5cm (5 inches). I have included plenty of tips and tricks that I have refined over the years, which all make for a perfectly plumptious cushion... and you know how I feel about plumptiousness!

Tools and materials

Paper or calico
Pencil
Ruler
Scissors (both paper and fabric)
Foam: 7.5–12.5cm (3–5 inches) deep
Foam saw or sharp bread knife
Upholstery contact adhesive
Polyester wadding (115g/4oz)
Upholstery stockinette (optional)
Top fabric of choice
Piping cord: the thickness depends on the piping foot on your sewing machine and the size it can fit; I suggest no thicker than 5mm (3⁄16 inch)
Dressmaking pins
Matching sewing thread
Sewing machine
Hand-sewing needles

Making the template

1. On a piece of paper or scrap of calico, mark out the desired size and shape of the finished cushion to fit your chair, bench, sofa or armchair.

2. Label the template with 'front edge', 'back edge' and any other information you may find useful.

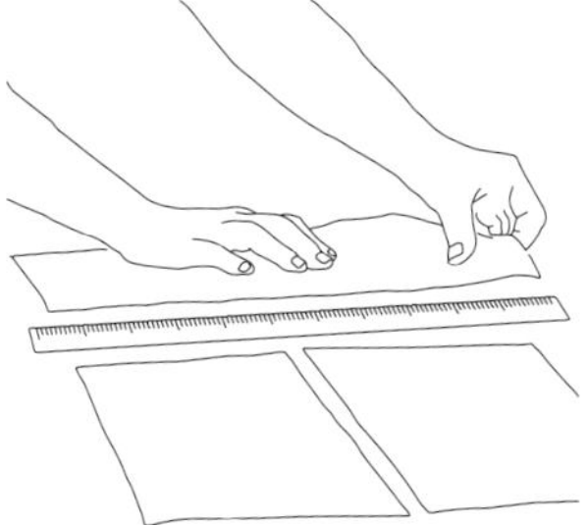

PRO TIP If you are using an existing cushion cover as your template, only use it as an exact guide if it's a perfect fit. If not, make any necessary adjustments to the size or shape to improve the cushion. Are the curves the right shape? Is the corner in the correct place? I never use existing covers as an exact template to work from, instead I use them only as a guide. I always add my own design tweaks and preferred shapes into my patterns.

Cutting out the foam

3. Make any necessary adjustments according to the fabric and foam padding you are using. I oversize the foam padding by 1cm (3⁄8 inch) all the way around to ensure the cushion cover is generously filled. The finished height of the foam determines the height of the cushion once sewn together. If I am using foam with a depth of 12.5cm (5 inches), then I make sure that my piped cushion will have a finished depth of 10cm (4 inches).

4. Using the adjusted template, cut out the foam padding with a foam saw or sharp bread knife. Consider asking the upholstery store to cut your foam padding for you if they have specialist tools. It can be tricky to achieve a neat finish when cutting through thick foam with a saw or blade.

Adding polyester wadding to the foam

5. Using an upholstery contact adhesive, glue a layer of polyester wadding to the base, top and sides of the cut foam. Do this by oversizing the wadding by 2–3cm (¾–1¼ inches), gluing it in place and trimming back to the foam or wadding layer if wadding has already been glued on to the foam.

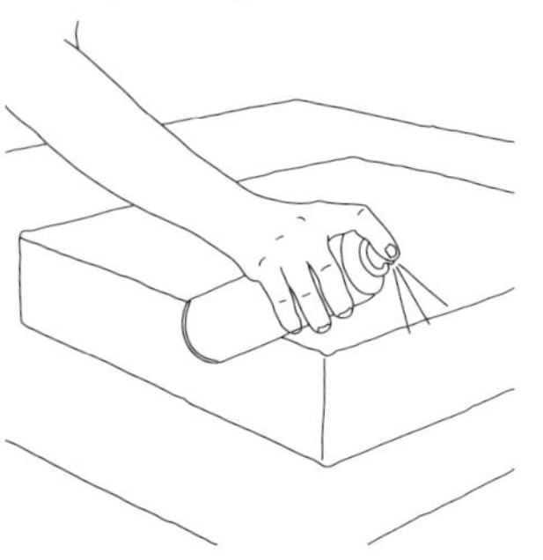

PRO TIP For a professional finish, add a layer of upholstery stockinette over the top of the wadding and foam. This elastic material stretches smoothly over the cushion, reducing friction inside the cover and preventing it from shifting out of place. To apply, lightly glue the stockinette along the sides of the cushion, avoiding the front and back edges. Trim away excess bulk to ensure a smooth finish. Secure the open ends by gluing them to the sides of the foam, taking care not to compress the polyester wadding. This will keep your cushion covers perfectly positioned and looking professional.

Cutting out the fabric

6. Prepare your fabric up to the same stage as though you are making a regular scatter cushion. For a neater finish, lightly press the fabric first. Then, lay the fabric face down on your workbench to mark on the back. Position your pattern on the fabric and use heavy objects to hold it in place.

7. If using a fabric with stretch, I recommend adjusting the template so the cut fabric pieces are slightly smaller to account for the stretch. To do this, take a length of fabric that is the approximate width of the template. Clamp or hold down the fabric at one edge and then gently pull it over the width of the template to see how much the fabric stretches. Measure the amount of fabric that stretches beyond the template with a ruler. Deduct this amount from the template size before cutting it. You can either include a seam allowance in your pattern or add it when marking the fabric. If you choose to include the seam allowance, add it to your new measurement before cutting.

8. Using the template, adjusted or not, cut out all the fabric pieces including the cushion top, cushion bottom, piping and borders. Make sure that you have added the seam allowance on each piece. To make the piping, see page 37 in Essential Techniques: Piping.

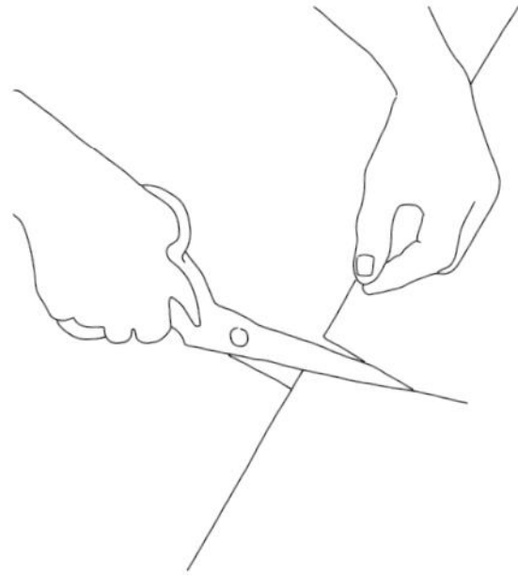

PRO TIP Depending on the perimeter of the cushion, you may need to sew two joins in the piping if your fabric is not wide enough to go all the way around the cushion. If you are using a plain fabric, cut the piping along the length rather than across the width so that you only need to make one join in the back corner. If this is not possible, then you will probably have to make one or two joins towards the back edges of the cover, one in each back corner.

Sewing the cushion cover

9. Add central marry marks to the wrong side of each cut fabric piece (see page 47). Using those marks, pin one long edge of the piping to the edge of the cushion face with right sides together and the raw edges aligned. If you are using a patterned fabric, pattern match the piping on the front of the cushion if necessary.

10. With the piping on top and starting approximately 5cm (2 inches) in from one back corner, machine stitch along the seam allowance to join the piping to the cushion top. Stop stitching at the next corner, leaving the needle down to hold the two layers of fabric in place. To help the piping wrap around corners easily as you sew it into place, cut into the seam allowance 3–4 times, spacing the cuts approximately 1cm (⅜ inch) apart. Whether you've cut your piping from the roll for sufficient length or on the bias, the starting position and technique remain the same.

11. To continue stitching along the next edge, turn the fabric 90 degrees and sew along the seam allowance, keeping the raw edges aligned.

12. Continue working in this way, stopping 5cm (2 inches) before the other back corner.

13. Pin the cushion base to the other edge of the piping with right sides together and raw edges aligned.

14. Stitch the piping and base together in the same way as you have just sewn the piping to the cushion top, easing the corners and opening up the seam allowance.

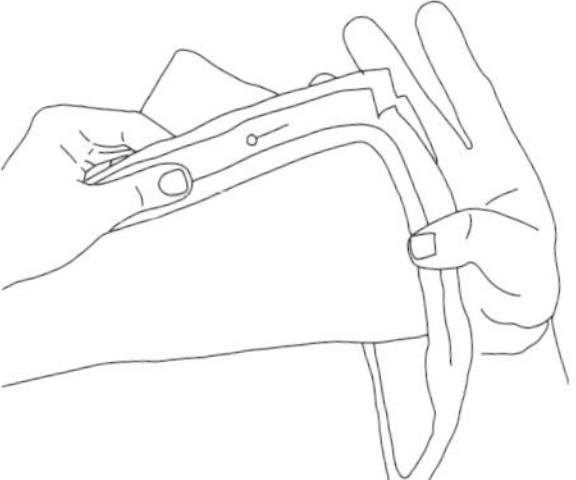

Attaching the borders and sewing the second face fabric

15. To attach the borders to the main panels, follow the instructions for steps 8–12 of the Box scatter cushion/with piping project on page 169.

Inserting the foam padding

16. Turn the cushion cover right side out and insert the foam padding into the cover. Ensure the foam fills each corner fully for a square shape.

PRO TIP Arrange the seam allowances over the piping of the cushion so they sit uniformly inside the cover, keeping the bulk away from the base or top. This gives the cushion a neat appearance.

Sewing up the cushion

17. Pin the turned-under edges of the opening in the cushion cover together along the cushion top, base and piping. Hand sew the opening closed using slip stitch (see page 35).

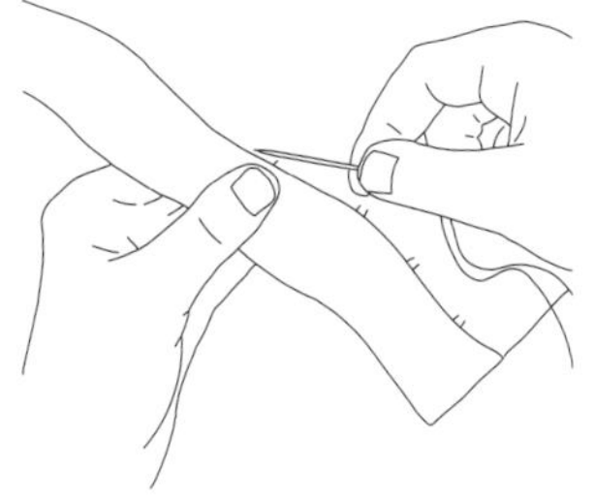

Box seat cushion / with ties for a dining chair

For a farmhouse-style seat with either a woven or wooden base, it is nice to have a soft box cushion filled with thick foam to sit on, rather than a thin scatter cushion. Additional ties are incorporated into the cushion cover so that the cushion does not slip off or move about too much when in use. With this project, I show you how to make a 5–7.5cm (2–3 inch) deep chair cushion, although you should adjust the height of the foam according to the existing height of the chair seat. For a high chair seat, use a 5cm (2 inch) foam, but if the chair seat is slightly lower, then you can afford to use a deeper 7.5cm (3 inch) foam. This will ensure the cushion height suits the chair's overall height and the person using it is comfortable.

Tools and materials

Paper or calico
Pencil
Ruler
Scissors (both paper and fabric)
Foam: 5–7.5cm (2–3 inches) deep
Foam saw or sharp bread knife
Upholstery contact adhesive
Polyester wadding (115g/4oz)
Upholstery stockinette (optional)
Top fabric of choice
Fabric for ties or ribbon (see Pro Tip, top of page 58)
Piping cord: the thickness depends on the piping foot on your sewing machine and the size it can fit; I suggest no thicker than 5mm (3⁄16 inch)
Dressmaking pins
Matching sewing thread
Sewing machine
Hand-sewing needles

Making the template

1. To make a template, follow the instructions for step 1 of the Box seat cushion/hand sewn closed with piping/no zip project on page 52.

2. Label the template with 'front edge', 'back edge' as necessary but also mark where the ties need to be sewn in order to match up to the uprights of the chair. Where the ties are best sewn into your cover is specific to the chair. For example, you could sew the ties into the corners of the border (see photo opposite), or you may need to position them further in from the corners so you can use the ties around the wooden upright rails of the backrest. If you opt for the latter, you need to choose whether to sew the ties to the top or bottom of the bordered edge. Be sure to make the ties long enough so that, if you were to flip the cushion on to its other side, the ties will still reach and tie securely.

Cutting out the foam

3. Make any adjustments to the template to account for the fabric and foam you are using, and then cut out the foam padding. Follow the instructions for steps 3 and 4 on page 52, but keep in mind the depth of the foam you are using and adjust the template accordingly.

Adding polyester wadding to the foam

4. To add the polyester wadding, follow the instructions for step 5 on page 54.

Cutting out the fabric

5. Prepare and cut out your main cushion cover fabric as instructed in steps 6–8 on page 54.

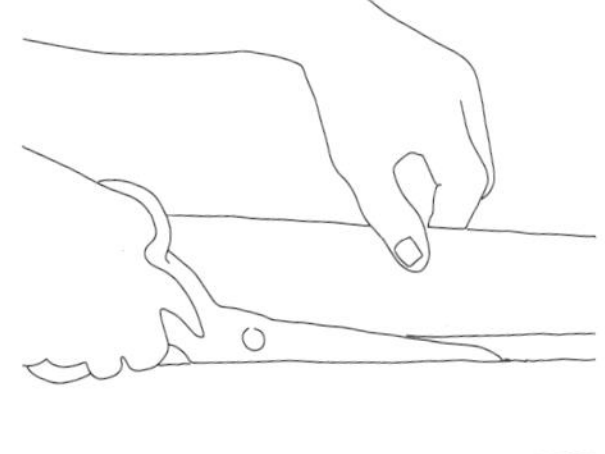

6. Next, cut out the fabric for the ties. Cut out two strips of fabric approximately 25–30cm (10–12 inches) long and 5–6cm (2–2½ inches) wide, depending on the weight of your fabric. Heavier fabrics might need narrower strips to make tying easier.

PRO TIP I prefer to make the ties out of the same fabric used for the main cushion cover, but you may want to use an alternative fabric or even a ribbon in a contrasting or complementary shade.

Sewing the cushion ties

7. Fold each tie in half lengthways, wrong sides together, press, then open out. Next, fold each long edge in to meet at the centre fold line and press again. At each end of the strip, fold the fabric in by 1cm (⅜ inch) and press. Fold the tie in half lengthways, pin and machine stitch together across the ends and all the way down the long, folded side of the ties, stitching 2-3mm (1/16-⅛ inch) in from the edge. (Folding the sides all the way to the centre will depend on the bulk of the fabric.)

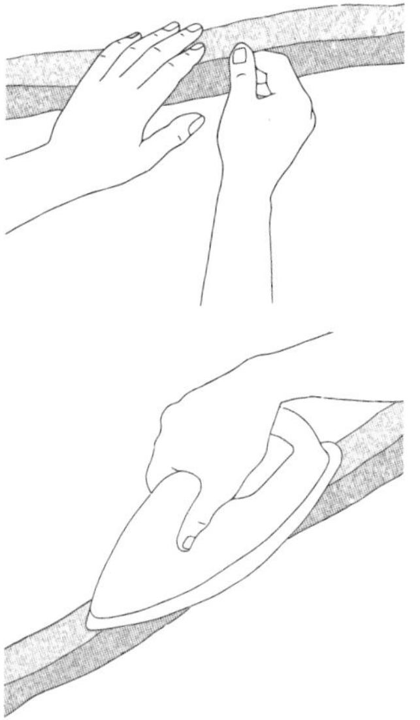

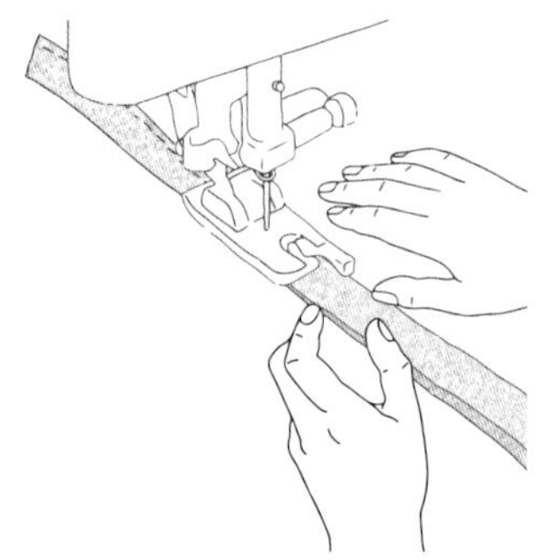

Sewing the cushion cover

8. Fold each tie in half to find the centre point (and create two 'legs'). Referring to the marks on your template, position the centre of each tie on the main cushion cover piece and pin it in place. If you are sewing your ties into the corners of the border because you are positioning the ties in a different place due to the frame, add them in when sewing the border. For the ties to sit well when the cushion cover is stuffed with the foam, it is best to sew the ties into the cushion cover once you apply the piping.

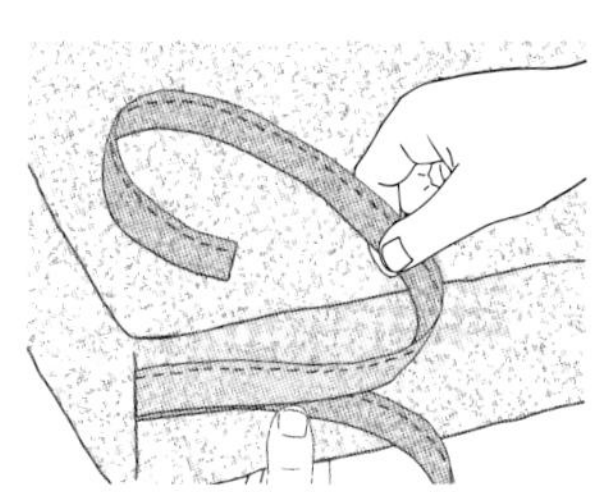

Attaching the borders

9. Sew the cushion together with the borders by following steps 8-12 of the Box scatter cushion/ with piping project on page 169.

Inserting the foam padding and sewing up the cushion

10. Fill the cushion cover with the foam padding and stitch it closed, following steps 16-17 on page 55.

PRO TIP For a thinner cushion without piping, you can follow these instructions to sew ties into the cover. Simply omit the piping and fill the cover with a hollow fibre cushion pad.

Shaped cushion / with ties for a dining chair

Sometimes, it's more convenient to make a thin seat cushion for a wooden based chair using a thin foam pad, rather than a thicker one that would require a border to be incorporated into the cushion cover. These thinner seat cushions are typically made with ties and are often for dining chairs or occasional chairs that are not used for extended periods of time. If you have this kind of chair in a bedroom, adding a seat pad can introduce a pop of colour and texture, even if it's not strictly for comfort.

To make this seat cushion, you will follow many of the same steps as for the Box seat cushion/with ties for a dining chair project on page 56. However, it's important to note that if you are using a very thick fabric, it's best to avoid piping the edges, as this can make the cushion too bulky inside, even if you do trim the bulk back.

Tools and materials

Paper or calico (large enough to overhang the size of the seat base)
Pencil
Ruler
Scissors (both paper and fabric)
Foam: 2.5cm (1 inch) deep firm seating-grade foam
Foam saw or sharp bread knife
Upholstery contact adhesive
Polyester wadding (55g/2oz)
Fabric for ties or ribbon (see Pro Tip, top of page 58)
Dressmaking pins
Top fabric of choice
Dressmaking pins
Matching sewing thread
Sewing machine
Hand-sewing needles
Piping cord: the thickness depends on the piping foot on your sewing machine and the size it can fit; I suggest no thicker than 5mm (3⁄16 inch)
5 or 6.5cm (2 or 2⅝ inch) small curved needle
Slip-stitching thread (or use the same thread as on the sewing machine)

Creating the template and cutting the foam

1. Follow steps 1–3 of the Box seat cushion/with ties for a dining chair project on page 56, using 2.5cm (1 inch) foam (no thicker). For this thin seat cushion, shape the foam edges to create a rounded softer edge, so you don't see the square edge beneath the fabric. To do this, lightly spray upholstery contact adhesive around the edge of the foam, wait 20 seconds for the glue to cure, then squeeze the edge on to itself, pinching it closed and rounding off the edge.

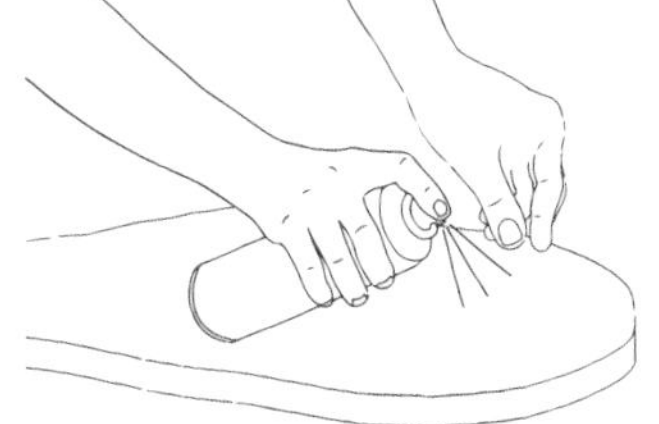

Adding the polyester wadding

2. To add the polyester wadding, lightly spray a layer of upholstery contact adhesive on to one side of the foam pad and press it on to the wadding. You don't need to spray the wadding itself. Repeat this process on the other side of the foam pad, then use scissors to trim the wadding back to the edge of the foam.

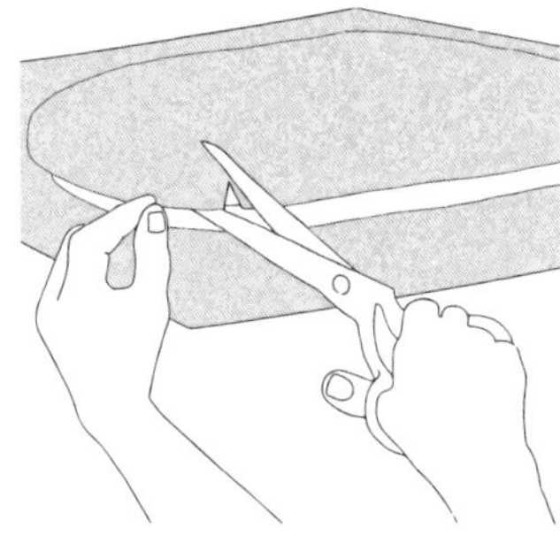

Cutting out the fabric

3. Once your foam is ready, follow steps 5–6 on page 56 to cut the fabric and ties (disregard anything relating to cutting border fabric as this cushion version does not include border panels). Cut V-shaped notches at the square corners and around the curved edges on both faces to achieve a neat shape when turned through. If you are opting for a piped finish, you will need to cut the piping fabric too (see page 37 in Essential Techniques: Piping).

Sewing the cushion ties and the cushion cover

4. Follow steps 7–8 on page 58 to sew the cushion ties. Once the ties are prepared, you'll be ready to sew the two faces of the seat cushion together.

PRO TIP If you have chosen a piped finish edge, then this is the stage where you will need to sew your piping around one of the cushion faces. To do this, follow steps 4–6 of the Scatter cushion/ machine sewn with piping/no zip project on pages 160 and 163.

5. Pin the two faces together, right side to right side, ensuring they are orientated correctly to one another by referencing your marry marks (see page 47). Referring to the marks on your template, position the centre of each tie on the main cushion cover piece and pin it in place. Position the pins 3–4cm (1¼–1½ inches) in from the edge so they do not get in the way of the sewing machine foot.

6. Machine stitch the two faces together just outside the ties. If you have a heavy-duty sewing machine, you can start inside the ties and sew over them. Sew around the cover, ensuring the two faces stay aligned edge to edge, and maintain a consistent stitched line along your seam allowance or along your piping stitched line.

7. When you reach the other side, either stop sewing just before the ties or sew over them, depending on how you started. Remember to leave a sufficient opening to insert the foam pad.

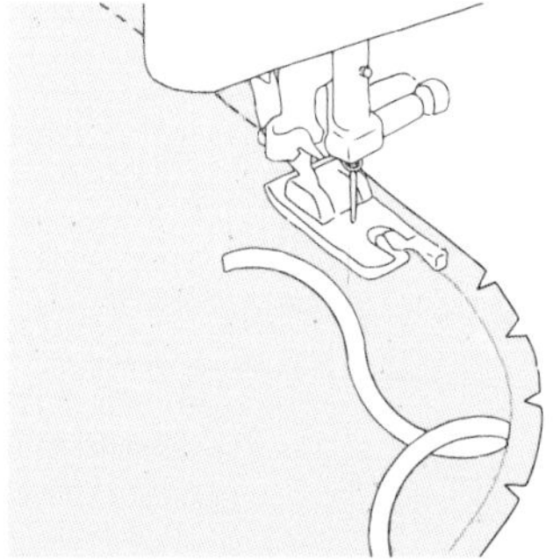

8. Turn the cover right side out, pressing the seams so that they lay flat.

Inserting the foam pad and closing up the opening

9. Stuff the foam into the cover carefully, smoothing the fabric over the foam to manipulate the cover into place. Make sure the bulk of the seam allowance is evenly distributed all around by using your hand from inside the cushion to adjust it to either the top or bottom side of the foam. This will help achieve a neater look and finish.

10. Once the cover is in place, fold the edges of the opening inwards along the seam allowance and pin together.

11. Use a curved needle and either slip-stitching twine or the thread from your sewing machine to slip stitch the cover closed (see page 35). If you are using the machine thread, double it up for added strength.

Once sewn, the cushion is ready to be placed on your chair and tied into place to enjoy!

Drop-in seat base for an occasional chair / modern technique

Nowadays, dining chairs frequently inhabit other spaces in the home and are put to alternative uses. They may be used as occasional chairs when extra seating is needed, but they may also be found in the bedroom, draped with clothes at the end of the day, or located in the hallway, as somewhere to perch while putting on shoes.

Tools and materials

Tack lifter
Mallet
Black-and-white webbing
Web stretcher
Scissors (both paper and fabric)
Pencil
Ruler
Hessian
Staple gun and staples
Foam: medium-density 2.5cm (1 inch) chip foam; seating-grade 2.5cm (1 inch) blue foam; 1.25cm (½ inch) foam (optional)
Foam saw or sharp bread knife
Upholstery contact adhesive
Polyester wadding (55g/2oz) (optional)
FR calico or Woolguard, for the base layer of fabric
Fabric of your choice, for the top of the seat pad
Fabric of your choice, for the underside of the seat pad (such as calico, hessian or Dipryl)
Regulator

Assessing the fit of the seat

1. First, check how tight the drop-in seat frame sits in the chair frame. Depending on how tight the fit, there are two options for finishing the foam. If there is a 3-4mm (⅛–³⁄₁₆ inch) gap between the drop-in seat frame and the chair frame, you can glue the foam so it covers the top of the seat base and carries over down the sides to the bottom edge. If the gap is smaller than this, you must glue the foam to the top edge of the frame with only 2-3mm (¹⁄₁₆–⅛ inch) down the sides. As you strip the chair back, look for any evidence of what was previously done on the old upholstery.

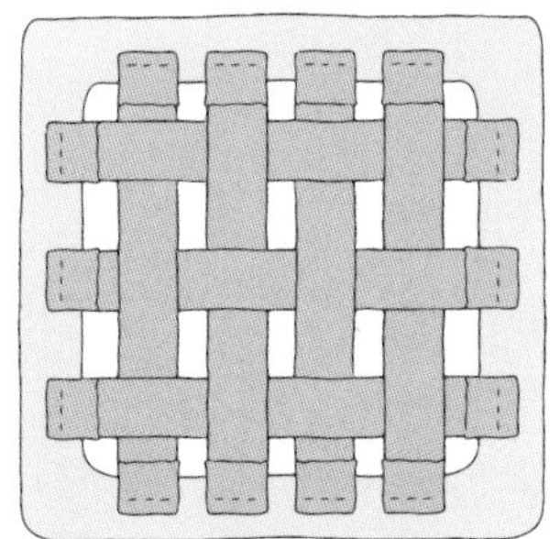

Stripping the chair and replacing the webbing

2. Following the instructions on pages 30 and 31 in Essential Techniques: Stripping Out and Webbing, strip out the existing upholstery from the chair and replace the webbing, if needed.

Covering the webbing with hessian

3. Cut a piece of hessian approximately 3cm (1¼ inches) larger than the drop-in seat base. A drop-in seat base frame often tapers at the back. You can either carefully measure the seat base frame and accurately transfer those measurements to the hessian before cutting out, or lay the seat frame on the hessian and draw around it as a template.

PRO TIP Make sure the weave of the hessian is lying as straight as possible so that you can use the lines of the weave as a reference point when securing the hessian to the frame. If the warp and weft threads are straight and in line with the front and back of the frame, it is easier to fold the edges down evenly and achieve equal tension.

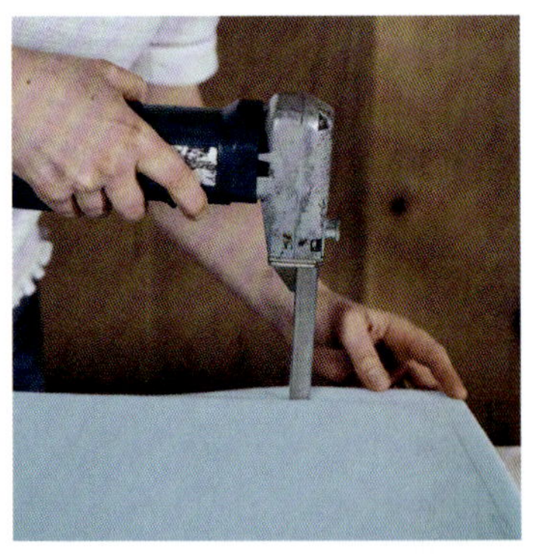

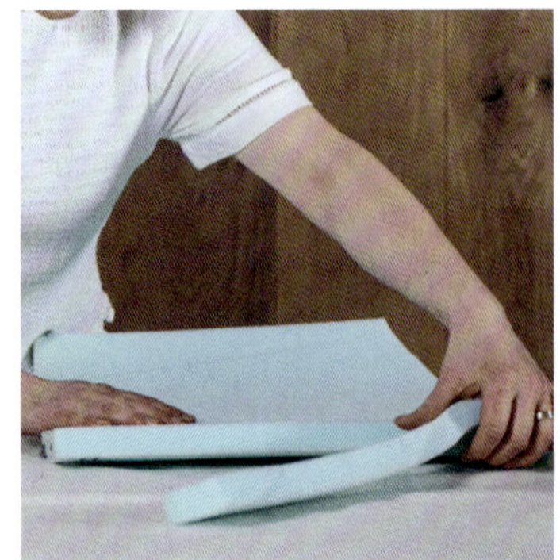

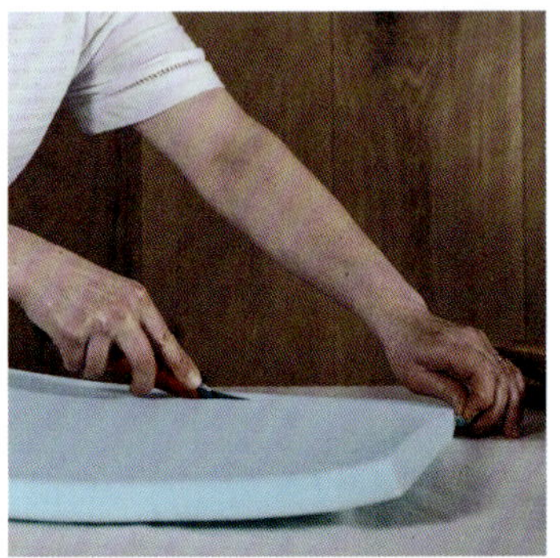

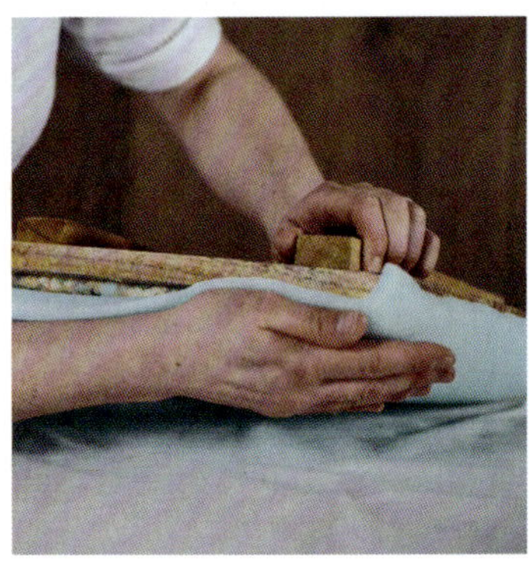

4. Starting with the back rail, secure the hessian to the frame. The edge of the hessian should sit just over the webbing line and not too close to the wooden frame edge. There are two ways to fix the hessian in place (for simplicity, follow Option 1):

Option 1: With the hessian evenly positioned over the frame and starting at the centre on each side, add a staple to hold the cloth in place. Working outwards to the corners and alternating between front edge, back edge and side edges, continue to add staples spaced approximately 3cm (1¼ inches) apart. Fold the hessian back over on to itself and add a staple in between each staple of the first round, then neatly fold the corners in on themselves and staple in place.

Option 2: Fold the top edge of the hessian back on to itself by 2–3cm (¾–1¼ inches) and secure it in place starting on the back rail with a line of staples, working from the centre out. Pull the hessian across to the front rail and, starting with the centre again, secure it with staples placed approximately 3cm (1¼ inches) apart. Fold the edge over and staple in between the first round of staples. Repeat this process on the sides, initially securing one side down already folded and then building tension on the other side to enable you to fold the edge over and staple it down.

Cutting out and fixing the foam

5. To create a comfortable seat base, layer up different densities of foam. The first layer is made up of a medium-density 2.5cm (1 inch) chip foam. Trace the outline of the drop-in seat on to the first layer of foam, and then measure and mark a line 5–7.5cm (2–3 inches) from the edge all around. This will be your chamfer cutting line.

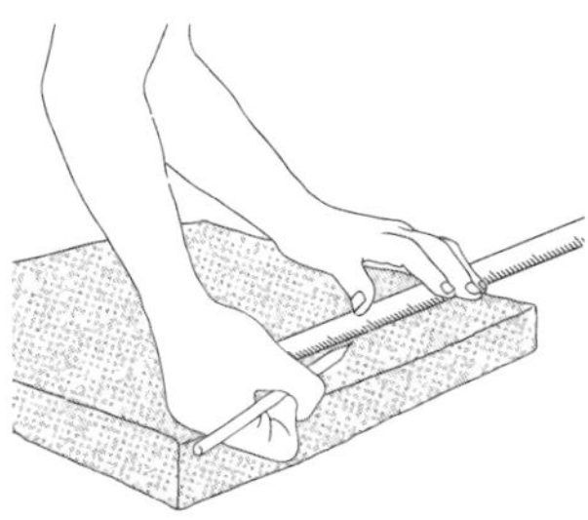

6. Following the marked outline, cut out the chip foam with a foam saw or sharp bread knife. Next, chamfer the edges of the foam by cutting back to the marked line that sits 5–7.5cm (2–3 inches) in from the edge at an angle to create a gentle slope. This will result in the removal of a long triangular section of foam, to create the chamfered edge.

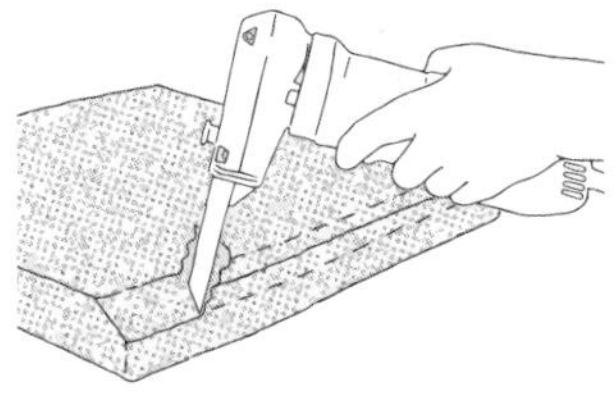

PRO TIP There a few different styles of layering up foam. Over time, you can experiment to achieve your preferred level of plumptiousness. You might try a shorter chamfer for a more squared edge, or add a small amount of wadding in the centre underneath the first layer of foam to create a more pronounced dome shape in the middle. Consider using a 1cm (⅜ inch) foam layer on top of the initial chip foam instead of a 3cm (1¼ inch) layer. As you gain experience and work on more furniture, you'll develop your own preferences.

7. Position the chip foam on the seat pad and stick it down using an upholstery contact adhesive.

8. The second layer is made up of a seating-grade 2.5cm (1 inch) blue foam. Depending on how tight the drop-in seat frame fits in the chair frame, this time the foam will either wrap over the sides of the frame towards the bottom edge or sit on the top edge of the frame. Once you have determined where the layer of foam should finish, measure and cut it to shape. Again, chamfer the edges of the foam, but this time by cutting back 2.5cm (1 inch) from the outer edge at a steeper angle than before.

PRO TIP If you are taking the foam over the sides of the frame and your seat base is 2.5cm (1 inch) deep, the chamfered edge will sit on the entire depth of the frame and the foam will fill the space without being too tight, which is perfect. If you are taking the foam to the top edge only, then the same distance chamfer works equally well.

9. Using upholstery contact adhesive, stick the second layer of foam to the frame and finish the edge accordingly.

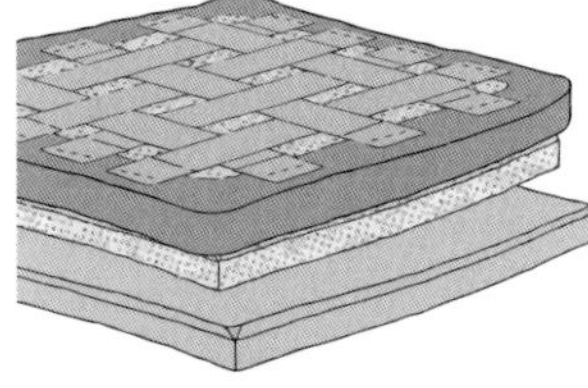

Cutting out and fixing the base layer of fabric

10. If you are using FR calico rather than Woolguard for your base layer, cut a piece of polyester wadding large enough to cover the seat top and just carry on over the top edges and down the sides. Place this centrally on top of the seat (there is no need to glue it into place). Now measure and cut out a piece of FR calico or Woolguard that is large enough to cover the top of the seat frame padding with the layers of foam you have applied.

11. Starting with the centre point of each side and applying a small amount of tension to keep the fabric taut, secure the base fabric with a temporary fixing on all four sides. Working outwards to the corners and, alternating between opposite sides, add more temporary fixings, stopping approximately 5–7.5cm (2–3 inches) in from the corners.

12. Once you are happy with the position of the fabric, secure it in place with permanent staples and remove the temporary fixings as you work.

Making box pleats at the corners

13. When you reach the corners, create box pleats. See page 36 in Essential Techniques: Box Pleats.

14. Temporary tack the edges on the bottom, positioning your staples towards the middle inside line of the frame and trim away the excess. Staple the fabric to the underside of the chair frame, ensuring it is securely attached to the seat. Position the staples closer to the inner edge of the wooden frame. This placement will ensure that, when you add the bottom cloth, the staples will be covered, as the bottom cloth will be stapled to the frame nearer to its outer edge.

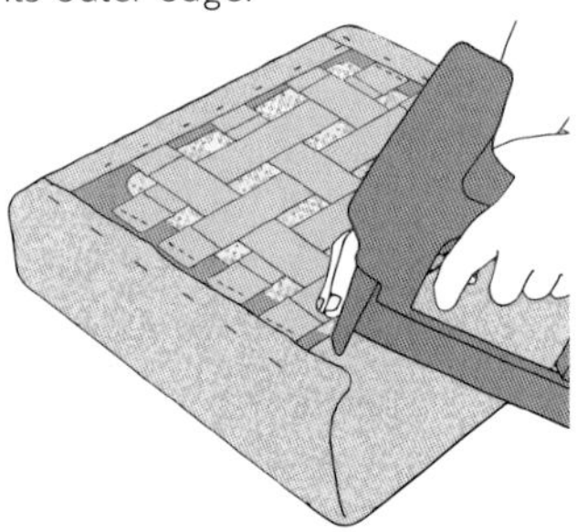

15. Drop the seat frame into the chair frame to check the fit. If you are using a heavy-weight fabric and the fit already feels tight, do not add any extra layers of padding. If the fit allows and you have used calico for the base layer of fabric, you could add an additional layer of polyester wadding. If you have used Woolguard for the base layer of fabric, extra padding is not necessary. If you are using a light-weight fabric and the fit is quite tight, you can still add a layer of polyester wadding but take it only to the top edge, rather than down the sides, of the seat frame.

Cutting out and fixing the top layer of fabric

16. If you are using a patterned fabric, position the pattern centrally on the seat pad. Cut out a piece of fabric that is approximately 4–5cm (1½–2 inches) larger all around than the seat pad frame to give you something to hold on to. Find and mark the centre points on each edge of the fabric, so that you can marry these up with the marks on the frame.

17. Position the fabric on the seat pad frame and temporary tack it in place, as you did for the base layer of fabric. The calico or Woolguard is holding everything in place, so the top layer of fabric does need to be tensioned, but not pulled too taut. Position the staples towards the inside edge of the underside of the frame to allow space for the bottom cloth to be attached.

18. Next, box pleat the corners as you did in step 13.

19. Once the fabric is well tensioned and in the correct position with neat box pleated corners, replace the temporary fixings with permanent staples, filling in the gaps, and trim away any excess fabric.

Cutting out and fixing the bottom cloth

20. Cut out a piece of either Dipryl, calico or hessian fabric that is approximately 2–3cm (¾–1¼ inches) larger all around than the seat pad frame. As before, find and mark the centre points on each edge of the fabric.

21. Working from the centre outwards to the corners, fold the edges of the fabric under to give a neat edge and staple the bottom cloth to the underside of the frame, leaving a 2–3cm (¾–1¼ inches) gap between staples and positioning the folded edge central to the rail.

22. Fold each corner under on both sides and secure with a staple for a neat finish.

23. Drop the reupholstered seat pad into the chair frame.

PRO TIP Some occasional chairs have a shaped wooden back, an oval wooden back or a square wooden back, while others have upholstered backs. To learn how to reupholster a chair back, see the Regular fixed back dining chair project on page 74.

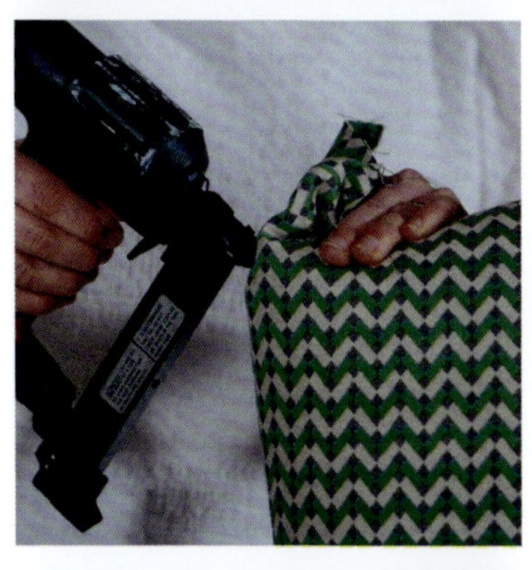

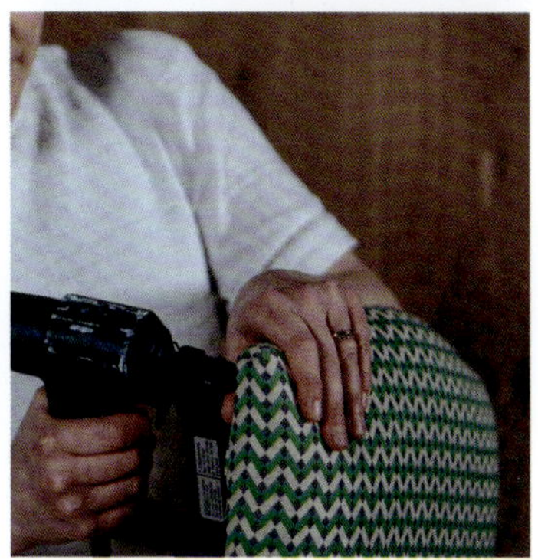

Drop-in seat base for an occasional chair / traditional technique

Building on the skills you have learnt from the modern method of reupholstering a drop-in seat base (see page 62), I am now going to walk you through the traditional technique. With this style of upholstery, you have the option to use a hammer and tacks as the more traditional tool and fixings. The use of horsehair stuffing adds durability and resilience, providing a firm yet comfortable seat that conforms to the body while retaining its shape over time.

Tools and materials

Tack lifter
Mallet
Black-and-white webbing
Web stretcher
Tacks: 16mm (⅝ inch) IMP (improved) tacks for the webbing, 13mm (½ inch) IMP tacks for the hessian, and 6mm (¼ inch) fine tacks for the calico
Magnetic upholstery hammer
Scissors (both paper and fabric)
Pencil
Ruler
Hessian
Upholstery twine/stitching cord
Curved upholstery needle
Horsehair stuffing
Cotton felt (optional)
FR calico
Soft tape measure
Regulator
Fabric of choice, for the top of the seat pad
Marking tool
Polyester wadding (55g/2oz) (optional)
Upholstery contact adhesive (optional)
Fabric of choice, for the underside of the seat pad (such as hessian or Dipryl)

Stripping out the chair, replacing the webbing and adding a base layer

1. Following the instructions on pages 30 and 31 in Essential Techniques: Stripping Out and Webbing, strip out the existing upholstery from the chair and replace the webbing, if needed. Note that in traditional upholstery you will be replacing the staples used in the modern upholstery project with tacks. Once the webbing is secure, cover it with a hessian base layer following steps 3 and 4 of the Drop-in seat base for an occasional chair/modern technique project on pages 62 and 64.

PRO TIP In traditional upholstery you do not add the foam layer. The sequence should be webbing > base layer of fabric (hessian) > horsehair stuffing > calico.

Creating bridle ties and adding the horsehair stuffing

2. Next you will create 'bridle ties' (see page 34) to hold the horsehair stuffing in place. First, mark the lines where you would like to stitch using chalk or a pencil to create a grid-like pattern as shown in the diagram on the right. Thread a large curved needle with approximately 45–75cm (18–30 inches) of upholstery twine or stitching cord. Secure your twine to the hessian with a slip knot (see page 35), 10cm (4 inches) in from the back corner of the seat.

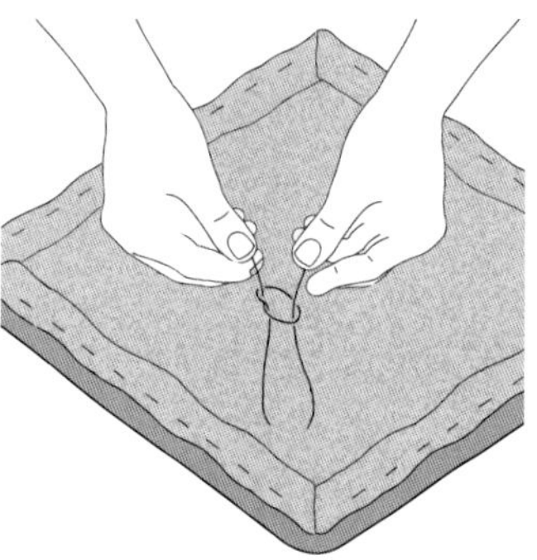

PRO TIP Estimate how much twine or cord you need to go all around the seat pad. You want to avoid running out too soon and having to stop and start again more than once.

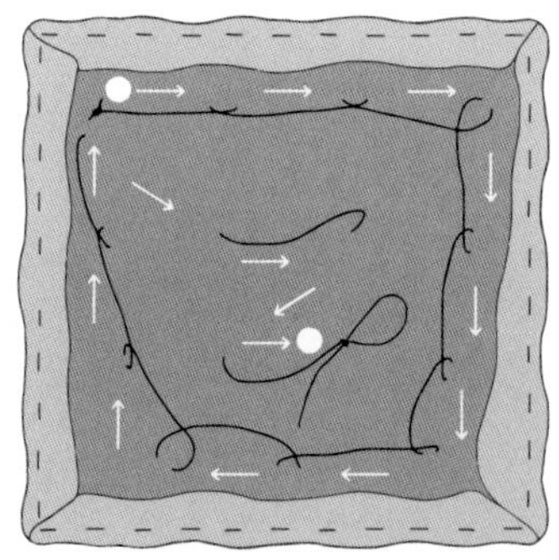

RAINER MARIA RILKE Selected Poems
VLADIMIR NABOKOV
Jean-Paul Sartre Nausea

3. From the knotted corner, you will sew around the frame and through the middle to add bridle ties between 2-3cm (¾-1¼ inches) high to hold the horsehair underneath. Position your needle about a hand's width away from the knot and stitch a small backstitch, leaving a loop about 3-4cm (1¼-1½ inches) long, into the hessian. Slip your hand under the larger loop to gauge how loose to leave it, ensuring there is enough space to stuff horsehair underneath. Continue this process, creating a series of small, evenly spaced stitches that form larger loops. Sew all the way around the frame and into the middle.

4. Now create a couple of stitches in the centre of the seat. If your thread doesn't reach this far, just tie on a new length to the hessian base layer. Some upholsterers leave the twine unknotted to allow for adjustment of the tension once the horsehair is stuffed within the ties. You may choose this method if you prefer.

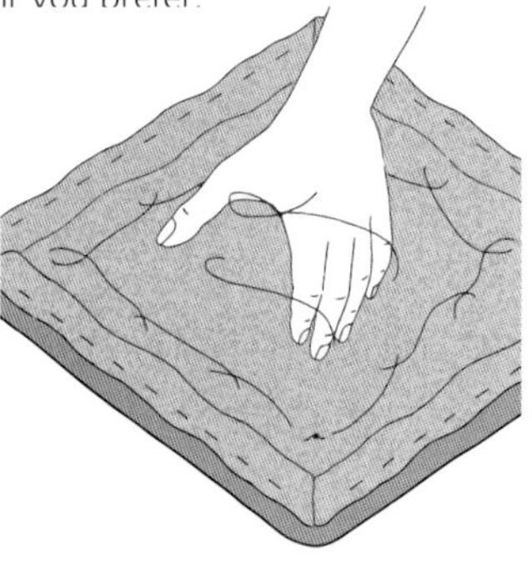

5. Check through the horsehair stuffing and extract any hard or lumpy bits. Take handfuls of the horsehair and, starting from the back corner, stuff it under the bridle ties. Being careful not to overstuff the back section of the seat, and leaving enough slack in the bridle ties at the front, continue stuffing the horsehair under the bridle ties. Keep checking to make sure you have an even distribution of stuffing over the seat, but also that you have a slightly more raised section in the centre of the seat pad for a domed shape. Bring the horsehair stuffing out to the edges, creating an even layer on all the side edges so that they do not feel too sharp. Use your regulator to 'tease' the horsehair, also known as 'regulating', to even out any lumps or higher sections. At this stage you have the option of adding a thin layer of cotton felt on top of the stuffing for additional softness. To do this, measure a piece of cotton felt that is 2-4cm (¾-1½ inches) larger than the seat pad, lay this on top of the horse hair and pull the edges back to sit flush with the edge of the seat, also known as teasing, thinning the thickness of the edge of the wadding so that it is not bulky.

Covering the stuffing with calico

6. Measure and cut out a piece of FR calico. Measure from the underside of the frame, up and over the padding, round and under the opposite side, adding 2.5-5cm (1-2 inches) to your measurements.

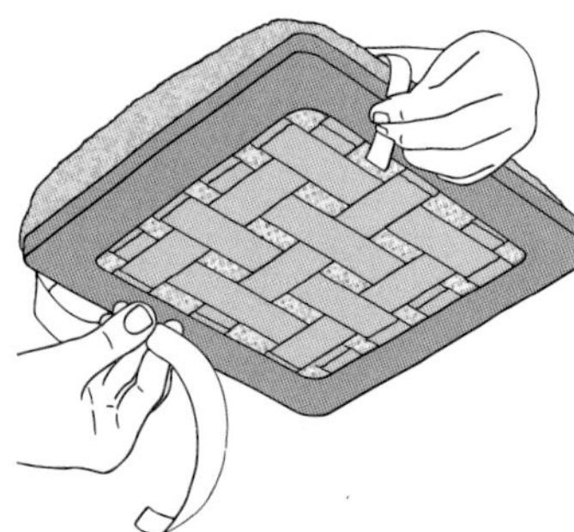

7. Starting at the centre of each edge and working outwards to the corners, temporary tack the calico to the side of the seat pad frame, applying a good level of tension to the fabric. Typically, this is done by positioning the seat frame under your free arm and using your hand to smooth out the fabric. You may want to add two or three tacks to the edge of the fabric as you will be applying a lot of tension and this will help to prevent the calico from ripping. Do not tack right up to the corners, instead stop 5–7.5cm (2–3 inches) before each one.

8. Once you have added temporary tacks on all four sides and to all corners, you need to apply further tension to the calico as you will not be able to get it tight enough the first time. Starting from the centre, smooth out the calico again, making it tighter, and reposition the temporary tacks. Repeat all the way around the frame.

9. Add more horsehair stuffing to any hollow areas and smooth out smaller lumps using a regulator to pierce the calico if needed.

10. Once the calico is tight and even along all four sides, hammer the tacks down.

11. Pull the calico tight over the corners, adding more horsehair stuffing if needed. Tack the corners down without folding the calico excessively.

12. Trim away any excess calico, trimming as close to the tacks as is possible.

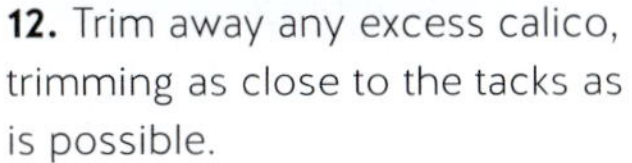

ALTERNATIVE TECHNIQUE FOR FIXING THE CALICO

While the instructions for this project reflect a more traditional school of thought, you can also attach the calico to the underneath of the frame in the same way you will with the top fabric. You may opt for this alternative technique if you have ample space between the drop in and the seat frame it sits in – assess this gap before you make your decision. If you do opt for this approach, you should box pleat the corners as you would for the top fabric to create more bulk. It's key that, whether you are tacking off the calico on the side or underneath, you use 6mm (¼ inch) fine tacks. This is especially important if tacking off on the sides as you do not want to risk splitting the wood.

Covering the seat with fabric

13. Find the centre of the rails on all four sides and mark the centre points using a pencil.

14. Using a soft tape measure, measure the seat to calculate the size needed for the top fabric. The top fabric will be tacked off on the underside, rather than the sides, so leave enough fabric (approximately 7.5–8cm/3–3¼ inches) to reach the underside and allow you to hold on to it adequately.

15. Fold the fabric in half both widthways and lengthways to find the centre and mark the centre point using a pencil.

16. You have the option to cut a piece of polyester wadding large enough to cover the seat top and just carry on over the top edges and down the sides. Check the fit of the seat pad in the chair frame: if it is already tight, cut the

wadding back so that it sits on top of the padding only and does not continue down the sides. If you're concerned about it shifting while you work on the seat, you can apply a light spray of upholstery contact adhesive to the top of the seat pad and press it into place.

17. Position the top fabric evenly over the seat base, matching up the central marry marks (see page 47). Temporary tack the fabric in place on all four sides as you did for the calico layer, but this time on the underside of the frame.

18. Re-tension the top fabric as necessary to ensure the weave of the fabric is sitting straight and is not wavy.

PRO TIP If the top fabric looks wavy, the fabric may have been pulled too tight in a particular area. If this is the case, release the fixing, smooth the fabric to re-tension it and replace the fixing.

19. Once you are happy with the tension of the top fabric, hammer down the tacks to make them permanent fixings.

Making box pleats at the corners

20. Take the side section of top fabric and fold it over to the front edge of the frame and fix it with a 6mm (¼ inch) tack. You will find that the fabric at the corner wants to fold over itself - encourage this to test the fold. Testing the pleat tells you whether or not you need to trim away any of the bulk from the fabric. To do this, open up the fold, then trim away the excess from inside the fold and inside the fixed point on the frame by cutting out a small V-shape (see the following Pro Tip). Fold the fabric back down, neatening up the fold, and fix the fabric to the bottom of the frame.

PRO TIP Start by cutting away a very small 'V' to test the fold, then continue to trim away a little more of the bulk in stages as needed. You can always trim more fabric away, but you cannot add it back on.

21. Fold the top section of the fabric (where you may have trimmed away the bulk) and fix it to the underside of the frame.

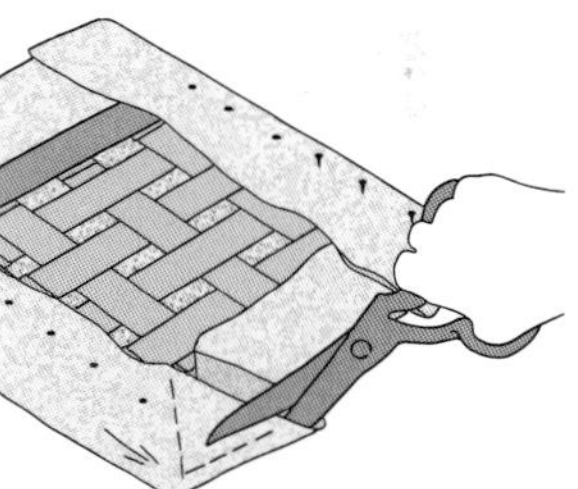

22. You may need to dress the fold using a regulator. To do this, use the pointed end and, applying some pressure, run the point up into the corner to neaten the fold.

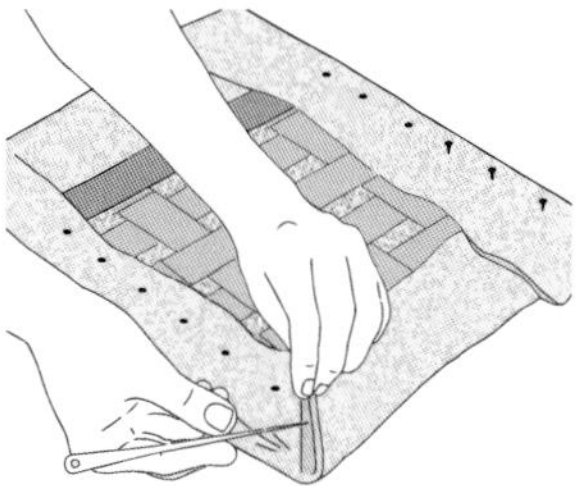

23. Repeat the box pleat at all four corners. See page 36 in Essential Techniques: Box Pleats, for more detail.

Cutting out and fixing the bottom cloth

24. Follow steps 20–23 of the Drop-in seat base for an occasional chair/modern technique project on page 67 to prepare and attach the bottom cloth to the underside of the seat pad.

Rectangular fixed back dining chair

Some styles of dining chair have square or rectangular backs and some have oval backs. The techniques are very similar but there are some key differences in the finishing.

For this project, we'll focus on upholstering just the back section of a dining chair with a rectangular back, using an individually studded finish as an example. These instructions cover both traditional and modern styles of upholstery and include finishing on the top, outside edges and bottom front of the frame. To upholster the fixed seat base, see pages 62–73 for either a modern or traditional method.

Tools and materials
Fabric scissors
Soft tape measure
Top fabric of choice
Staple gun and staples
Polyester wadding (55g/2oz)
Jute webbing (optional)
Hessian (optional)
Foam: medium-density 2.5cm (1 inch) foam
Foam saw or sharp bread knife
Upholstery contact adhesive
Regulator
Stud hammer
Dome-headed studs
Staple lifter

Attaching the top fabric without support

1. Cut a piece of your top fabric 2-3cm (¾–1¼ inches) larger than the opening of the back. This fabric will go on to the frame first, facing outwards and the rest of the upholstery is built on top of this.

2. Starting in the middle and working towards the corners, building a small amount of tension into the fabric, temporarily staple the piece of fabric in place, positioning the staples centrally to the rails and then 3–4cm (1¼–1½ inches) apart, working towards the corners.

3. Check that the weave is straight and the tension is even across this panel, then replace the temporary staples with permanent ones.

4. Trim the excess fabric back to the staples and position a layer of polyester wadding over the top of the fabric.

Adding support

5. Tall seat backs may benefit from extra support, compared to shorter backs. For backs taller than 20cm (8 inches) I suggest adding one or two vertical rows of jute webbing positioned evenly across the back. Add these as described on page 31 of Essential Techniques: Webbing.

6. If not adding webbing, staple a layer of hessian over the top of a polyester wadding layer, fixing it either centrally to the rail or slightly closer to the outside edge, close to the line of staples used to fix the first piece of fabric in place. Start with the centres and work your way to the corners in the same way you did for the fabric in step 2.

Preparing the foam

7. Measure the size of the back on the front edges (not taking the foam over the edge) and cut a piece of 2.5cm (1 inch) thick foam accordingly.

8. Mark a 2.5cm (1 inch) chamfer on the foam (see step 6 of the Drop-in seat base for an occasional chair/modern technique project on page 65) and cut this using a foam saw or sharp bread knife.

9. Glue the foam on to the back using upholstery contact adhesive, securing the chamfer to the front edge of the frame.

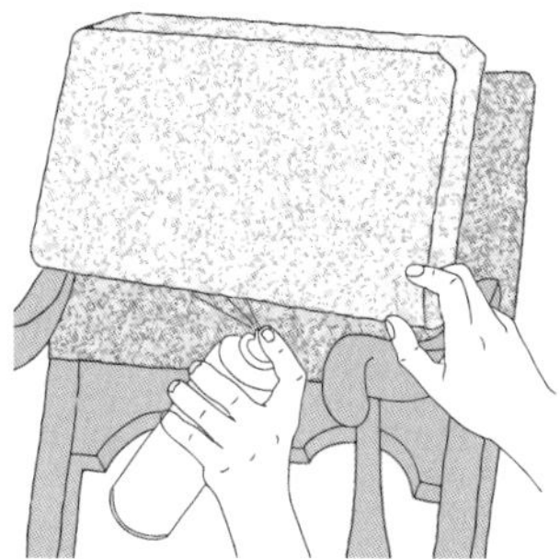

10. Cover the foam with a layer of polyester wadding and trim it to match the edge of the foam.

Adding the top fabric layer

11. Measure the frame to the outside back edge of the top, sides and to the bottom inside edge of the back. Cut your top fabric 2cm (¾ inch) larger than these measurements.

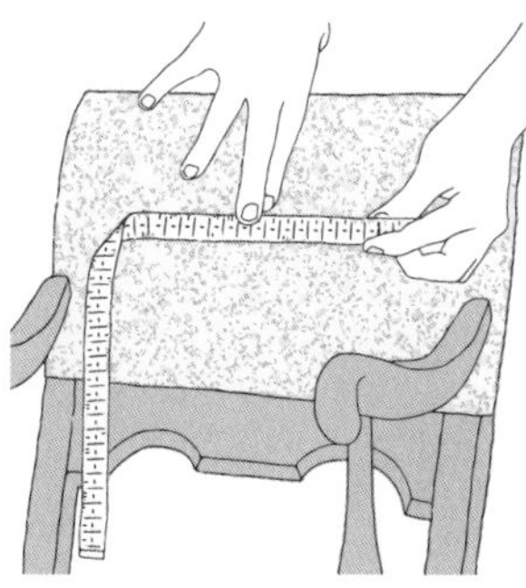

12. Position your chair on its back with the chair legs facing away from you so that you have the back closest to you. Starting with the bottom inside front edge, turn your fabric under and secure it with temporary staples spaced approximately 2cm (¾ inch) apart.

13. Set the chair upright and pull the fabric up towards the top of the back, folding it under and securing it along the top edge, in line with the back edge of the wood, with temporary staples spaced 2cm (¾ inch) apart. Work towards the corners stapling 3–4cm (1¼–1½ inches) away from the corners. If the fabric stretches too much and gives you too much fabric to fold under easily then cut away some of the excess until it feels manageable to work with.

14. Repeat the process for the sides, working towards the top and bottom. For the bottom side, fold the fabric over on to itself to create a crisp square corner.

15. For the top corners the technique is similar to steps 20–23 of the Drop-in seat base for an occasional chair/modern technique project on page 67 except that, instead of tacking the fabric underneath the frame, you fold the edge under to give a neat finish and then tack it off ready for studding (see photo, page 75). Use the sharp tip of a regulator to manipulate the fabric into the fold, ensuring the fold sits on the top of the chair. The side fabric folds up and is tacked off on the top corner and the top part of the fabric folds over this once the bulk is cut out. Use the regulator to help position the fabric with tension to enable you to staple it down and create a square finish.

Adding studs

16. Using a stud hammer with a nylon tip, start studding the top edge, removing the temporary staples as you go. Begin at one end and work towards the other, being sure to keep an eye on the spacing so that you end up with a whole stud positioned at the end without any gap or overhang.

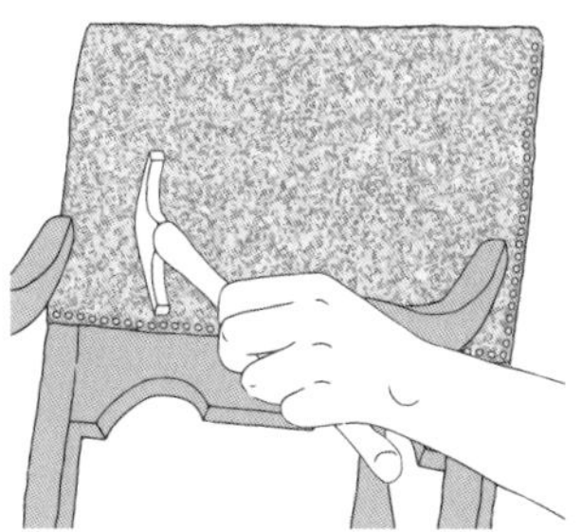

17. Repeat this process down the sides and along the bottom front edge of your chair back.

Fixed seat base for a dining chair / modern technique

There are two types of finish for a fixed seat base. One style, shown here, is where the fabric wraps over to the underside and the other style, on pages 84–85, is where the edge of the fabric sits on the visible side edges, usually above a decorative 'show wood' wooden trim, and is finished with an individual stud or braid finish.

Tools and materials

Tack lifter
Mallet
Scissors (both paper and fabric)
Black-and-white webbing
Web stretcher
Staple gun and staples
Hessian
Foam: medium-density 2.5cm (1 inch) chip foam, seating-grade 2.5cm (1 inch) blue foam, 12mm (½ inch) foam (optional)
Foam saw or sharp bread knife
Upholstery contact adhesive
Soft tape measure
Pencil or chinagraph pencil
Ruler
Polyester wadding (55g/2oz or 115g/4oz) or Woolguard
FR calico (optional)
Regulator
Top fabric of choice
Hot melt glue gun
Braid (see third Pro Tip, page 82)
Dressmaking pins
Bottom cloth

Stripping out the chair and replacing the webbing

1. Following the instructions on pages 30 and 31 in Essential Techniques: Stripping Out and Webbing, strip out the existing upholstery from the chair and replace the webbing, if needed.

Covering the webbing with hessian

2. Follow the instructions in steps 3 and 4 of the Drop-in seat base for an occasional chair/modern technique project on pages 62 and 64, to cover the webbing with hessian.

Cutting out and fixing the foam

3. To create a comfortable seat base, I like to layer up different densities of foam. The first layer is made up of 2.5cm (1 inch) chip foam. Trace the outline of the drop-in seat on to this first layer of foam.

4. Cut out the chip foam with a foam saw or sharp bread knife. Next, chamfer the edges of the foam by marking approximately 3-4cm (1¼-1½ inches) back from the outer edge and cutting along that line at an angle down to the bottom edge to create a gentle slope (see also step 6, page 65). This will give a dome-shaped look to your seat as well as adding extra comfort.

5. Position the chip foam on the seat, chamfer cut facing down, and secure using upholstery contact adhesive.

6. The second layer is made up of a seating-grade 2.5cm (1 inch) blue foam. Measure and cut the foam to the size of the top edge, but add an extra 5mm (³⁄₁₆ inch) that overhangs the seat frame. This will give a soft edge to the seat. Again, chamfer the edge of this piece of foam, cutting 3-4cm (1¼-1½ inches) back.

7. Using upholstery contact adhesive, first apply an even coat of glue to the top of the first layer of chip foam. Then, spray the surface of the second layer that will come into contact with the chip foam. Once both surfaces are coated, carefully position the top layer of foam on to the chip foam, ensuring it is aligned evenly all around. Apply pressure across the

entire top layer to ensure it adheres properly. If there is any overhang, gently roll down the edges to fit.

PRO TIP You might consider adding an extra layer of foam, either 12mm (½ inch) or 2.5cm (1 inch) thick, between the layers of chip foam and the blue foam top layer. Experiment with these different thicknesses to determine which provides the look and feel you prefer. Cut this additional piece slightly larger than the chip foam, by about 5–10mm (3⁄16–⅜ inch), to ensure a good fit. Ultimately, this is a matter of personal preference - whether you want a slightly softer seat or a more domed appearance.

8. Position a piece of polyester wadding or Woolguard over the top of the foam, making sure there is sufficient to hang down the sides of the frame. Use contact adhesive to just glue the top centre section of this layer as you only need to keep it in place while you work on the top fabric. Spraying such a small patch also mitigates any risk of over-spraying on to the frame of the chair. If you have used polyester wadding rather than Woolguard, add a layer of FR calico to cover the wadding.

Cutting out and fixing the base layer of fabric

9. If you have used polyester wadding, measure a piece of FR calico that is large enough to cover the seat. Note that the calico will be attached to the side edge of the frame above the visible wood, not underneath. Using a soft tape measure, measure up and over the frame, adding 2.5cm (1 inch) to both sides. Repeat front to back. Cut the calico to size, fold in half and mark the centre point on two of the edges, repeat this for the other two edges and you will have a centre mark on all four sides to reference.

If using Woolguard, hold the fabric in position on the front edge, above the show wood section, and mark a line approximately 1cm (⅜ inch) above the show wood. Trim the Woolguard along this line, then repeat for the remaining three sides. Cut the Woolguard around the shape of the backrest rails so that it sits flat.

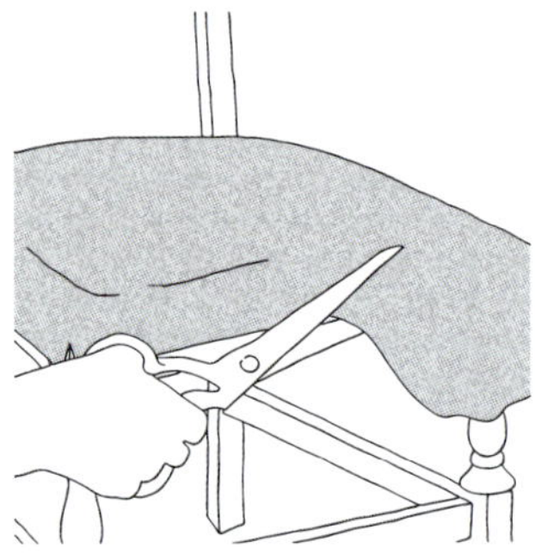

10. Measure the sides of the seat frame and mark the central points on the sides with a pencil. Ensure the marks are on a place that will be covered, and not on the show wood. Position the calico on top of the seat, aligning the marry marks with those on the seat edges.

PRO TIP The calico is used here to stop the top fabric rubbing on the foam or wadding, not to form the shape of the seat. I recommend treating the calico layer as if it were the top fabric. This means it should be applied with the same level of neatness, tidiness and even tension as the final fabric and should be securely fixed to the frame over the padding.

11. Starting at the centre point of each edge and working outwards toward the corners, fix the calico in place along all four sides with temporary fixings to the side of the chair frame and central to the height of the seat rail, leaving approximately 2.5cm (1 inch) gaps between each temporary staple. Adjust the tension as needed, smoothing out the calico over the foam by hand as you work along the edges, using the weave of the fabric to gauge the evenness of the tension (see Pro Tip, below). Reposition the temporary tacks as required. Continue this process along all four edges, leaving a 5–7.5cm (2–3 inch) gap from each corner. Once you are satisfied with the tension and position of everything overall, replace the temporary fixings with final fixings.

PRO TIP To gauge the evenness of the fabric tension, check if it looks wavy. If so, the fabric may be pulled too tight in a particular area. If this is the case, release the fixing, smooth the fabric to re-tension it and replace the fixing.

Making box pleats at the front corners (calico layer)

12. For the front corners, you will need a pencil, scissors and a staple gun. This stage can be tricky, so I'll break it down into simple steps. Trim the edge of the fabric to follow the staple line, stopping at the corners. This leaves a flap of fabric that you can bring to the front of the rail. Create the pleat by folding the side section of calico round to the front edge of the frame. Staple it 4–6mm (3⁄16–¼ inch) in from the edge. Now fold the flap of fabric under itself to create a neat pleat. Test the pleat; it should sit flat with the fold vertically aligned with the side of the frame. Make sure that the fabric inside the fold is smooth (use a regulator to ease it flat, see step 19), and staple it in place just above the show wood on the front edge. Repeat this process on the opposite front corner.

Addressing the back corners (calico layer)

13. Since you haven't stapled the fabric all the way to the back leg corners, there's a gap that allows you to fold the fabric back on to itself. Flatten the fold as much as possible. If needed, remove a couple of temporary staples to gain more fabric to work with. Use a pencil to mark a 45-degree angle from the inside corner of the back to the edge of the calico. Make this mark on the back of the fabric, which will not be visible when folded back. Cut along this line towards the upright rail, taking care not to cut too far. Cut little by little, checking by pulling the fabric through to the back and side to assess. The cut should be discreet enough to hide between the padding and the upright.

Finishing the back corners (calico layer)

14. Fold the excess triangular section under itself so that the folded edge sits neatly where the side rail meets the back upright. Pull the fabric taut and staple it on to the side rail where other staples are placed. Repeat on the back edge and the other side. Trim any remaining excess fabric as close to the staples as possible.

Cutting out and fixing the top layer of fabric

15. To cut your top fabric repeat the measuring, cutting and marking stages as you did with the calico base layer. If you are using a patterned fabric, make sure to position the cuts so that the pattern appears where you want it on the chair. For geometric patterns, ensure the design is evenly aligned on the chair.

16. Repeat the same process of temporarily fixing the fabric to the frame as you did for the calico, this time placing your fixings inside from the centre of the underside of the rail, covering the calico fixings and leaving 6–8cm (2½–3¼ inches) from the corners.

PRO TIP Check THRICE, not twice! As a general rule, I check everything three times to avoid making mistakes. It's free and quick to check measurements one more time, while the cost and inconvenience of ruined materials and time wasted is not!

17. Before securing the top fabric with final staples, triple-check that the tension and positioning are just right. If needed, remove the temporary staples, make adjustments and then replace them with properly fixed staples. If you're still unsure, recheck and adjust as necessary before committing to the final staples. Secure the fabric with final tacks all the way around the edge in the same way as you did with the calico. Work up to the corners and the back legs, leaving a 3–5cm (1¼–2 inch) gap so that you can work the fabric around the corner and back after properly securing the sides. If you intend to use studs to finish the edge, refer to the Stud finish instructions on page 85 first before continuing.

PRO TIP Some upholsterers prefer to fold the edge of the fabric under before stapling, which can be more challenging and is not recommended for beginners. You might need to add a second row of staples at the end to ensure the fabric stays securely in place before attaching the braid.

Finishing the front corners

18. There are usually two types of front corners to a chair:

Option 1: A decorative wooden raised corner to cut around.

Option 2: A straight edge finish.

The method for finishing the front corners is the same for both options, although with Option 1 you must cut into the fabric so that it sits around the raised wooden shapes on the corners. You do this by following the same technique as though you were cutting the fabric to sit around an arm for a carver or back leg (see steps 19–21 of the Carver chair project on page 91). For a straight edge finish, follow steps 12 and 13 up to marking the line on the corner of the chair where you will be cutting so that the fabric can be folded around the leg. Repeat for the other side. Once you have cut along the line, bring the fabric around to the front edge of the corner, fixing it into place with a staple. Make sure there is no puckering on the section of fabric that is wrapped around the corner of the frame. The fabric at the front of the corner will want to fold under itself – encourage this to test the fold, creating a box pleat. If you are using a thick fabric, you will be able to see whether there is too much bulk as this will be visible from the front of the folded fabric. If you have to cut the bulk out, use a pencil to mark on the inside of the fold and the inside of the stapled point, which will form a V-shape. Cut this away (see Pro Tip, below).

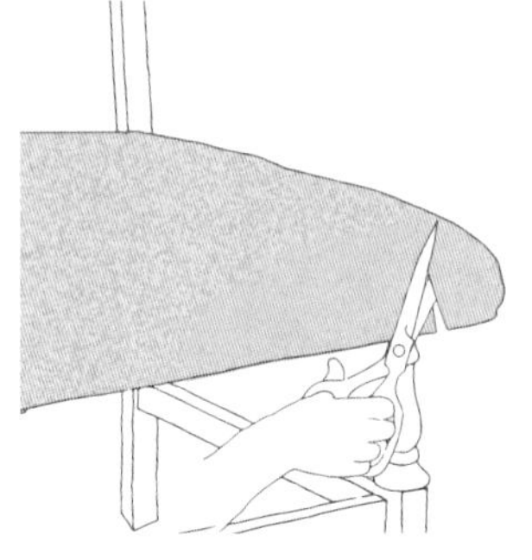

PRO TIP Start by cutting away a very small V-shape to test the fold, then continue to trim away a little more of the bulk in stages as needed. You can always trim more fabric away, but you cannot add it back on.

19. Fold the fabric under itself (where you may have trimmed away the bulk) forming a neat folded line 1–2mm (1/16 inch) in from the vertical line of the upright edge of the corner and staple down just above the show wood section. You may need to dress the fold using a regulator. To do this, use the pointed end and, applying some pressure, run the point up into the corner to neaten the fold.

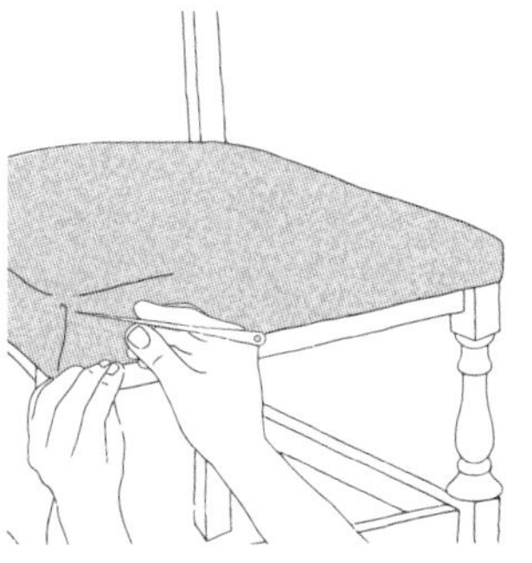

20. Repeat the box pleat for the opposite front corner and trim off the excess.

21. For the back corners repeat the same process as you did in step 14 with the calico, this time not necessarily cutting as far. You can tuck the excess down into the space between the foam and the back upright rails. You will still be able to fold the sides under to create a neat edge, staple down and cut away the excess.

Attaching the braid

22. Ensure the fabric is securely stapled. If needed, add an extra row of staples to prevent the fabric from pulling away. You are now ready to attach the braid finish.

PRO TIP There are a number of factors to consider when choosing a braid (or 'gimp trim'), and there are many different types to choose from. I recommend you opt for one that measures 1–3cm (3/8–1¼ inches) in height. Choose a pliable braid if you need it to sit around tight curves neatly. Go for an accent shade that will highlight a colour from your chosen fabric or a matching colour that will blend with it. If you are opting for an accent shade, ensure your braid is applied perfectly straight as any wobbles will be very obvious!

23. Using a hot melt glue gun and a regulator, attach the braid, beginning on one side of the seat base and working your way around the chair, leaving the back edge, which you will finish separately. Fold the end of the braid back on itself (wrong sides together) to form a clean edge. Fold about 3cm (1¼ inches) and then trim the braid to 1cm (⅜ inch) to prevent fraying.

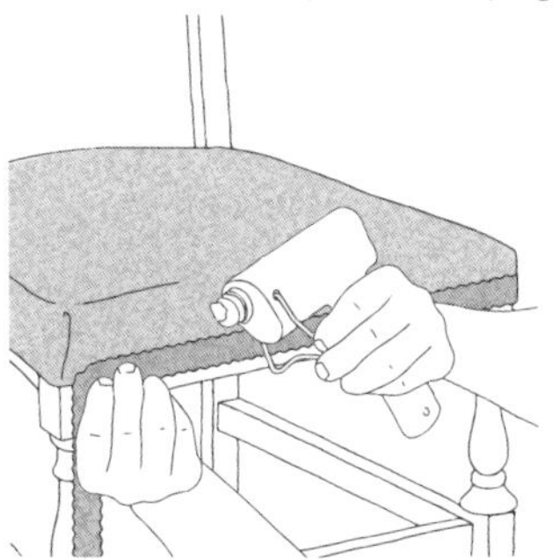

24. As well as being a decorative embellishment the braid acts as a cover for the line of staples on the chair. It is important to position the braid so that it totally covers the staples and hides the edge of the fabric that you have cut back. The braid sits above the show wood rail.

PRO TIP Less is more here. Use a small amount of glue to avoid excess seepage, which can be visible and difficult to remove. I prefer hot melt glue over liquid fabric glue as it prevents bleeding into the fabric.

---

25. Start by placing a small dot of glue on the folded end of the braid and attach it to the very back side edge where the base meets the back upright section. Press the end firmly for a few seconds to ensure a strong bond.

26. Apply a thin line of glue in 5–7cm (2–2¾ inch) increments along the centre of the braid. Gently pull and position the braid into place, pressing it on to the fabric. Check the bond by gently pulling back; if it holds, continue. If not, reapply the glue and adjust.

27. Continue gluing the braid around the chair until you reach the other side, leaving a gap of 5–7cm (2–2¾ inches) at the end before finishing.

28. Match the end of the braid and pin it to mark where it needs to be trimmed. Apply a small dot of glue to the marked area, fold the braid under (wrong sides together), and ensure the fold has enough glue to prevent fraying. If the braid has loops, ensure they are glued down securely.

29. Trim the folded and glued end to 1cm (⅜ inch) and attach it to the chair.

30. Repeat the process for the back edge, using a shorter distance for the braid application.

Cutting out and fixing the bottom cloth

31. Follow steps 20–23 of the Drop-in seat base for an occasional chair/modern technique project on page 67, which explain how to prepare and attach the bottom cloth to the underside of the seat.

Fixed seat base for a dining chair / alternative finish around legs

If your dining seat has a visible decorative wooden trim at the seat base, follow these instructions to upholster the seat in either a traditional or modern style. The principles are the same, but these key steps will ensure a professional finish.

Additional tools and materials
Braid
Hot melt glue gun or dressmaking pins, or a hand-sewing needle and matching sewing thread

Braid finish

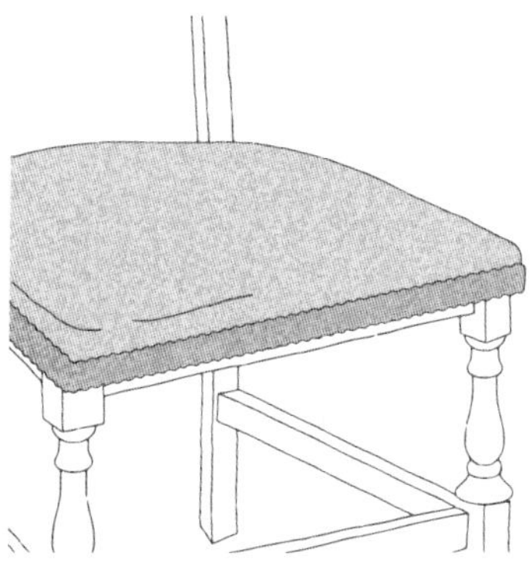

Fixing the base layer
1. When temporarily fixing and permanently fixing your calico or Woolguard into place, attach it to the side of the rails two-thirds up from where the decorative trim will sit instead of on the underside.

Fixing the top fabric
2. Temporarily fix the fabric to the edge of the decorative rail, then trim off the excess, leaving 1.5–2cm (⅝–¾ inch) of fabric. Starting from the centre front, remove the temporary fixings, turn the fabric under, and refix permanently into place. Work your way to the corners. You may find that you can turn the fabric under and create the box pleat at the corners simultaneously. If not, staple the corners down without folding the fabric under, then trim the excess as close to your fixings as possible.

Adding the braid
3. Once the fabric is fixed all around the chair, follow steps 22–30 of the Fixed seat base for a dining chair/modern technique project on pages 82–83. As you gain more experience you will notice that similar techniques for attaching the braid will apply to different projects yet you will adapt these techniques depending on the specific shapes and decorative carvings you have to work around.

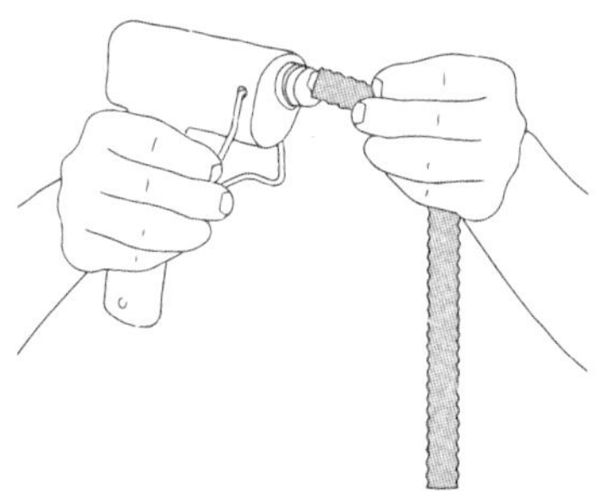

PRO TIP If your chair frame has curved sections, choose a braid that will bend to the shape without puckering. Test the braid out beforehand to make sure it is suitable before committing to it.

Additional tools and materials
Dome-headed studs
Stud hammer

Stud finish

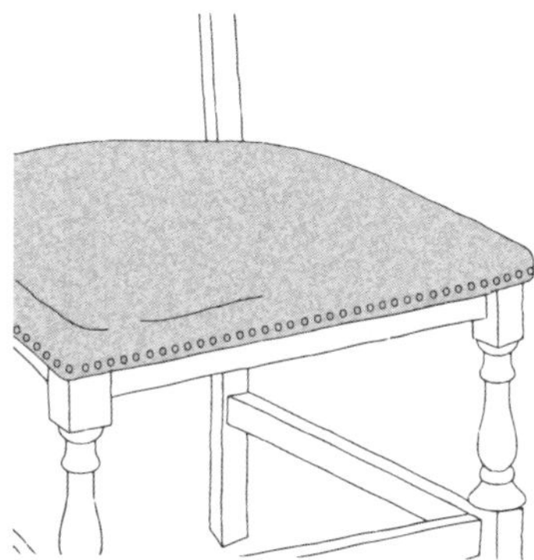

For this finish, fold the edge of the fabric under while fixing it in place. If you simply staple the fabric and trim it back, the frayed edges will be visible and poke out between the gaps of the dome-headed studs. By folding the edge, you ensure a neat appearance without frayed edges showing through.

Stapling the fabric

1. When you get to the stage of stapling off your fabric with permanent fixings, instead of stapling the fabric at the very bottom edge close to the show wood, bring the fixing position up by 2–3mm (1/16–1/8 inch). You could leave large gaps between the staples of 2.5–5cm (1–2 inches) because the studs will act as a fixing for the fabric once applied, reducing the chance of seeing the staples between the heads of the studs. Some upholsterers even remove the staples as they go, ensuring that no staples are at risk of being seen.

Hammering the studs

2. Using a stud hammer, hammer your studs in one by one. As the staples are 2–3mm (1/16–1/8 inch) higher, they should not be visible between the studs.

PRO TIP Before studding your actual chair, practice on a piece of scrap wood. There is a 1–2mm (1/16 inch) 'play' with the stud head, so if you hammer it into place and it's not touching the previous stud or the bottom edge, you can carefully knock the head over into place.

Spacing the studs

3. When you are around 6–7cm (2½–2¾ inches) away from reaching the end of a section, check if the studs will fit perfectly into the space left. You may need to space the remaining studs out slightly.

Carver chair

A carver chair, traditionally used at the head of the dining table, is distinguished by armrests that are jointed into the seat. The instructions below will help you to navigate upholstering around the uprights for the arms, which require careful attention to detail. Note that not all carver chairs have fixed seats, some may have drop-in seats and others may include an upholstered backrest, too.

Tools and materials

For the seat:

Tack lifter
Mallet
Scissors (both paper and fabric)
Black-and-white webbing
Web stretcher
Staple gun and staples
Hessian
Foam: medium-density 2.5cm (1 inch) chip foam, seating-grade 2.5cm (1 inch) blue foam, and 12mm (½ inch) foam (optional)
Foam saw, craft knife with retractable blade or sharp bread knife
Upholstery contact adhesive
Calico or paper for template (optional)
Soft tape measure
Pencil or chinagraph pencil
Ruler
Polyester wadding (55g/2oz)
Top fabric of choice
Regulator
Small curved hand-sewing needle (optional)
Matching sewing thread (optional)
Bottom cloth

For the upholstered backrest (optional):

Foam: back-quality 2.5cm (1 inch) blue foam

Stripping out the chair, replacing the webbing and covering the webbing with hessian

1. Follow the instructions on pages 30 and 31 in Essential Techniques: Stripping Out and Webbing, and page 34, Essential Techniques: Stuffing, to strip out the existing upholstery from the chair, replace the webbing, if needed, and cover the webbing with hessian.

Cutting out and fixing the foam

2. To create the first layer of foam padding, follow steps 3–5 of the Fixed seat base for a dining chair/ modern technique project on page 78, except for a carver seat you will need to cut the foam around the arm uprights following the traced outline of the seat base – use a craft knife with a sharp blade for cutting small shapes from the foam.

3. The second layer is made of 2.5cm (1 inch) blue foam. Measure from the front to the back and from one side of your chair seat to the other, taking the measurement from the bottom edge of the wood down the sides. Add 4cm (1½ inches) on all sides when transferring these measurements to your foam. You could also make a calico or paper template, if you prefer. Cut the foam following your markings.

4. Spray a 12.5cm (5 inch) square of upholstery contact adhesive in the centre of the seat on the chip foam and the centre of the blue foam. Once the glue has become tacky, carefully position the top layer of the foam on the chip foam. Apply pressure across the area to ensure it adheres properly (pull the foam up to test; you should feel some resistance).

5. Gently roll the corner of the foam that is not stuck down out towards the inside of the left-hand corner of the back upright. Once the foam has made contact with the inside corner, use a pencil to mark a line from the upright corner to the corner of foam in your hand. Cut along this line, stopping short of the corner to allow some extra padding to press up against the wood for a nice tight finish. Keep making small cuts to shape the foam around the upright, pushing the foam down either side of the wooden upright to see where it sits.

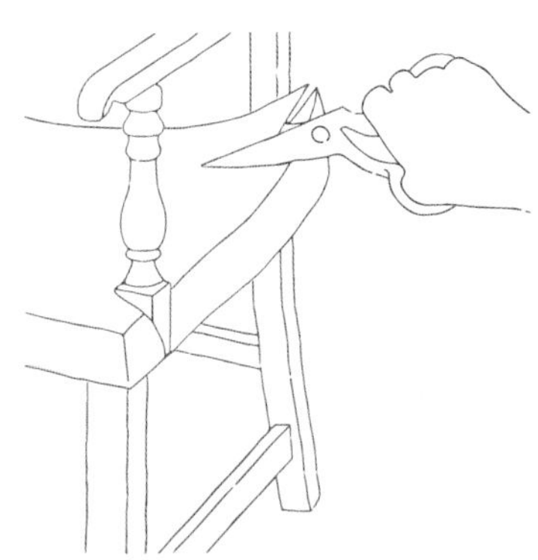

6. Once you are happy, spray the corner of the seat base and the underside of the foam layer with a light spray of adhesive and glue it down to the inside corner. Repeat on the right-hand side back corner. This will help to keep the foam in place while you work on cutting the foam to the right shape.

Shaping the foam around set-back uprights and the sides

7. If the joinery for the arms of your carver chair is flush to the front of the frame, then repeat steps 5 and 6 for the two front corners. However, the style of most carver chairs has the front uprights set back slightly and these need to be treated differently. Instead of approaching the corner at an angle, square the foam up to the inside edge of the wooden arm upright, pushing it against the woodwork.

8. Mark the middle of the upright on the foam and draw a straight line out towards the edge of the foam that runs parallel to the front edge of the chair. Make two diagonal marks from the inside corners of the upright to the straight line (to make a V-shape), connecting the lines to form a Y-shape. Cut along the straight line, using scissors, then make small cuts on the V-line, testing the tightness of the foam around the wooden upright with every cut. Only cut out the full V-shaped excess if necessary. Follow step 6 to glue the foam to the corner. Repeat for the opposite side.

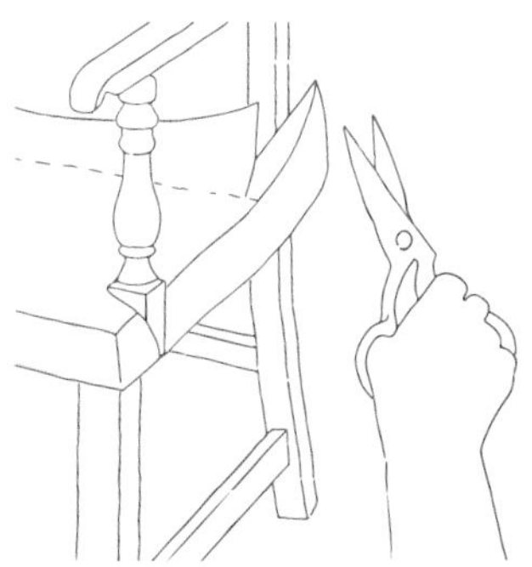

9. Now you can glue the sides down before cutting away the excess foam. Start with the back edge of the chair and lightly spray the centre back of the wooden seat frame and do the same for the corresponding section of foam. Once the glue has gone off slightly, glue the foam into place.

10. To cut the foam to sit neatly between the back upright rails, mark and cut the foam in a similar way to step 5 for the front. Starting at one side, fold the foam back on to itself so that you can see the inside edge of the back rail and the underside of the foam. Mark a cut line which, when cut, will allow the foam to lay flat over the back edge of the seat. Mark this line 2–3mm (⅛ inch) in from the edge, making the foam slightly bigger, so that it sits tight to the rail. Now cut a small 1 × 1cm (⅜ × ⅜ inch) chamfer (see step 6 of the Drop-in seat base for an occasional chair/ modern technique project on page 65) along that edge to reduce the thickness slightly and give you a neater finish. Repeat for the side edge of the other side, and then for each corner of the back right upright, on the back and side.

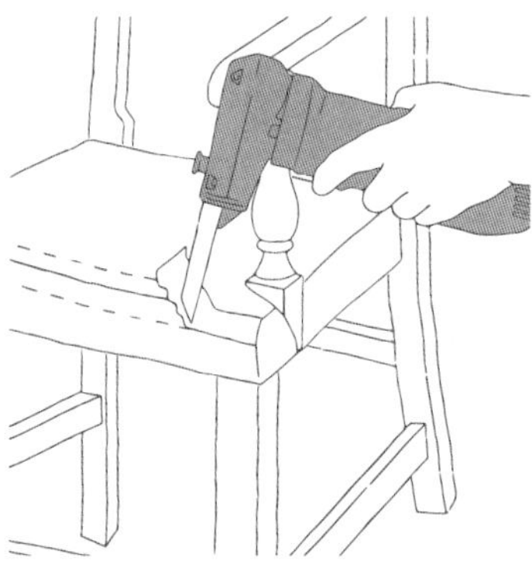

Cutting the excess foam

11. Move to the front section. The method for cutting away the excess foam around the uprights is the same as for the back in step 8. Once you have glued the sides down you will notice that the foam on the side overhangs the front corner of the chair. We will address this next.

12. Mark a line as for step 10 to the front edge out from the corner and cut with scissors, allowing 3mm (⅛ inch) extra. Glue this section of the foam into place. Repeat on the other corner.

13. On the front straight edge of the chair, lightly spray the centre of the wooden frame and the corresponding section of the foam and glue together.

14. Position the foam flat on the front and towards the corner, as if it has been glued down, so that you can repeat the same marking and cutting procedure for the foam to finish on the corner of the wooden seat frame. This time once you make the cut, allowing 3mm (⅛ inch) extra on each side again, don't glue this corner down as we will be fixing the fabric on to the front of this rail first and securing the foam down after for a neater, less bulky finish. Repeat on the other front corner.

Cutting out and fixing the wadding and top fabric

15. Cut a piece of polyester wadding large enough to cover the seat top and down to the underside of the frame. Centre this on top of the foam and glue the top section only to keep it in place while you work with the top fabric. Cut around the arm uprights and back rails following the method for cutting foam in steps 7–10.

16. Using a soft tape measure and pencil, mark the middle of each side of your chair on the polyester wadding. These marry marks (see page 47) will be references for you to follow when applying your fabric.

17. For your top fabric, measure from underneath the frame where the fabric will be tacked off and add 5cm (2 inches) on all sides to give you enough fabric to hold on to when fixing it into place. If you are using a patterned fabric, make sure to position this centrally or where you want the pattern to sit on the chair. Cut out then find and mark the middle points on each edge of the fabric, so that you can marry these up with the marks on the wadding.

PRO TIP
Upholstering a carver chair seat base where set-back arm uprights need to be worked around requires a little more time and careful planning than a standard seat. If you are not feeling confident, practise the top cover stage with a piece of scrap fabric to understand the process before attempting it with your actual fabric.

18. Position the fabric on the wadding, with the central marry marks aligned. Temporary tack in place (see page 32) along the back and front edge only (not the sides), approximately 5–7.5cm (2–3 inches) apart. If the padding is too thick on the back edge you could chamfer the foam using a pair of scissors.

19. Fold the back corner fabric back on to itself and in the same way as you did with the foam, mark a cut line on the fabric so that it will divide around the corner. Cut along the line, stopping short of the corner by 1.2cm (½ inch) – keep trying the fabric around the upright to make sure you don't cut too far. Make small snips so that the fabric fits against the wood when pulled taut.

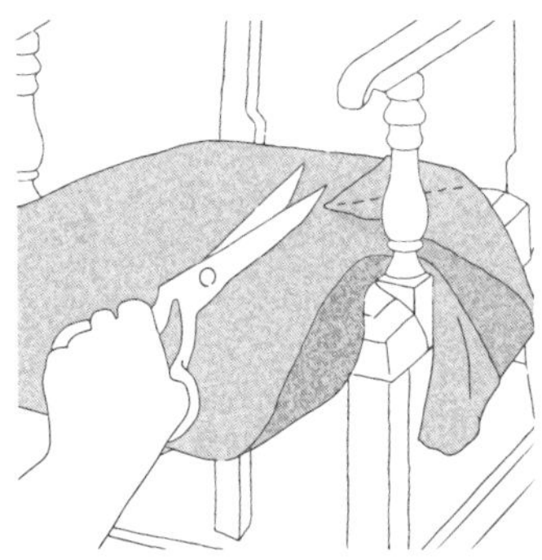

20. Pull the fabric on each side of the upright to sit around it, fold the edges under to make a neat straight edge against the upright and secure with a tack on the underside of the frame.

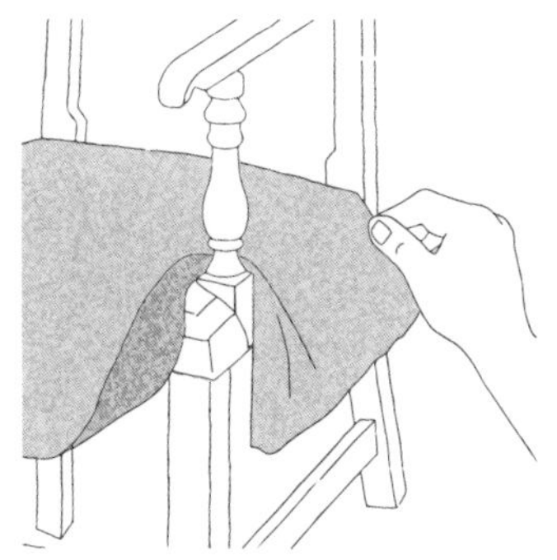

21. On the back or side edges of the frame, fold the excess fabric under itself into a straight line and hold in position to test for fit. The fabric fold should follow the straight line of the frame and sit neatly up against it so that no padding shows underneath. If there is too much fabric or if it's quite a thick fabric, cut the excess away leaving 2–2.5cm (¾–1 inch) of folded fabric. Temporary tack in place and repeat this on the back edge of the other corner.

22. Repeat steps 19 and 20 for the inside edge of the arms. Fold the fabric back on to itself, roll it up towards the inside face of the wooden arm upright. Mark the centre of the wooden rail on to the fold and again mark the V-shape from the width of the rail to the line creating the same Y-shape as for cutting the foam in step 8.

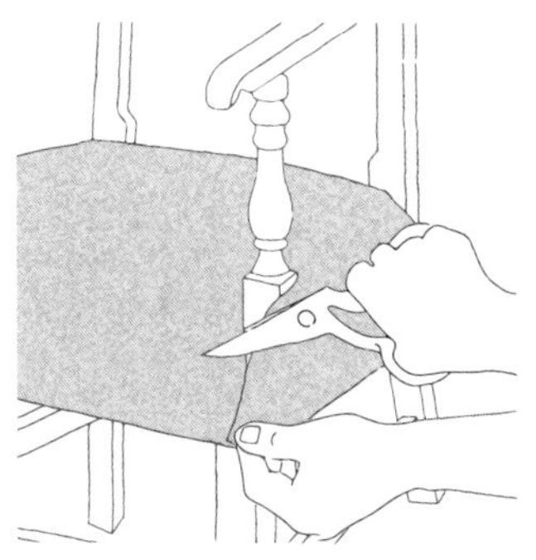

PRO TIP
It's important at this stage to make sure you are happy with the tension front to back. If not, then tighten the temporary tack through the front. If you cut the fabric and then tighten the tension, your cut will be in the wrong place.

23. Cut these lines and keep testing the cuts around the upright to make sure you don't cut too far. Once cut, fold the two sides under in the same was as in step 20 for the back fold, assess the excess, cut if necessary and temporary tack into place. Use a regulator to tuck the fabric neatly between the foam and the upright. Repeat for the other back corner of the chair.

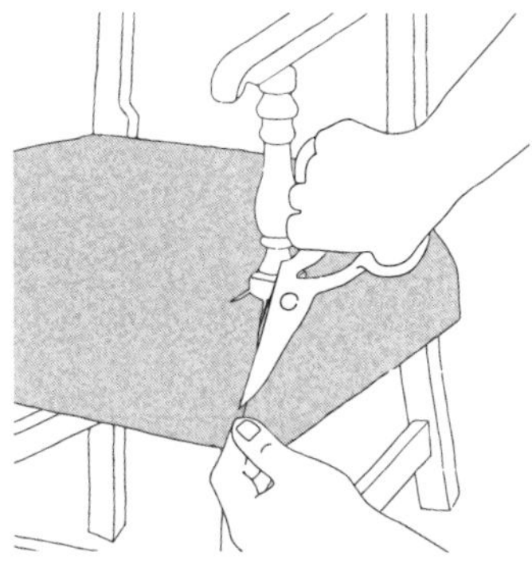

24. Repeat steps 19–23 to shape and tack the fabric around the front uprights, leaving just the front corners to finish.

Box pleating the corners

25. Now box pleat the corners (see page 36 in Essential Techniques: Box Pleats). Take care not to pull the fabric too hard from around the sides to the front edge to be tacked as this can create a gap. You may want to slip stitch your box pleat closed with a curved needle and matching thread (see How to slip stitch, page 35).

26. Once the fabric is well tensioned and in the correct position with neat box-pleated corners, replace the temporary fixings with permanent staples, filling in the gaps, and trim away any excess fabric.

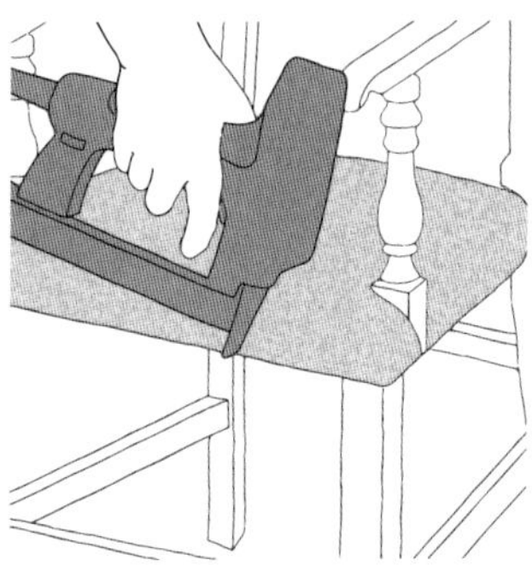

Cutting out and fixing the bottom cloth

27. Follow steps 20–23 of the Drop-in seat base for an occasional chair/modern technique project on page 67 to prepare and attach the bottom cloth to the underside of the chair.

Preparing the top fabric and adding support for the optional upholstered backrest

28. Follow steps 1–6 of the Rectangular fixed back dining chair project on page 74, if your carver chair has upholstery on the back of the backrest.

Preparing the foam

29. Depending on how confident you feel, you may want to make a paper template as a guide to cutting the foam, which you can also use when cutting the fabric. Measure the size of the backrest on the front edges (without taking the foam over the edge) and cut a piece of 2.5cm (1 inch) thick back-quality foam accordingly. Measure around the armrests, transfer these measurements to your foam piece and cut out.

30. Follow steps 8–10 of the Rectangular fixed back dining chair project on pages 74 and 77, but do not cut the chamfer on the cut-out arm sections.

Adding the top fabric layer

31. Measure and cut the top fabric following step 11 of the Rectangular fixed back dining chair project on page 77. If you made a template for the foam, you can use this as a guide for the fabric but don't forget to oversize the fabric by at least 2cm (¾ inch) all the way around.

32. Centre the top fabric over the seat. Temporarily staple the fabric at the top, bottom and sides, maintaining even tension.

33. Find the middle point where each arm connects to the back and mark this on to the fabric with a pencil. Cut the fabric up to this marked line, stopping 1cm (⅜ inch) away from the arm.

34. Twist the fabric around the top of the arm and make another incision, which will create a V-shape. Repeat underneath the arm and then manipulate the fabric around the arm by smoothing the fabric to the side.

35. Use a regulator to tuck the fabric smoothly in between the foam and arm. If there is still some puckering, make a few more incisions until the fabric sits completely flat. Be careful not to cut too close to the edge of the initial straight cut as you need the fabric to fold under itself to sit neatly above and below the arm.

Finishing around the arms

36. Once you have folded the fabric under itself around each arm, fold the outside edges under and temporarily staple them in place. Make any final adjustments, ensuring the fabric is smooth and neat around the arm. You can add a trim to finish (see Braid finish, page 84, or Stud finish, page 85), or permanently tack the fabric in place.

Straight back dining chair

/ all covered recover

The humble upholstered dining chair is the workhorse of any busy household. Used almost daily, it becomes the centre of activity for breakfast, lunch, dinner and social gatherings. In some homes, the dining table is where all the action happens.

I've reupholstered many dining chairs that have endured spills, sticky hands, stains, general wear-and-tear and even discoloration from home cleaning products. When reupholstering chairs for a busy household, the fabric choice is crucial for their longevity. You may also need to replace the webbing of the bases, which can become slack with frequent use.

These instructions are for a tall/straight back dining chair but can be modified if you have a different variation.

Tools and materials

Top fabric of choice
Soft tape measure
Pencil or chinagraph pencil
Tack lifter
Mallet
Scissors (both paper and fabric)
Black-and-white webbing
Web stretcher
Hessian (280g/10oz)
Staple gun and staples
Foam: 2.5cm (1 inch) chip foam; seating-grade 2.5cm (1 inch) blue foam or 12mm (½ inch) foam
Foam saw, craft knife with retractable blade or sharp bread knife
Upholstery contact adhesive
Metre ruler
Woolguard (optional)
Set square or roofing square
Dressmaking pins
Tailor's chalk
Polyester wadding (55g/2oz) (optional)
Regulator
Back-tacking strip
7.5cm (3 inch) curved needle
Matching sewing thread
Coloured fixings
Bottom cloth

Preparation

1. First, decide on your fabric, taking into account the width of the panels. If you are thinking of using a patterned fabric with a large-scale design, ensure that it fits on each panel and suits the scale of the chair. I recommend either choosing a plain fabric, which you won't have to pattern match, or a fabric with a very small pattern repeat that is simple to match.

2. Measure each panel of the chair, oversizing each measurement by 6–9cm (2½–3½ inches) all around. Use this information to create a cutting list. Label each panel piece as follows: I/B (inside back), O/B (outside back) and BS (base). Be mindful that the inside back may taper at the top, and the cover will need to return to meet the outside back. Include the side measurements for the inside back, taking the measurement from the bottom of the back.

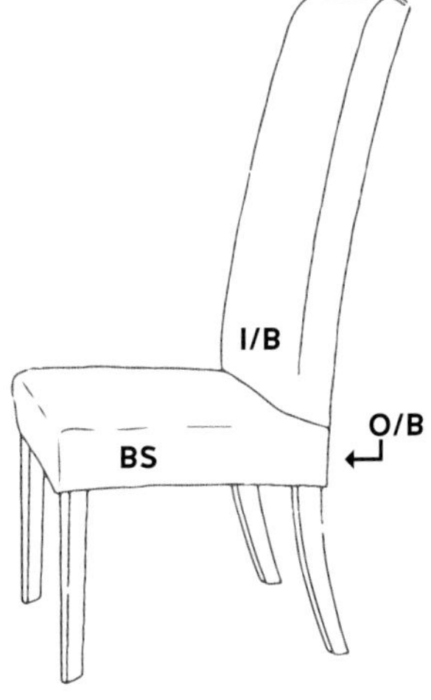

PRO TIP If you are using a patterned fabric be sure to centre the pattern on each panel and allow extra fabric for pattern matching. Patterned fabrics are less economical, as you'll need to cut away more waste to ensure the panels align correctly.

Stripping back and webbing

3. Once you have stripped the original cover off the chair following the instructions on page 30 in Essential Techniques: Stripping Out, assess the existing webbing on the base and the back. While the foam is still attached, sit on the chair and test it out. If it doesn't feel supportive, or if you can feel the edge of the wooden rails under your legs, then the webbing will need replacing.

4. If you need to replace the webbing, follow the steps on page 31 in Essential Techniques: Webbing.

Replacing the hessian layer

5. Cut a piece of hessian about 3cm (1¼ inches) larger than your seat base. Seat base frames tend to taper towards the back, so keep this in mind when measuring. You can either measure and cut your hessian or lay the hessian on top of the seat frame, mark around it and cut it out accordingly. Try to align the weave of the hessian as straight as possible with the front and back edge of the frame; this helps you to fold the edges down more accurately and maintain equal tension when securing the hessian to the frame.

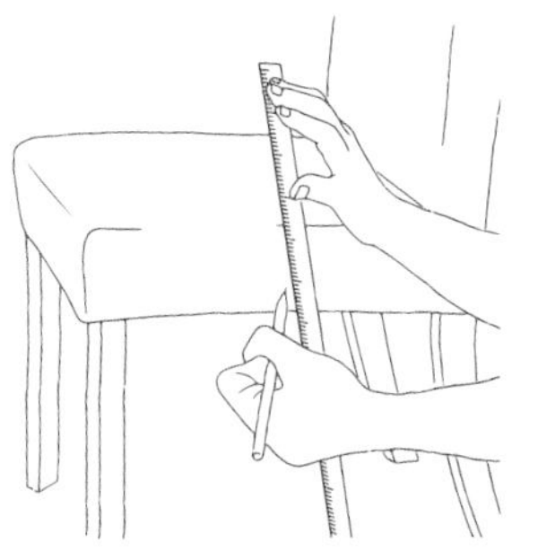

6. Starting with the back rail, you can secure the hessian in one of two ways, ensuring that the edge of the hessian sits just over the webbing line and not too close to the wooden frame edge.

Option 1: Starting with the middle on each side, place a fixing, making sure that the hessian is evenly positioned on the frame. Place fixings approximately 3cm (1¼ inches) apart along each side, working in opposite directions to the corners. Fold the hessian over on to itself and staple in between each first layer of staples, neatly folding the corners into themselves.

Option 2: Fold the top edge of hessian on to itself by 2–3cm (¾–1¼ inches) and secure with a line of staples.

Covering the back of the chair

7. For now, leave the base foam off to give good access at the back of the chair, allowing you to cover the inside back first. If you are replacing the webbing on the back, follow the instructions on page 31 in Essential Techniques: Webbing. For backrests of tall dining chairs, the webbing is often only stretched horizontally across the two upright sides of the chair. Use what you stripped out as a guide for replacement. If you feel the webbing was too far apart, reduce the gap between each strip and add a few more. The minimum space between web strips should be 2cm (¾ inch) and the maximum 4cm (1½ inches).

8. Next, cover the webbing on the back with hessian, using the same process as you did for the base.

Adding the foam

9. If you are replacing the foam on the back, assess what has been used so you can replicate it. If the foam has disintegrated or you think it was insufficient, follow these guidelines for dining chair backs.

10. Use a soft tape measure to determine the size of the chair back, adding 5mm (3⁄16 inch) all around. Mark this measurement on a piece of chip foam. Alternatively, you could cut the foam to the exact size of the back.

11. Cut the foam using a foam saw or a very sharp knife. Lay the chair down on your bench with the inside back facing up for easy access. Test the size of the foam on the back to ensure it fits properly.

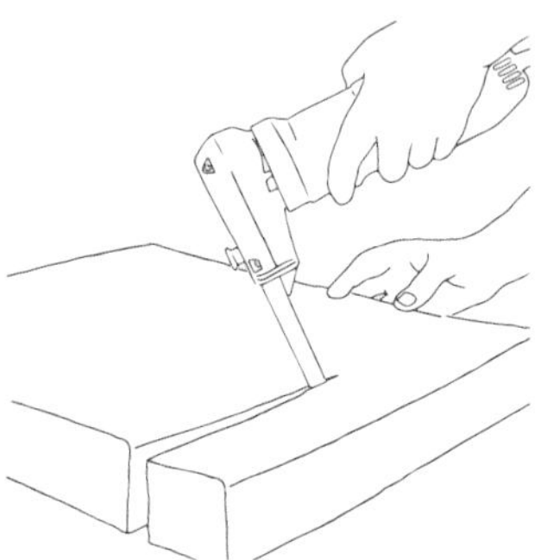

12. Spray a good layer of upholstery contact adhesive on both the hessian on the inside back and the foam. Wait for the glue to become tacky and then lay the chip foam on to the inside back. Ensure the foam sits at the base of the bottom back rail or high enough for the seat base to sit under the back foam if your chair does not have a bottom back rail. Look at how it was upholstered before and refer to this to inform the new upholstery you are making.

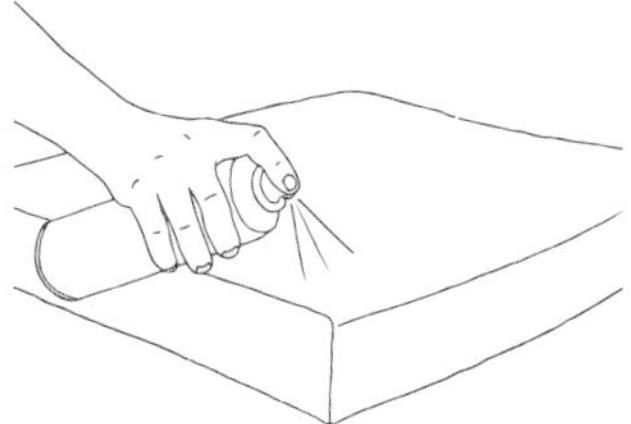

13. Measure the width of the inside back from the side return, across the chip foam to the other side return. Be sure to take the measurement across the lower section as chair backs often taper slightly at the top. For the height, measure from where the chip foam sits above the base of the inside back, up and over the top return. Allow an additional 2.5cm (1 inch) all around so that you have some excess to trim back to the wooden frame. Mark these measurements on the 12mm (½ inch) chip foam, using a metre ruler. Cut out with a foam saw or sharp knife.

14. Use upholstery contact adhesive to stick the foam to the chip foam, wrapping and gluing it around the sides and top edge, overhanging the back edge of the frame.

15. As you glue the foam to the two sides, work up to the top corners. When you reach the top, cut into the foam in line with the top of the wooden frame across the depth of the corner. Spray a small amount of upholstery contact adhesive on the tops of the foam you have just cut and stick the top section along the top of the back rail.

Adding Woolguard (optional)

16. If your top fabric is not FR coated you will need to add a layer of Woolguard to the foam. Measure and cut a piece for the I/B panel following the instructions in step 2. Spray a light layer of upholstery contact adhesive on to the inside back front and lay the Woolguard on top of this, applying pressure to help it attach. Spray the sides and top of the chair and smooth the Woolguard over these to stick it in place. A triangular-shaped flap of excess fabric will form at the top corners; trim this off level with the foam. Wrap the Woolguard on the sides around to the outside back of the frame by 2–3cm (¾–1¼ inches), where the fabric will be tacked off. Cut any overlapping Woolguard on the top corners on the back of the frame. At the bottom of the inside back, trim the Woolguard around the uprights 5mm (3/16 inch) higher than the foam, leaving a flap that will be pushed through and tacked off on the back rail.

Cutting the top fabric

17. Transfer your measurements taken in step 2 to the back of the fabric using tailor's chalk, making sure to use the fabric as economically as possible, using the whole width of the fabric. For example, you could place the inside back and base next to each other on the width.

18. Use a set square (or roofing square, which is larger), a metre ruler and tailor's chalk to mark the sizes of the panels on to the fabric. Triple-check your measurements before cutting the panels out and labelling them.

Creating marry marks

19. Using a soft tape measure and a pencil, on the inside back mark the middle on the top edge of the frame and where the back meets the base. Fold the fabric panel in half lengthways and mark the middle top and middle bottom with tailor's chalk. These will be the 'marry marks' (see page 47) that you will use as a reference for positioning your fabric on the back frame to ensure your panels are central.

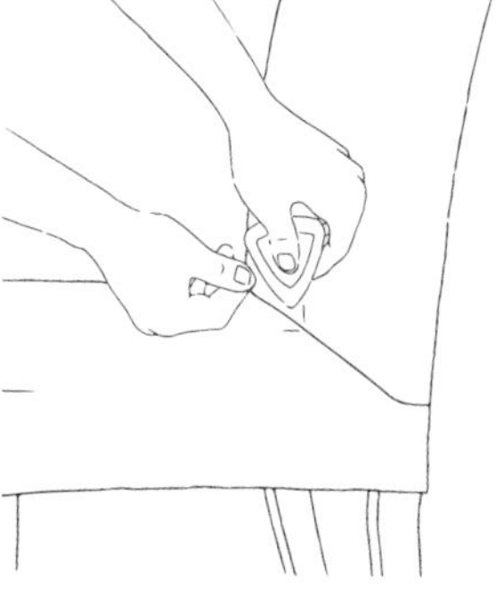

Attaching the inside back fabric

20. Start with the inside back of the chair. Lay the fabric on to the chair centrally, checking that the overhang you have allowed for is even all around. Ensure the bottom of the inside back fabric reaches through to the back rail where it will be tacked off.

PRO TIP It's always wise to keep a record of how the original cover was attached before you strip it back. This is useful information to have to hand regarding the order and positioning of components.

21. Starting in the middle of the top of the inside back, secure a temporary fixing in place and repeat this on the three remaining sides. Start to work your way to the top corners of the chair and to where the back meets the base fixing, placing temporary staples approximately 3–4cm (1¼–1½ inches) apart. Make sure the fabric is straight and square by assessing the weave on the front. Adjust where necessary by taking out any temporary staples and repositioning the fabric.

22. Once you have double-checked the position of the panel, replace the temporary fixings with final fixings approximately 1cm (⅜ inch) apart leaving 5–8cm (2–3¼ inches) from the top corners and the bottom near the base. Place your permanent fixings towards the inside of the back rail edge so that your outside back panel will cover them.

Box pleating the top corners

23. Box pleat the top corner by wrapping the side section of fabric across the top edge of the top rail and fixing a staple 2–3cm (¾–1¼ inches) in. Staple up to the top corner on the back, tapering the line of staples into the corner on the back edge. With the fabric left loose at the top, staple this small section off in the same way on the back. Trim away the excess as close to the staples as possible. If you are using a thick fabric, hammer this section down to flatten any bulk as much as possible. Replace the temporary fixing on the top with a permanent one. Fold the top fabric under itself into the corner to create the initial fold for where the fabric will finish. Open up the fold and trim out the excess from the inside of the fold and the inside of the fixed point on the frame. Cut out a V-shape. Now fold the flap of fabric back under itself to create a neat pleat. Test the pleat: it should sit flat with the fold vertically aligned with the side of the frame. Make sure the fabric inside the fold is smooth (use a regulator to ease it flat), and staple it in place on to the back of the frame 2–2.5cm (¾–1 inch) down from the top edge of the wood. Repeat on the other side.

24. For the bottom section of the back, release the temporary staples and use a pin to find the corner where the upright rail meets the bottom back rail. Cut up to this point 5mm (³⁄₁₆ inch) away from the pin at a 25–30-degree angle. Repeat this on the other side and temporary tack the back on to the bottom back rail.

25. Pull the sides of the cover round and down and tack off on the side lower than the height of the horizontal back rail. Trim off the excess.

Adding the foam to the base

26. Measure and cut out the chip foam following the measurements taken in step 2. Refer to steps 2–14 of the Carver chair project on pages 86–90 for guidance on how to finish off the foam around the sides of the seat frame. Attach the base foam pad on to the seat using upholstery contact adhesive and staples if you used staples before. Spray both the top of the hessian on the frame and the foam. Ensure you position the foam tight to the back.

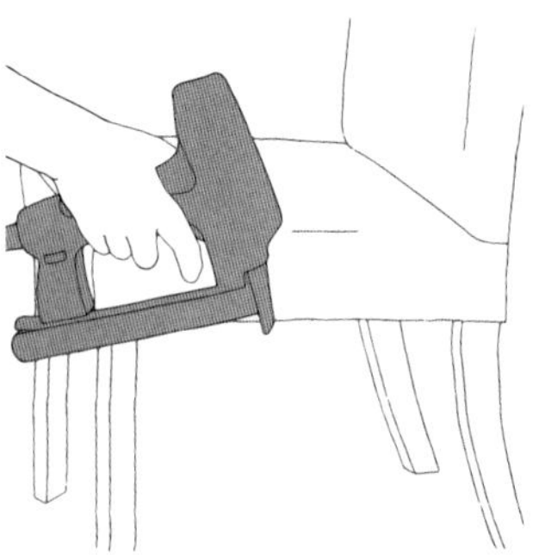

PRO TIP If the original foam is still in good condition but lacks plumptiousness, you can add a layer of 2.5cm (1 inch) foam to the base before replacing the original foam. Measure the top of the base frame, reduce this measurement by 3–4cm (1¼–1½ inches), and transfer it to the foam using a chinagraph pencil. Cut the foam to size then trim the very top edge of the foam to create a 'mini' chamfer (see step 6 of the Drop-in seat base for an occasional chair/modern technique project on page 65). Test the fit by placing the new foam on the base and covering it with the original foam. If the edge of the new foam is visible, cut a larger chamfer.

Attaching the base fabric

27. If your top fabric is not FR treated, add a layer of Woolguard as you did in step 16. If your fabric is FR treated, use a layer of polyester wadding instead. Apply it in the same manner as the Woolguard, cutting around the upright rails at the back and the legs as before.

28. Position your fabric on the base centrally, just as you did for the inside back. Mark marry marks (see page 47) on the fabric to use as a reference for positioning your fabric on the seat frame, ensuring your panel is central when attaching the cover. Temporary tack the fabric into place, tacking on to the underside of the frame and leaving a gap of 5–8cm (2–3¼ inches) from the corners.

29. Repeat the same process as you did for the back, replacing your temporary fixings with final fixings towards the inside of the rail underneath following step 22.

Finishing the front corners on the seat base fabric

30. You will need to create box pleats on the two front corners. Follow the instructions on page 36 in Essential Techniques: Box Pleats.

Finishing the back corners on the seat base fabric

31. Moving to the back corners, release the temporary staples holding the back section in place. Pull this fabric through and fold it on to itself, positioning it up against the back padding and tucking it into the padding slightly. Use a regulator to poke into the gap between the base and the back to find the inside rail edge, keeping the regulator in place. Mark with a pencil at a 30–35-degree angle up to the inside front edge of the rail where the regulator is. Cut to this line and push the fabric through to test how it fits. If the fabric stops and there is some puckering on the top, then cut a little further. If you can pull the fabric through without resistance and it sits smoothly, then the cut is in the right place. Pull the fabric back out into its original position folded on to itself.

32. To get the fabric to sit neatly around the side of the backrest section, make another cut into the fabric. Position the fabric up against the width of the back upright, as you did when making your first cut. This time, use your marking tool to mark from the outside edge front corner of the rail towards the cut you just made, forming a V-shaped cut. Cut in smaller increments and test the cut by pulling the fabric around the side to check for puckering.

33. When the fabric is sitting smoothly, temporary tack the bottom of the back (on the side you have cut) into position. Move to the side of the chair, fold the excess fabric under itself to create a neat line, then pull the fabric back and down slightly. Tack the fabric off on to the back rail, positioning the fold of the fabric as horizontally as possible.

34. Find where the inside of the upright leg rail meets the bottom of the seat rail. Mark this point with a pin and cut up to this point at a 45-degree angle from the outside of the leg, allowing you to fold the excess fabric under and tack it on to the back of the frame. This creates a folded edge from front to back along the side. Fold and tack the fabric on the side into place. Assess the cuts and folds to make sure you are happy with the tension and positioning before final tacking. Repeat on the other side, checking that all sides are level with the bottom of the base rail. This ensures that when the outside back is attached, both sides finish level with one another. Tack off the back of the base on to the rail and then tack off the bottom edge of the inside back fabric that has been pushed through to the back on top of the line of staples you have just fixed into place.

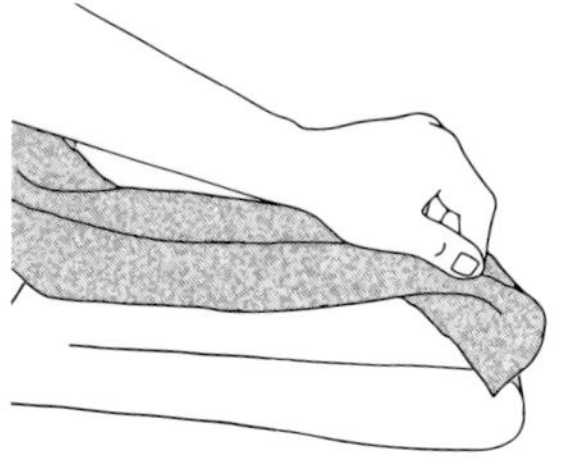

Attaching the fabric to the outside back

35. Repeat step 19 to add marry marks to the top and bottom of the outside back and find the centre of the fabric panel. Cut out a piece of hessian to the outside back measurements noted in step 2, oversizing by 2–3cm (¾–1¼ inches) all around. Follow the weave of the hessian to cut out.

36. Turn the chair over so that the top of the back slants down towards you. Position the hessian centrally on the outside back of the chair and, starting from the middle top, place a staple towards the inside edge of the rail. Next, place another staple at the bottom and also on the sides, being careful not to distort the weave. Use the weave to guide the evenness of the tension. Working towards all four corners, place temporary staples 3–4cm (1¼–1½ inches) apart.

37. Once you are satisfied with the tension, replace the temporary staples with permanent ones, 2–3cm (¾–1¼ inches) apart. Depending on the space and the bulk of fabric you have on the back rail, cut the hessian on all four corners by cutting diagonally across the excess flap of hessian.

38. Fold the hessian back on to itself all around, overlapping on the corners, and staple this excess down positioning the staples 3–4cm (1¼–1½ inches) apart.

39. Turn the chair upright and use tailor's chalk or a pin to mark the centre top on the outside back. The outside back will be positioned using back-tacking strip, which is a special tape to give you a perfectly straight line (see page 26). Cut a piece of back-tacking strip 3–5mm (⅛–3⁄16 inch) smaller than the width of the top of the back. The fabric will be fixed behind the strip and will cascade over the top of it. Put the back-tacking strip to one side. Lay the top edge of the outside back fabric face down on the top edge of the back (don't worry, it's not the wrong way around and all will make sense soon!). Position the cut edge 3–5cm (1¼–2 inches) below the top of the frame. Temporary staple the fabric on the cut edge, gently pulling the fabric to create a little tension across the width. Leave a gap of 5cm (2 inches) from the sides.

40. Flip the fabric over from the inside back of the chair so it is now on the outside back of the chair, right side facing out, and assess where the sides will finish. This fabric will cover the previous layer of fixings on the hessian layer. Flip the fabric back on to the inside back of the chair.

41. Measure and cut a piece of polyester wadding to match the width of the back of the chair. This wadding provides aesthetic padding between the fabric and the hessian. Position the wadding in the same way and on top of the flipped-over outside back fabric, lining up the cut edge of the wadding with the cut edge of the fabric 5cm (2 inches) down from the edge of the top of the backrest frame.

42. Position the back-tacking strip on top of the fabric and wadding layers so that the top of the tape sits 5mm (3⁄16 inch) down from the top of the chair frame. It shouldn't foul any of the temporary staples; if these staples are in the way, remove them for now. Starting from the middle, place temporary staples every 3cm (1¼ inches). Check the line by flipping the fabric back over. Make any adjustments where necessary. Flip the fabric back to the inside back. To final fix, staple the back-tacking strip 2–3mm (⅛ inch) down from the top of the tape and no more than 3mm (⅛ inch) apart. Place staples vertically to ensure the ends of the strip are held in place securely.

43. Flip the fabric over again to the outside back, and pull it down over the wadding. Secure temporary staples on the underneath of the bottom rail, leaving a 4–5cm (1½–2 inch) gap from the legs. Be sure to marry up the centre line on the fabric with the centre line on the rail.

44. Using chalk, mark the sides of the fabric at intervals no more than 5cm (2 inches) apart, making the marks 1.5–2cm (⅝–¾ inch) wider than the chair back. Cut off the excess fabric. Fold the sides under, pin them into place, pin at 5cm (2 inch) intervals from the top, leaving a 5cm (2 inch) gap from the bottom.

45. Check the tension for any ripples or bagginess. If everything looks smooth, replace the temporary fixings on the bottom with permanent staples.

46. Use a regulator to fold the top corners neatly into place. If you are using a thicker fabric you may need to trim out some bulk by cutting across the corner, similarly to how you did with the hessian layer, only this time leave about 5mm (3⁄16 inch) from the back-tacking strip.

47. Using a 7.5cm (3 inch) curved needle and cotton thread that matches or complements your fabric, slip stitch the sides closed (see How to slip stitch, page 35), finishing 4–5cm (1½–2 inches) above the bottom corners. Ensure the needle exits the fabric where the outside back fabric has been folded to keep the stitches hidden. If the thread becomes visible, remove the stitches and re-do that section.

PRO TIP You can use waxed Barbour twine (see page 23), which is thicker than cotton thread and works well with thicker fabrics. However, keep in mind that Barbour twine comes in a limited range of colours.

48. If you run out of thread, secure it by stitching over the same area three to four times. Start a new thread in the same manner as you did at the top, working your way down to within 4cm (1½ inches) of the bottom edge. Finish off securely and repeat the process on the other side of the back.

49. On the outside back fabric, locate where the bottom of the base rail meets the leg and place a pin at this point. Cut up to this point at a 45-degree angle from the outside edge, creating a small V-shaped cut. Mark 1.5–2cm (⅝–¾ inch) below the bottom of the back rail and trim off any excess. Using the point of a regulator, fold the remaining excess fabric under and secure the corner in place with a coloured fixing, in the same way you did for the front. Repeat this on the other side/leg.

50. Fold the remaining excess (where you'd cut into the fabric at an angle) under itself to form a neatly folded line. Pull this down and underneath the chair frame, staple it in place and secure it, positioning the staples in the same way as you did for the seat base. Repeat on the other side and secure the in-between section, replacing any temporary staples with final ones.

Attaching the bottom cloth

51. Use a soft tape measure to determine the size of the bottom cloth, adding 3–4cm (1¼–1½ inches) extra all around. Mark these measurements on to the bottom cloth with tailor's chalk and a ruler, then cut it out. Position the chair upside down on your work surface, with the back extending over the edge of the bench where you are standing.

PRO TIP The purpose of the bottom cloth here is to neatly cover the underside of the chair and also to cover the staples that have fixed the top fabric in place.

52. Start with the middle of the back of the chair. Fold the edge of the cloth under and secure it with a temporary staple if you're unsure about achieving even tension around the entire edge. Pull the cloth taut towards the front and staple it in place. Repeat this process for the sides. Work your way to the corners/legs leaving a 5cm (2 inch) space away from the legs.

53. On a corner, fold the bottom cloth back on to itself and cut at a 45-degree angle towards the leg leaving 5mm (³⁄₁₆ inch) space away from the leg. Fold the excess under on both sides of the leg, trim away any excess or bulk, and staple into place.

54. Repeat this on the remaining three legs. If you have used temporary staples, now is the time to replace them with final staples.

Straight back dining chair
/ chair slipcover

If you already have loose covers on your dining chairs, you can use an existing cover as a template for creating a new one. Simply take apart the old cover and use its pieces to cut out your new fabric. Making loose covers for your chairs offers several benefits; by choosing a machine-washable fabric, you can easily clean the covers without worrying about shrinking or distortion, especially if your chairs are prone to spills, stains or sticky fingers. You can also change the colours or textures of the covers to suit different seasons or occasions, such as switching to a bright summer palette or a cosy winter texture.

Additionally, if you're celebrating a special event, you can coordinate your chair covers with your table runner and placemats for a unified look.

Tools and materials

Top fabric of choice
Soft tape measure
Metre ruler
Paper
Pencil
Scissors (both paper and fabric)
Set square or roofing square
Tailor's chalk
Dressmaking pins
Matching sewing thread
Sewing machine
Regulator

PRO TIP You may also need some Paper, calico or remnant fabric if you are planning to make a pattern before cutting your fabric panels.

Choosing your fabric

1. First, decide on your top fabric. Opt for a plain fabric or a small repeat pattern to simplify pattern matching. Avoid large patterns that may not fit well on the panels.

Measuring and cutting the fabric panels

2. Measure each panel of the chair (see the Seat base pattern, right), adding 4-6cm (1½-2⅓ inches) to all sides. Create a cutting list with the labels I/B (inside back), O/B (outside back) and BS (base). If you decide to add a skirt to the chair (see Straight back dining chair/chair slipcover with skirt on page 108), label this measurement SKT.

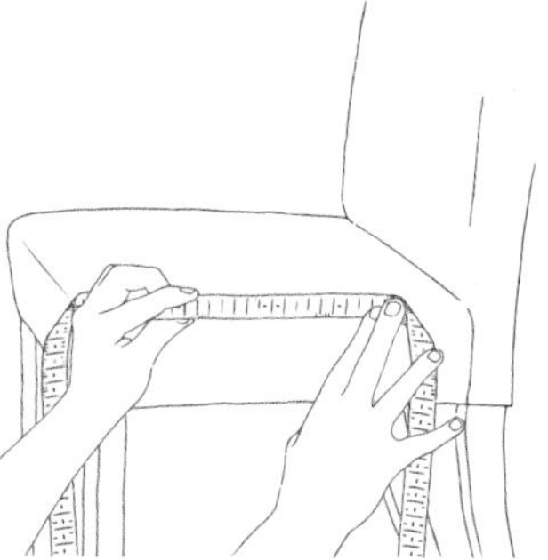

SEAT BASE PATTERN

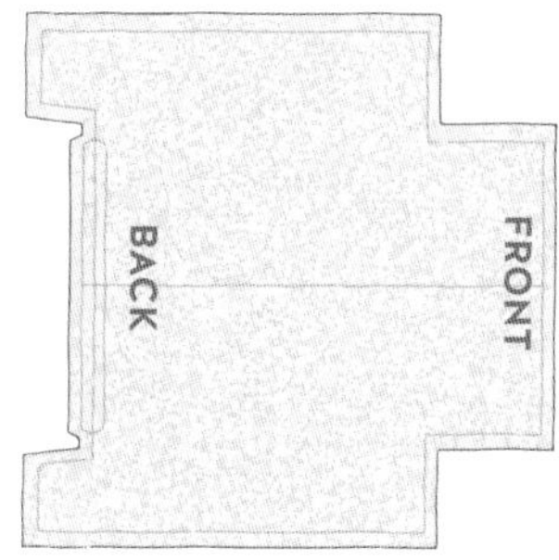

3. In your measurements, take into account whether the chair back tapers at the top and ensure that the inside back measurement extends to the lower edge of the side and over the top edge to the outside back.

Preparing the fabric

4. Use a set square or roofing square, a metre ruler and tailor's chalk to mark the dimensions of the panels on to the back of the top fabric, excluding the skirt. Ensure you use the fabric as efficiently as possible. For instance, you might place the pieces for the inside back and base side by side to maximize fabric usage.

TABASCO
BRAND

5. Triple-check your measurements before cutting the panels out and labelling them.

Marking and pinning the panels

6. Position pins on the chair. Measure and pin the middle top, inside back bottom middle (where the back meets the base) and the middle front on the base. To find the centre of your fabric panels, fold the fabric sections in half lengthways and use tailor's chalk to mark the middle top and middle bottom. These 'marry marks' (see page 47) will help ensure the panels are centred when you assemble the cover.

Fitting the inside back panel

7. Start with the inside back of the chair. Place the fabric inside out on to the chair so you can make any notes directly on the fabric. This step is helpful for beginners but may not be necessary for more advanced sewers. Marry up the middle marks on the chair with those on the fabric to ensure the fabric is central. Leave a 3cm (1¼ inch) overhang of fabric at the top and an additional 3-6cm (1¼-2⅓ inches) at the bottom. Tuck the fabric into the area where the back meets the base, smoothing and pinning the rest of the panel into place. Unlike with upholstery, you are not looking to build lots of tension into the fabric; the finished loose cover should 'sit' perfectly tailored to the back. You will repeat this same process with the other panels, pinning and marking in the same way.

Securing the inside back and back panels

8. Starting from the middle of the inside back side, smooth the fabric around the sides, placing pins through the fabric into the upholstery as you work up and down. Leave a space of 5-6cm (2-2⅓ inches) up from the base.

9. At the top of the inside back, again working from the middle to the corners, smooth the fabric over and pin into place. A triangle-shaped flap of excess fabric will form on the corners – pin along the line where the pinched fabric sits along the depth of the corner of the back frame (front to back), which will become your stitching line. Repeat on the other corner on the other side. Repeat this process again for the outside back panel, which will not wrap around the side but meets the sides when sewn together.

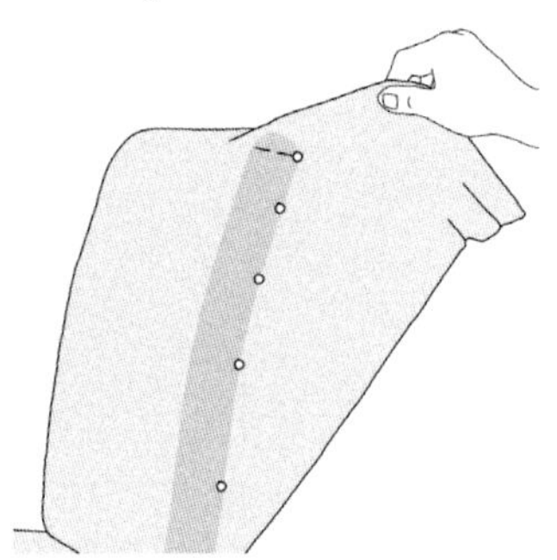

Cutting and sewing the front and back panels

10. Before taking the panels off the chair, use a pencil to mark where the pins are positioned so you have a reference to follow when you mark the stitching line in the next step. Take the panels off the chair and remove the pins as you go. Use the pencil and a ruler to mark the stitching line on all three sides (left, right and top) of both the inside and outside back panels and the top corner folds of the front panel where you pinned, then mark a seam allowance line of 1 or 1.5cm (⅜ or ⅝ inch). Cut along this line. Begin by sewing the corners of the inside back. Then, sew the front and back panels together right sides facing. Start from the top centre, working your way to one corner and side first, then return to the middle and sew towards the other corner and down the other side. Sew as far down as it was pinned, leaving the bottom of the cover open and unsewn. This will allow you to work around the legs later.

11. While the back cover is still inside out, place it on to the chair to test the fit and make any necessary adjustments. If the cover is too large, take in the seam slightly; if it's too tight, sew a slightly smaller allowance on that side to loosen the fit. The cover should slip on with minimal resistance.

Once the cover fits correctly, tuck the inside back fabric into the tight space between the seat base and the backrest. Use a regulator or your fingers to locate the backrest rails by poking into the gap and moving it over until you feel resistance to the outside corner of the frame. Mark this inside corner of the frame to the outside corner of the frame on to the fabric with a pencil. Repeat this on the other inside corner.

Next, pull the tucked fabric slightly out so it rests on the seat base, keeping it close to where the back meets the base. Mark from the inside corner to the outside corner to the edge of the seat, and repeat on the other side. Add a seam allowance line to these marks but do not cut yet.

12. Mark a line, 2-3cm (¾-1¼ inches) long on both sides from the inside edge of the corners you have just marked at a 45-degree angle towards the centre of the seat base.

13. Use your ruler to mark another line horizontally to connect the two 45-degree lines. This extended section will help form a shape that will enable you to tuck the cover into the space between the back and base upholstery, creating a neat finish.

Now mark where the fabric will wrap around the side of the backrest. To determine this stitching line, fold the section you are working on on to itself, untucked, then pin the middle of the fold into the chair upholstery to secure it. Continue the fold around the side of the chair frame to the back edge horizontally. This fold line will be your stitching line. Mark the line on the fabric, then repeat on the other side. Place a pin in the upholstery to mark where the horizontal line sits so it can be referenced for the seat base.

14. Next, place the base fabric on to the seat base with the back edge folded back. Tension and smooth the fabric, pinning it into place in the same manner as you did for the inside back, including pinning the front corners similarly to the top corners of the back. Note that you will only be able to pin the fabric up to the inside back, as it needs to be cut to wrap around the sides.

If the tension is satisfactory, use a pencil to mark the bottom edge of the seat base frame on to the fabric on all three sides (left, right and front edges), as far back as possible on the sides. Gently tuck the back edge of the base fabric into the gap between the back and the base, and mark the corners, across the corners and the space between the corners, as you did for the back, including the 45-degree angled lines. The lines you have just marked on the fabric will be referenced again later in this project.

PRO TIP If there is any slack around the front of the seat base, pull the fabric towards the back to create additional tension. This will ensure the cover fits snugly around the upholstery when sewn.

15. Pin the outside back panel on to the chair using the same technique as for the previous two panels. Centre the panel, smooth out the excess fabric and pin it into place. Ensure the panel is straight and square by referencing the weave alignment. Check that the excess fabric at the bottom matches the excess on the bottom of the back sides.

16. Use a pencil to mark the top and side edges where the inside back meets the outside back on the back edge of the chair. Repeat this for the inside back and where the base wraps around the side to meet the outside back.

17. Add two or three marry marks to the sides of the panel (see page 47), transfer and make sure the marks are on each of the three sides of the back.

18. Remove the panels from the chair and add a seam allowance. Cut along this line and sew the panels together making sure the marry marks match as you work your way around the panel. Snip into the corner of the inside back to help the fabric sit around the corner.

19. Using the same technique as for the back (see steps 8–9 on page 104), fold the sides of the seat back to the pin and mark the stitching line from the front edge of the inside back frame to the pin. This line will mirror the stitching line on the inside back panel.

20. Remove the panels from the chair and take out all the pins. Referring to the Seat base pattern diagram on page 102 you can see how the sides extend back towards the back edge of the chair. Add a seam allowance along all of the cutting lines and cut along these lines.

21. This beginner's guide suggests sewing the panels together in stages and fitting them to the chair as you go. This approach helps to ensure the best possible fit and reduces the likelihood of mistakes. First, check the panels against each other to make sure they are correct and align; adjust where needed. Sew the base corners closed and then sew the flap and inside back panel together in one continuous stitching line. You now have the inside back, base and outside back sewn together. If necessary, close up the open sections on the back part of the cover where you have previously sewn down to and kept open.

PRO TIP If I am ever sewing something that is symmetrical, I always start from the middle and work my way down either side. This approach helps prevent the sewing machine from 'pushing' or shifting the top layer of fabric, which can cause pattern misalignment.

22. Fit the cover on to the chair, right side out, and pin it into place to check the fit. You will have some overhang of fabric all along the bottom edge of the base and the back edge of the back; we will address this later. If you are happy with the fit take the cover off and re-pin it back into place inside out.

PRO TIP We need to re-pin the cover back on to the chair inside out as we will continue to make marks on all the panels. Working on the cover inside out ensures more accurate placement and adjustments. If you choose to keep the cover right side out, simply follow the same instructions for steps 23 to 25.

23. Re-fit the cover on to the chair, ensuring it fits snugly but comfortably (much like a well-fitting pair of gloves, the cover should be secure but not overly tight). Dress the cover into place, tucking the flap into the space where the inside back meets the base at the inner front edge of the chair.

24. While keeping the cover in place, mark the bottom edge of the chair frame, again checking against your previous marks, all around on to the excess fabric. Take the cover off and decide how far down you want the cover to extend on the chair - about 2-3cm (¾-1¼ inches) below the bottom of the framework is recommended. Measure down another 2.5-3cm (1-1¼ inches) so that the cover extends past the bottom of the seat frame. Use a pencil and ruler to draw a hem line at this depth. Then, add an additional 1.5-2cm (⅝-¾ inch) to create a cut line. If you wanted a double-fold hem to encapsulate the raw edge, add a 2-4cm (¾-1½ inch) seam allowance. Consider the thickness of your fabric, the strength of your sewing machine and the added bulk that thick fabric will create if you choose a double hem. Take the cover off and cut along this line.

25. Starting from the front side, 10-14cm (4-5½ inches) in from the corner, fold your fabric under and sew the hem in a continuous stitching line, pressing your seams in the correct direction as you go around. I suggest pressing the bulk of the seams into the chair on both the front and the back. Since the hem will be a visible stitch line, don't back tack at the start and finish. Instead, finish in the same stitch hole as you started, then pull the threads through and tie them off to the wrong side for a cleaner finish.

Your cover is now ready to slip back on to your chair for good!

Straight back dining chair

/ chair slipcover with skirt

You have two main skirt styles to choose from when designing your slipcover for a square back dining chair. You can either extend the skirt drop from the sides, being mindful of how the back legs taper out, or add a pleated skirt for a more tailored look. The following instructions will guide you through creating a pleated skirt with minimal bulk at the seams.

Tools and materials
Top fabric of choice
Soft tape measure
Pencil
Dressmaking pins
30cm (12 inch) ruler
Fabric scissors
Tailor's chalk
Iron
Matching sewing thread
Sewing machine

Marking the skirt length

1. Follow the Straight back dining chair/chair slipcover instructions up to step 24, where you mark the bottom of the frame. Since some chair bases taper backward, it's best to measure from the floor to determine where the skirt should start. I recommend marking just above or at the same level as the front of the seat. With the cover still on the chair, measure and pin this point at each corner and at 4–6cm (1½–2½ inch) intervals along the sides. Note these measurements for reference when making your skirt.

Preparing the cover

2. Remove the cover and mark the pin locations with a pencil on the inside. Use a ruler to connect these marks and draw a straight line all around the cover. Add a 2–2.5cm (¾–1 inch) seam allowance to this line and cut along it, stopping at the seams (do not cut through the seams). Begin the cut line on the next panel and continue around.

Measuring for panels

3. Measure the width of the front, sides and back of the seat seam to seam. Decide if you want the skirt to reach the floor or finish slightly higher. I suggest finishing 1–2cm (⅜–¾ inch) higher to accommodate any movement in the cover. Deduct 2cm (¾ inch) from the height measured in step 1.

Cutting the skirt panels

4. Transfer the final width and height measurements for your four panels to your fabric with tailor's chalk and a ruler, adding a 2–2.5cm (¾–1 inch) seam allowance all around.

Adding the corner panels

5. For each corner, sew in an additional narrower panel, giving you a total of eight panels. The width of these corner panels should be between 18–20cm (7–8 inches). Transfer these measurements to your fabric, including a 2–2.5cm (¾–1 inch) seam allowance.

Sewing the hems

6. Cut out all the panels, press the hems on the two sides and the bottom only, and fold and press the corners neatly. Machine stitch the hems.

Attaching the larger panels

7. Pin the four larger panels around the seat and sew them into place, starting at one corner and continuing all the way back around to the same corner you started on.

Attaching the corner panels

8. Pin the smaller corner panels to the skirt. Find the middle of the top of each panel by folding it in half and marking it with a pencil. Pin this mark to the larger panel on the wrong side.

Sewing the panels together

9. Sew along each panel's top edge, positioning the stitching line just below the first line by 1–2mm (1/16 inch) to avoid distorting the original stitch line.

Making the final touches

10. Turn the cover right side out, press the hems flat from the inside and then re-fit the slipcover to your chair.

Restuffing sofa seat cushions and backs

This is great way to refresh your cushions without the expense of new inserts. The following method for restuffing sofa cushions is effective for both feather and hollow fibre cushions, and it also works well for conservatory cushions. However, if you're allergic to feathers, it's best to avoid doing this yourself. If the cushion insert's lining is too old, brittle or disintegrated, it may be impossible to restuff. Assess your cushions before you start and consider an alternative method if necessary, such as adding a new insert.

Tools and materials
Feather or hollow fibre stuffing
Dust mask
Stitch unpicker or sewing snips
Dressmaking pins
Hand-sewing needle
Matching sewing thread
Fabric scissors

1. Look for cushions that have lost their plumptiousness, typically in areas that are sat on the most. Cushions often have sewn-in channels to keep the filling evenly distributed. Remove the cushion cover and set it aside.

2. Whether your cushion is feather or hollow fibre, the process is more or less the same. For feather cushions, wear a dust mask and handle carefully to avoid feathers spreading everywhere. Once you have your cushion in hand you will notice a series of channels inside the cushion that resemble the channels in a duvet, and you will also notice a closed seam around the edges; first try to push as much of the feather or hollow fibre back away from whichever channel you want to begin with and then simply and gently open up the seam using a stitch unpicker or small pair of sewing snips.

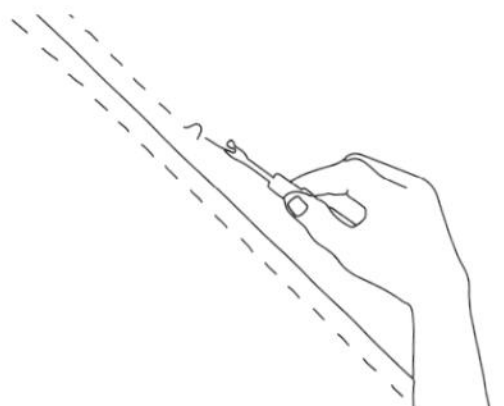

3. You can recycle stuffing from old scatter cushion infills that you are no longer using – open them up and gently transfer the feathers or hollow fibre from the old cushion to the cushion you are restuffing. Using old cushions is a great way to recycle stuffing material. Both feather and hollow fibre fillings are available for purchase online or from you local supplier's store.

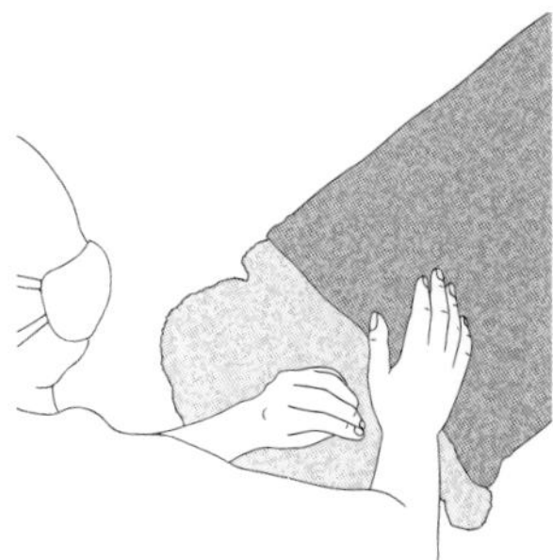

4. Be careful not to overstuff the cushions to maintain comfort and support. After filling the desired number of channels, pin the seams together and use a blanket stitch to close the opening. This stitch is strong and less likely to slip open compared to a slip stitch.

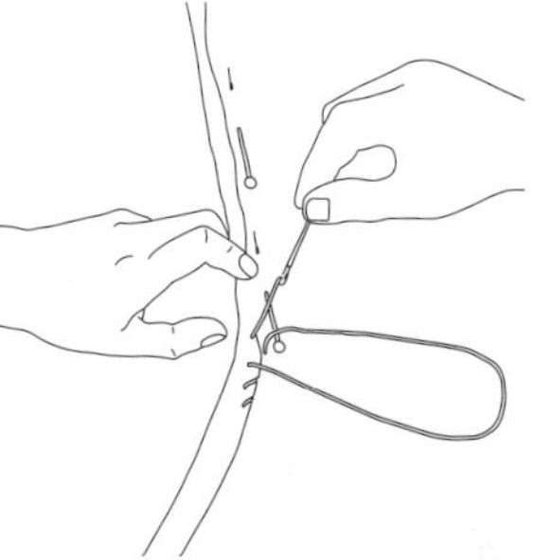

5. Once done, place the cushion back into its cover and enjoy its renewed plumpness and comfort.

PRO TIP Regularly turning your cushions and re-plumping them every week or each time you use them, is a great way to ensure they maintain their body for as long as possible. Rotating cushions around the home can also help them to maintain their shape and prolong their lives.

Room divider

Room dividers, often referred to as partitions or screens, have a rich history spanning various cultures and civilizations. Originally thought to have originated in China and Japan, these beautiful and functional wooden pieces were adorned with intricate carvings and paintings. Room dividers gained popularity during the 18th and 19th centuries in Europe, where they were used to divide large rooms into more intimate conversation areas, conceal changing spaces or dressing areas, and even enhance the overall aesthetics of interior spaces.

To start, decide where your screen will go and how you will use it; this will determine its height and length. The length is determined by the number of panels (a minimum of three) and their width. If you choose a patterned fabric, you may want to consider the position of the pattern on your panels to ensure they match across the screen. A large motif or pattern repeat may also determine the width of the panel.

For this project, I suggest a height of 180cm (71 inches) and a width of 40cm (16 inches) per panel, allowing you to get three front panels out of the fabric width.

Tools and materials

Jigsaw or hand saw (with dust mask and eye protection)
Wooden lengths to make the frame: at least 2.5 × 4cm (1 × 1½ inches)
Pencil or tailor's chalk
Rulers
Power drill with 2mm or 3mm (1/16 or ⅛ inch) drill bit for pilot holes, and corresponding screw bit
Wood glue
Wood screws: 4.0 × 50mm (0.15 × 2 inches)
Staple gun and staples
Set square or roofing square
Hessian
Upholstery contact adhesive
Polyester wadding (55g/2oz) or Woolguard
Fabric of choice for front and back
Regulator
6 x hinges: no longer/wider than 5cm (2 inches)/2.5cm (1 inch)
Braid: 1–1.5cm (⅜–⅝ inch) wide
Hot melt glue gun
Gliders/feet (optional)

Planning and preparation

1. Cut out wood pieces and corner braces following this cutting list:

- 6 × 180cm (71 inch) wooden lengths
- 9 × 35cm (14 inch) wooden lengths (top, bottom and centre bars)
- 18 × wooden corner supports with 45-degree angles at each end

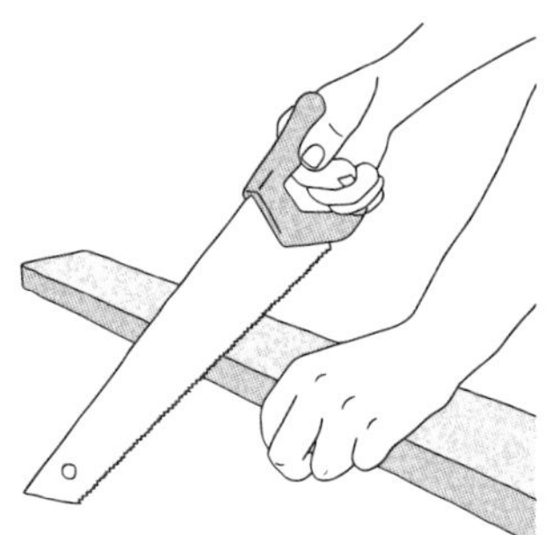

Assembling the frame

2. Align an upright piece with a bottom or top piece and mark where to drill pilot holes using a 2mm or 3mm (1/16 or ⅛ inch) bit. Repeat this on all of the top and bottom ends of the uprights.

3. Apply a small amount of wood glue to the ends of the smaller pieces and screw all the top and bottom pieces in, giving you three tall rectangular panels.

4. Measure the height of each panel and find the centre. Position the central bar off-centre by 7.5cm (3 inches) to avoid overlapping with the position of the hinge. Drill pilot holes and screw in the last shorter pieces on all three panels.

5. Next, repeat with the corner supports, following the diagram below. Drill a pilot hole, making sure that the position of the hole, which will be the position of the screw, is going to allow for the whole length of the screw to go into the wood without it showing through on the other side.

Adding the case fabric and padding

6. Once your three panels are ready, staple hessian or a similar material to both sides of each panel, ensuring it is centrally positioned on the wooden frame. Pull the fabric taut to prevent sagging over time.

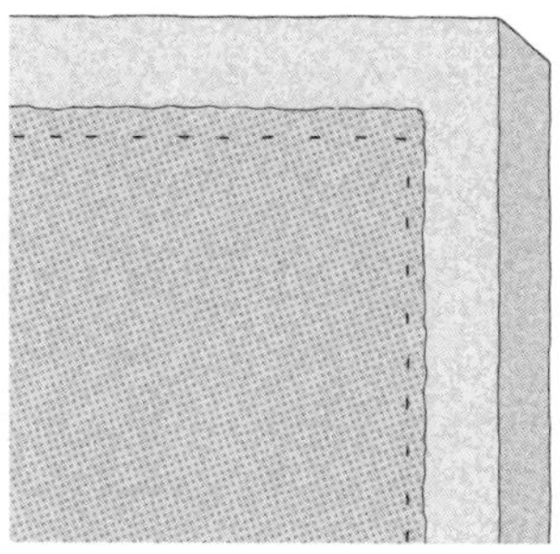

7. Now use upholstery contact adhesive to add a layer of polyester wadding or Woolguard to the front of each wooden panel. This glue is really to hold the padding in place so that it doesn't move while you are working with the panel, so it doesn't have to be heavily glued into place. Allow the wadding to overhang the wood edges by about 1.2cm (½ inch) or so to give the sides a small amount of padding.

Attaching the fabric

8. For this screen I am using a plain fabric for the back and a heavily patterned fabric for the face. You could, of course, use the same for both the front and back.

9. Starting with the back fabric, cut three panels so that you have plenty of excess to staple on to the edge of the frame.

PRO TIP One width of fabric can often cover all three panels, making the process more economical.

10. Start in the middle of each side and secure the fabric with temporary staples, working towards the corners. Apply an even tension to avoid wrinkles.

PRO TIP Temporary staples are staples that go all the way in on one side and halfway in on the other side (see also page 32). This way they are really easy to take out without damaging the wood surface.

11. If you are happy with the fabric position, replace the temporary staples with permanent ones, spacing them closely for finer fabrics. Leave a raw edge at this stage so as not to create bulk.

12. Once you are satisfied with the tension, box pleat the corners following the instructions on page 36 in Essential Techniques: Box Pleats, trimming excess fabric if that is required (thicker fabrics will require the excess removed while thinner fabrics will lay much flatter). Repeat this for all the panels.

Padding and covering the front

13. Now it's time to pad and cover the face of the panels starting again with the polyester wadding or Woolguard. Test whether to wrap the padding over the edges based on fabric thickness.

14. Lightly glue the padding in place in the same way you did on the back of the panel. Again this is really just to help you work with the panel so the panel doesn't move around while you are adding your top fabric.

PRO TIP If you have decided to take the padding over the edges I recommend you don't try to glue these sections. There is a high risk of the glue spraying on to the fabric.

15. To determine the width and depth of the front fabric, measure across the width from the side returns, and down the length from the return of the top frame to the bottom. Add a small allowance of 1.5–2.5cm (⅝–1 inch) all around.

Finishing the fabric

16. Start with one of the long sides of the panel, fold the fabric under and secure the first temporary staple in the same way as you did with the back, starting in the middles and working your way to the corners. This time, fold the fabric under itself to avoid a raw edge. Staple it along the folded edge, positioning the fold centrally on the width of the frame.

17. Staple all four sides, positioning the staples close to one another. Pleat the corners in the same way as you did for the back fabric, cutting out the bulk where needed. You may need a regulator to help hold the fold in place while you staple it down.

18. Repeat on the remaining panels, final fixing the staples in place as you go.

Attaching the hinges and braid

19. You will need six hinges if you have three panels – three for each join. Measure the centre of the panel height and then about 20–30cm (8–12 inches) in from the top and bottom edges for the other two hinges. Because you have offset your middle wooden bar you will not obstruct any screws when attaching your middle hinge (see step 4).

20. Drill pilot holes and attach three hinges to one panel with their corresponding screws. Once these are in place, position the second panel on top, face to face or back to back depending on the way around you have attached your hinges, making sure the two panels are level with one another. Now join the hinges to the second panel.

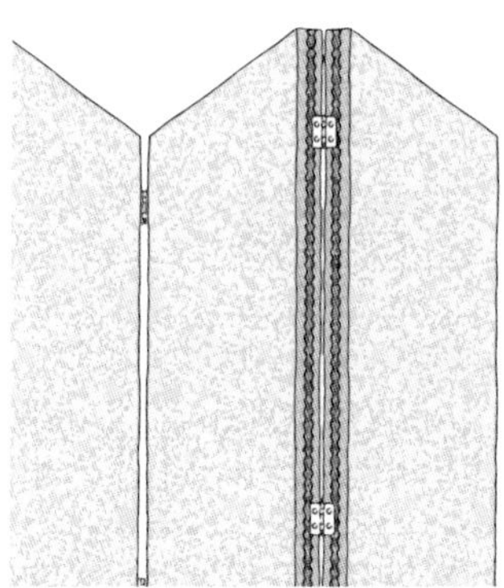

21. To enable the screen to open in a 'zig-zag' shape the hinges on the third panel will have to open the opposite way to the way you have attached them to the first and second panels, so keep this in mind when you are fixing them to the last panel.

22. To attach the braid, fold the screen up and lay it on a large flat surface. You can fix the braid in one of two ways:

Option 1: Visible hinges

23. Using a hot melt glue gun, attach your braid starting from the middle of one of the panels. Fold the end of the braid under itself to create a tidy starting point and glue the braid in a central position covering the line of staples.

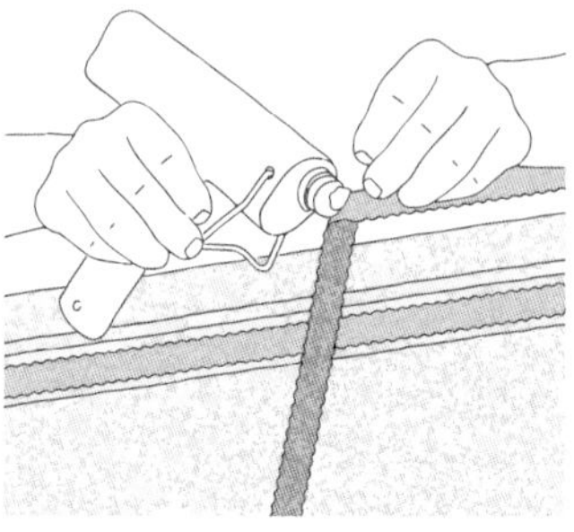

24. Continue up to the hinge then finish the braid by trimming it and turning the end under. Glue the end down.

25. Start the other side of the hinge again by turning and gluing an end under and carry on with the braid around the edge of each panel until you arrive at another hinge. Repeat this process until you reach your original starting point again. Finish the braid on the bottom edge by turning the end under and gluing down so it butts up closely to the starting braid edge. Repeat on all three panels.

PRO TIP Keep tension on the braid and avoid excess glue to prevent seeping. Small coloured upholstery pins can complement the braid.

Option 2: Covered hinges

26. Instead of stopping the braid at the hinge you could carry it over. Avoid gluing the braid to the hinge itself as it won't stick due to the shiny nature of the hinge's surface.

27. Once complete, you may choose to add small plastic nail-on gliders to the very bottom edge of the frame. This step is optional.

Rectangular headboard for beginners

Headboards can transform a bedroom space. In fact, on occasion, I have designed entire rooms around a headboard. The simplest way to make a headboard is to start with a rectangular shape, especially for a double or a queen-size bed. From there, you can work your way up to more complex shaped headboards (see page 120).

Tools and materials

MDF or plywood (18mm/ $^{11}/_{16}$ inch) thick
Jigsaw or hand saw (with dust mask and eye protection)
Foam: 2.5–5cm (1–2 inches), depending on desired thickness
Ruler
Pencil or tailor's chalk
Rasp tool (optional)
Foam saw, craft knife with retractable blade or sharp bread knife
Upholstery contact adhesive
Fabric scissors
Polyester wadding (55g/2oz) or Woolguard
Top fabric of choice
Staples and staple gun
Bottom cloth

PRO TIP There are a number of ways to make split battens. Search for 'how to make a split batten or French cleat' online for step-by-step instructions, or buy ready made.

Planning and preparation

1. Decide how you will fit the headboard – to the bed or the wall. Some divan-style beds have existing bolts that headboard legs can slot into. If that's the case, you can reuse these. If fixing the headboard to the wall, a split batten fixing (see Pro Tip) is a good method, meaning no legs are required.

2. Consider the fabric width when designing the height of your headboard. Double-height fabrics are available, but most upholstery or soft furnishings fabrics are made up to 137cm (54 inches) wide. If your headboard is taller than this, you may need to join your fabric together, especially if there is a pattern to match. If using plain fabric and the headboard is shorter than the fabric width, you can run the fabric left to right without joins.

Determining dimensions

3. Decide on the height and width of the headboard. It can extend beyond the width of the bed to include bedside tables, creating a unique look, or align with the bed frame or divan.

4. With regards to height, usually the larger the bed the taller the headboard. For example, a double bed may only require a headboard that is 35cm (14 inches) tall, whereas a queen-size bed will need one around 71cm (28 inches) tall and a king-size bed is suited to a headboard 147cm (58 inches) tall. You also want to consider the visible height of the headboard above the pillows. The headboard typically sits at the top of the mattress level.

Cutting the board

5. Cut a piece of MDF or plywood to size. Make sure you use a dust mask and goggles for this. A jigsaw is ideal, but a hand saw can also work. Alternatively, have the wood retailer cut the board to size. I recommend plywood over MDF as it holds staples better.

6. Cut the foam for the front to size, oversizing by 1.5 times the depth of the wooden board you are using.

PRO TIP Use 2.5cm (1 inch) foam for easier handling and neater corners, though you can opt for 5cm (2 inch) foam for a thicker look. Thicker foam can be more challenging to work with, though, and is more expensive too.

Preparing the foam and board

7. Use a rasp to smooth off the edges of the wood if necessary.

8. Chamfer the edge of the foam by marking 2.5cm (1 inch) back from the front edge and cutting the edge along that line at an angle down to the the bottom edge to create a gentle slope (see also step 6 of Drop-in seat base for an occasional chair/modern technique project on page 65).

9. Lay the foam down on a flat surface and place the wooden board on top, centring it.

10. In a well-ventilated space, use upholstery contact adhesive to glue the foam to the board – lift one side of the board up, spray glue on both surfaces, and then lay the board back down.

11. Spray the chamfered edge and the board edge, and once the glue has become tacky enough to stick, roll the foam over to cover the edge, sticking towards the back edge of the sides.

12. When you reach the corners, stick the foam as far as you can and cut off the excess overhanging the corner with a pair of scissors – cut it 5mm (3⁄16 inch) away from the corner of the wood. This will help fill out the fabric on the corners.

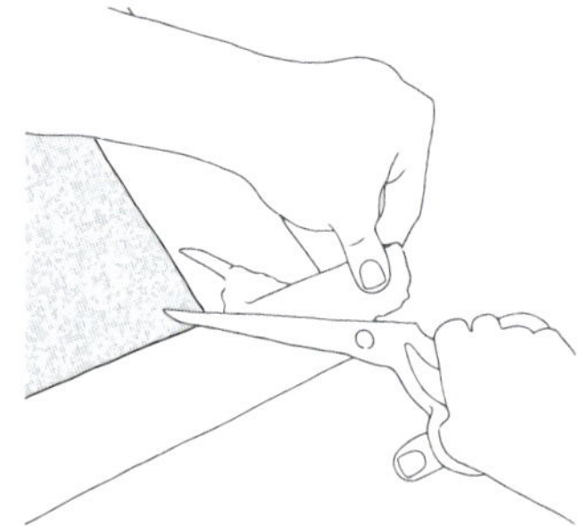

13. Cover the foam with polyester wadding or a layer of Woolguard, depending on whether your top fabric is FR treated. A very light layer of glue will help to keep this in place. Depending on the size of your headboard you may need more than one width. Glue the widths as close together as possible and try not to overlap the layers as the overlap will be visible when the fabric sits on top of it.

Covering with the top fabric

14. Cut the fabric with an additional 12.5cm (5 inches) all around. Unless you are using a double-width fabric, you will have to add joins to your fabric and the traditional way to do this is to add the additional sections to either side of a full-width section, which will result in two smaller sections and one main section.

15. Lay the fabric on the board and use a staple gun to place temporary staples in the centre of each side, working outwards to the corners to build tension.

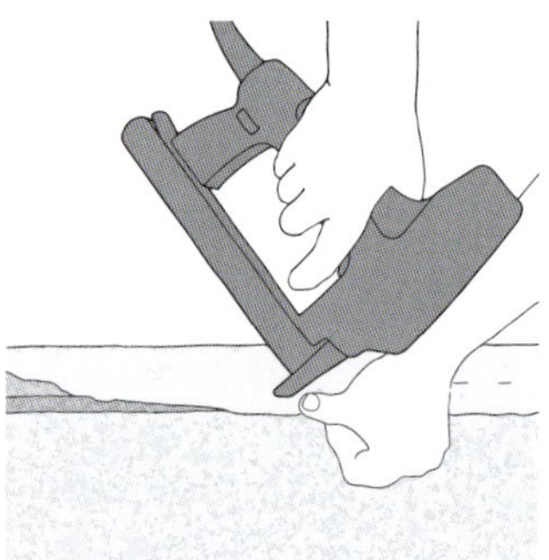

16. Ensure even tension and adjust by removing and repositioning temporary staples as needed.

PRO TIP: Use temporary staples to allow for adjustments (see page 34). They can be easily removed without damaging the fabric.

Final fixing the fabric

17. Once you are happy with the tension, secure the fabric with permanent staples, spaced 3-5cm (1¼-2 inches) apart.

18. Once you have reached the corners, tension the fabric on the side sections up to each corner and staple down on the back of the board. You will find that the weave of the fabric will glide back as the foam dips on the corners. Follow the dip and smooth the fabric out so the tension remains even across the whole headboard.

19. Take the side section of fabric and fold this across and back over the top edge of the corner and fix into place with a staple. You will find that at the corner the fabric will want to fold over itself - encourage this and fold and staple it down, trimming the excess fabric.

Adding box pleats

20. Before folding and fixing the fabric on the top corner of the headboard into a small box pleat (see Essential Techniques: Box Pleats on page 36), assess if any bulk needs to be cut out, especially when using thick fabric. Start by folding the excess fabric under itself and pulling it around to the back edge where you have stapled the other sections of fabric. Check if the fabric sits flat and evenly in line with the rest of the top of the headboard. If it lies neatly without raising up and you can easily fold a box pleat, you can staple it off on to the back in the same way as the rest of the fabric.

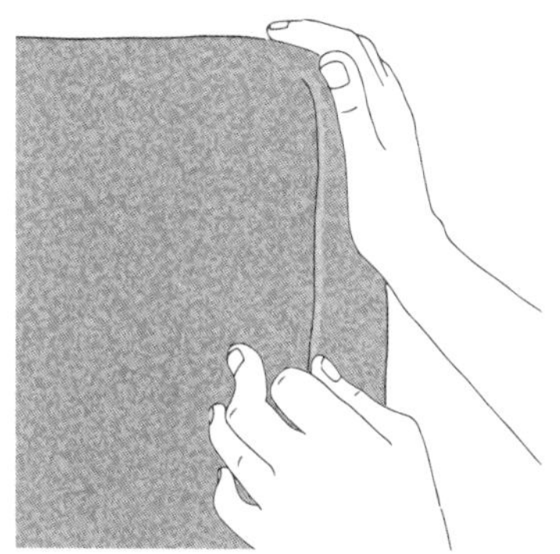

If the fabric is thick and creates too much bulk, causing it to sit higher than the rest of the top edge, you will need to cut out some bulk. Fold the excess fabric under itself to form a neat edge 1-2mm (1/16 inch) from the corner, then use a pencil or chalk to mark 3-4mm (1/8-3/16 inch) inside the fold on the inside of the pleat. Cut along this line to reduce the bulk.

PRO TIP: Cut out smaller sections of excess fabric initially. You can always cut more, but you can't add it back!

21. Fold the top section of the box-style pleat fabric over and staple on to the back with a folded neat edge. Repeat this on all four corners.

Finishing touches

22. Add a bottom cloth to the back to cover all of the staples, following steps 20-23 of the Drop-in seat base for an occasional chair/modern technique project on page 67.

23. Install split battens to fix the headboard to the wall, ensuring it sits above the mattress.

24. Fit the headboard to your bed or wall, and take pleasure in your custom creation!

Shaped headboard

Building on the techniques for a rectangular headboard, creating a decoratively shaped headboard can elevate your bedroom interior to another level. While most of the same principles apply, a shaped headboard is typically thicker in depth due to the construction of the frame. For this project, you will also pipe the edge and finish with a border stapled on the top of the headboard.

Tools and materials

Paper, calico or remnant fabric for patterning (large enough so that you don't have to join the paper or, if you do, with minimal joins)
Ruler
Marking implements
Low-tack masking tape
MDF or plywood, 18mm or 2.5cm (11/16 inch or 1 inch) thick
Jigsaw (with dust mask and eye protection)
Foam: 2.5–5cm (1–2 inches) depending on desired thickness
Rasp tool (optional)
Foam saw, craft knife with retractable blade or sharp bread knife
Upholstery contact adhesive
Staples (including some at least 10mm/3/8 inch long for stapling off the fabric towards the back edge of the headboard)
Staple gun
Top fabric of choice
Polyester wadding (55g/2oz) or Woolguard
Bottom cloth
Matching sewing thread
Sewing machine with piping or zip foot option
Piping cord
Back-tacking strip
Hand-sewing needle (optional)

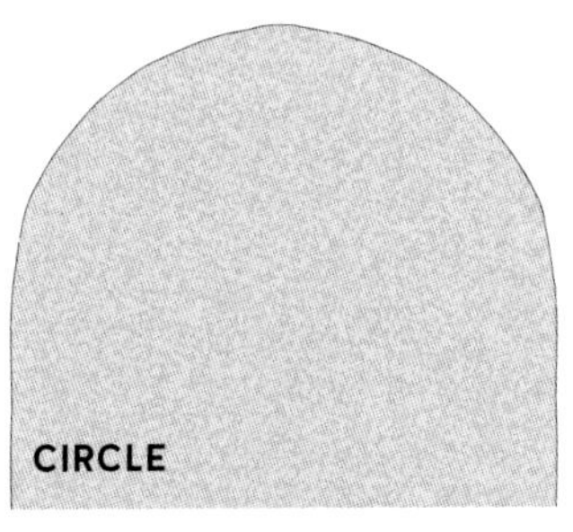

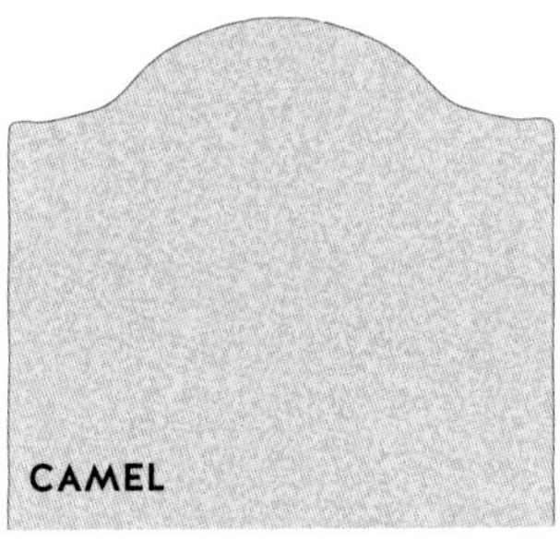

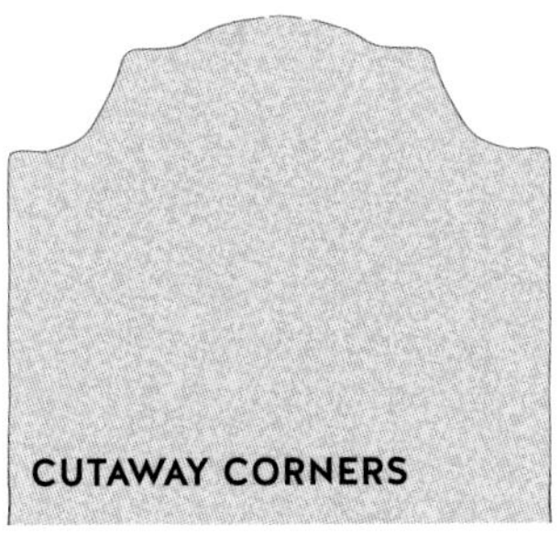

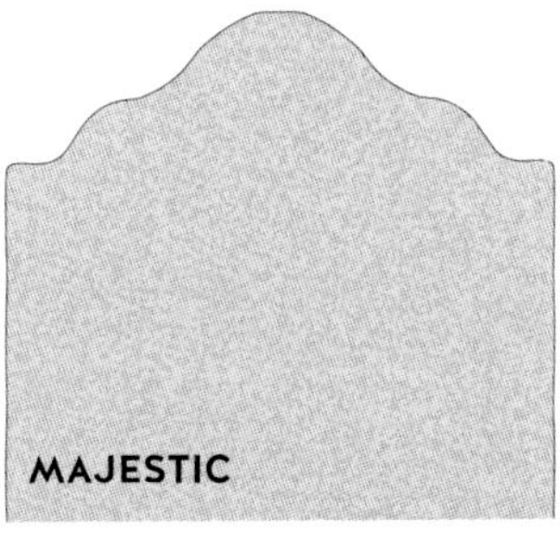

Designing the shape and fixing

1. Use a large sheet of paper, calico or remnant fabric to design the shape of your headboard. On the left are some shape suggestions you could recreate, scale and adjust to your preference.

2. When deciding on the height of your headboard, take into account the space pillows will occupy. You may want to keep that area free from shaping.

3. Decide how the headboard will be fixed in place: headboard legs attached to the divan or a split batten to the wall (see Pro Tip, page 116). Consider the size of the room; you might want the frame to sit behind the entire bed and rest on the floor.

4. Using a low-tack masking tape, stick your pattern to the wall above your bed. This helps you to check that you are happy with the scale and design.

Cutting the wood

5. Once you are happy with the design, cut a piece of MDF or plywood to size. Make sure you use a dust mask and goggles for this. A jigsaw is ideal. Alternatively, have the wood retailer cut the board to size. I recommend plywood over MDF as it holds staples better.

PRO TIP You might consider making the headboard thicker by using a batten between two sheets of wooden board. You may need a craftsperson to assist with this.

Preparing the foam and board

6. Follow step 2 of the Rectangular headboard for beginners project on page 116, to choose your fabric. You may have to join two sheets of foam together to cover the surface area required.

7. Follow steps 7–13 on page 118, to prepare your foam and attach it to the board, gluing it to the top edge of the wood, not the sides. The thinnest edge of the chamfer may slightly overhang; that's okay.

Covering with fabric

8. Follow steps 14 and 15 on page 118 but use staples that are at least 10mm (⅜ inch) long and staple off the fabric towards the back edge of the wooden board so they are not visible when the top border is added.

9. For concave curves, snip V-shaped notches into the fabric to help pull it tight over the curve and tack it to the edge, ensuring any puckering is smoothed out of the curve. You may need to cut more notches into the fabric 1cm (⅜ inch) apart to get the fabric to sit flat.

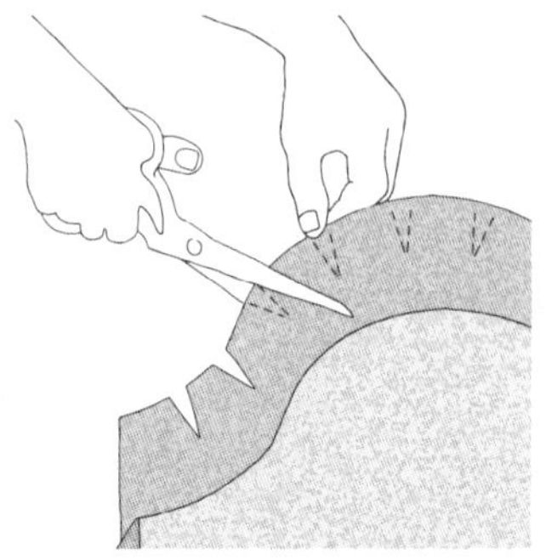

10. Staple off the fabric at the bottom edge of the headboard around to the back, rather than on the underside.

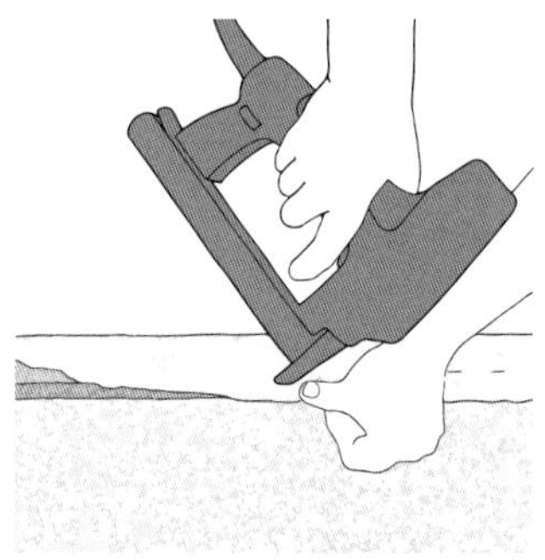

PRO TIP Ensure the fabric weave on the face remains straight and horizontal as much as possible.

11. After working to all the corners, curves and shaped sections, check the fabric's tension. The larger the headboard the more challenging it will be to build tension. Tighten as needed by adjusting temporary staples by taking them out, re-tensioning the fabric and putting another temporary staple back in its place.

12. Once you are happy with the tension, start to fully fix in staples into the back of the board. Again start from the middle and work out to the corners.

Adding the piping and border

13. If you are using the same fabric for the piping and border, cut the piping on the bias long enough to start and end at the two bottom corners. You may need a few lengths sewn together to create your desired length. This process is applicable to all headboard shapes (see Essential Techniques: Piping, on page 37).

14. Cut a fabric border 7.5cm (3 inches) deep, the same length as the piping. Using a piping foot or zip foot, sew the piping to the edge of the border fabric. Align the piping's selvedge edge with the edge of the border, and sew along the same stitch line you used when initially sewing the piping. Sew the piping to the face of the border fabric.

PRO TIP When sewing the piping together, don't sew too tightly at first. Sew closer to the piping when attaching the border to hide the stitching. Triple-check the stitched edge before attaching this to the headboard. If any stitches are visible or inconsistent, go over that section again.

15. Back tack the border and piping to the edge of the headboard using 12mm (½ inch) or 14mm (⁹⁄₁₆ inch) staples. See steps 39–42 of the Straight back dining chair/ all covered recover on page 100 for how to position the backing-tape strip and attach the border fabric. Cut the back-tacking strip to match the edge of the headboard, positioning the tape slightly back from the edge by 2–3mm (¹⁄₁₆–⅛ inch). Alternatively, use a hand-sewing needle and matching thread to slip stitch the border in place (see page 35). This prevents staples from showing through on the face and ensures that you are stapling into enough wood to get a good fixing. Pull gentle tension into the border as you work your way around the edge, first temporarily stapling on to the back of the headboard 2–4cm (¾–1½ inches) in from the edge and then, once checked, final fixing with staples.

16. Cut a piece of polyester wadding or Woolguard to pad out the border section. Depending on the fabric's thickness, add one layer up to the back-tacking strip, flush with the back of the headboard, and then another layer over the top of that. This second layer will overhang the back edge to soften the edge of the wood.

17. Pull tension into the border and tack this off on to the back of the headboard, again snipping into the fabric where there are any concave sections as you did in step 9. Follow the same practice of temporarily stapling into place, checking and adjusting where necessary, and then stapling down permanently. Cut the bulk of the fabric away tight to the staple line.

18. If you have a thicker headboard, consider adding another line of piping to the back edge as this gives a better look.

Final steps

19. Add a bottom cloth to cover all the staples on the back, following steps 20–23 of the Drop-in seat base for an occasional chair/modern technique project on page 67.

20. Determine the height for your split battens (see Pro Tip, page 116), noting that some large headboards may need both top and bottom split battens). The headboard should ideally sit above your mattress.

Once you have fitted your fixings, install the headboard to your bed and wall, and enjoy!

Headboard slipcover

This method transforms your existing headboard quickly and effectively without needing to construct a new one. Ideal for straight-sided headboards (shaped headboards are not recommended), this approach works for both patterned and plain fabrics. In this example, we are creating a slipcover for a double bed in order to demonstrate how to join fabric sections – for a single bed headboard the same principles apply but without the need to join the fabric.

Tools and materials

Top fabric of choice
Soft tape measure
Pencil or chalk
Fabric scissors
Matching sewing thread
Sewing machine
Paper, calico or remnant fabric for patterning
Dressmaking pins or masking tape
Ruler
Set square or roofing square
Regulator (optional)

Choosing fabric and measuring

1. First, it's important to to decide whether you are going to use a patterned or plain fabric. For a patterned fabric, it's at this stage that you need to plan the pattern placement, ensuring it won't be obstructed by pillows.

2. If the headboard is bolted to the bed frame you could remove it at this stage to make measuring easier. Measure the width and the up-and-over dimension of the headboard. Add an extra 10cm (4 inches) to these measurements all round. This is the amount of fabric you will need.

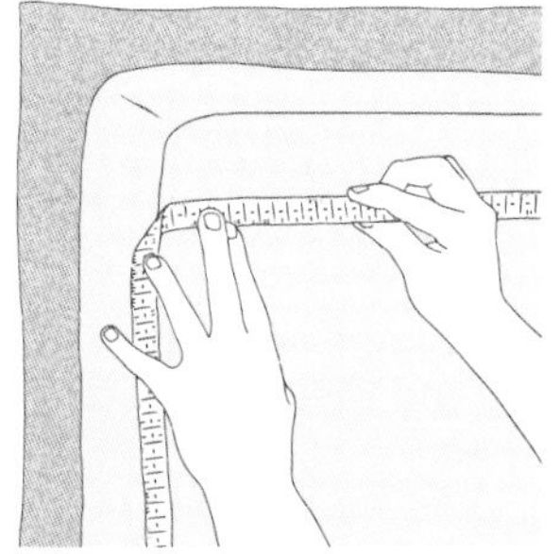

Cutting and sewing the fabric

3. Unless you are using a double-width fabric, you will have to add joins to your headboard slipcover and the traditional way to do this is to add the additional sections to either side of a full-width section, which will result in two smaller sections and one main section.

4. Sew these three pieces together and set them aside – we will come back to this once we have created a pattern for your end profile, which is used for both ends/sides. A shaped end or a shaped cushion side is referred to as a 'profile'. When referring to the end profile in this set of instructions I am referring to the left-hand and right-hand sides of the headboard, not the top or bottom.

Creating the end profile

5. To pattern the end profile, use a piece of calico or scrap piece of fabric or paper, and secure this to one end of the headboard (either the left- or right-hand side). If it's a fabric-covered headboard use pins, if it's a leather or vinyl one use some masking tape.

6. Mark the stitching line onto the pattern along the existing seam line or where the cover will sit better.

Mark from the front and up-and-over down the back.

7. Add marry marks around the edge of the patterned profile (see page 47), spacing them 3–4cm (1¼–1½ inches) apart. These marks will serve as a guide to ensure both shaped sides are sewn to the main fabric panel accurately, preventing the cover from being twisted or uneven. If you were to draw a line between opposite marry marks on the left and right sides, it would be horizontal, ensuring that the orientation of the side profile remains even.

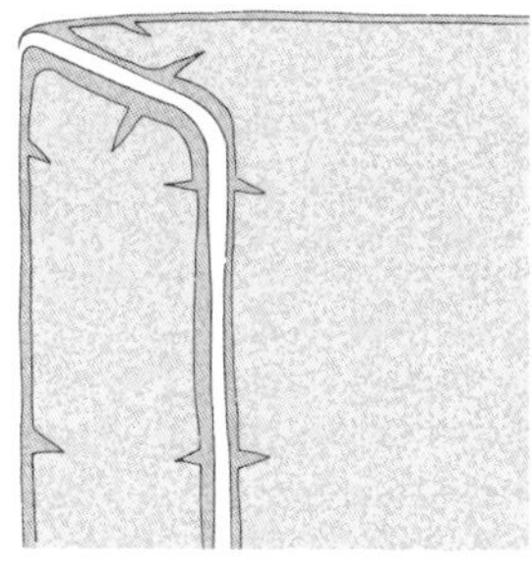

Determine where you would like the slipcover to finish at the base. If the headboard is integral to the bed frame, it's easiest to finish the slipcover where the headboard meets the side base frame. If the headboard has its own legs and is bolted to the bed frame, you can finish the slipcover at the bottom edge of the headboard.

8. Remove the pattern and add a seam allowance of 1.2–1.5cm (½–⅝ inch), or more if you prefer a bigger seam allowance around the edges, including a double allowance at the bottom for a double hem that will hide the raw edge of the fabric. Cut this pattern ready to transfer to your fabric.

9. Use your end profile pattern to cut out two ends. Flip the pattern over to make sure you have two mirrored sides. Don't forget to transfer the marry marks you have previously marked on the pattern on to the fabric. Be sure to mark lines within the seam allowance so that they won't be seen when everything is sewn together. Its good practice to only mark small lines even when marking on the reverse of your top fabric.

Joining the main section and end profiles

10. Measure the headboard width to the existing seam line, or where you think the seam should be. Take into consideration how stretchy your reverse is (see Pro Tip, page 130).

11. Allowing for any stretch, transfer this measurement to your main section of fabric and mark on the stitching line, adding your seam allowance.

12. Now it's time to start sewing everything together. Starting with your end profiles, hem the bottom edge of each one, turning the fabric allowance twice to form a neat hem with no raw edges of fabric showing. Next, hem the bottom front edge of the main panel. Don't hem the other edge at this stage.

PRO TIP If you are using a thick fabric you may not be able to use a double hem here as it may cause problems sewing through the bulk on the machine.

Attaching the end profiles

13. Before sewing the side profiles to the main section of the cover (the front and back) you need to transfer the marry marks to the edge of the cover where the profile will be sewn. This is done by 'walking' the profile along the edge. This term is used when you offer up the edge of the profile to the edge of the main fabric and run it along the edge as if it was being sewn together as a test to see how it fits and also in this case as a way to transfer the marry marks to the main fabric.

Lay the main fabric out on to a large flat surface right side up and then lay the profile on to the fabric right side down (so that they are face to face) at the beginning of the edge it will be sewn to. Position the end profile on the main fabric where it has been hemmed.

Use a pin or regulator to act as the sewing machine needle and position it on the stitching line with one hand, transfer the marry marks from the profile to the main section using a pencil or chalk with the other hand, be sure the mark is within the seam allowance.

Roll the profile edge along the edge of the main panel, repositioning the regulator/pin along the line as you go and transferring the marry marks as you work along the edge. The regulator/pin stops the profile from drifting away from the edge and helps to keep the fabrics in place as you work along the edge. Work all the way around to the other side and mark the end point of the side profile on to the main fabric.

Add a double seam allowance mark to the main fabric on the front and back, as you will fold this edge under twice to give you a neat edge. If you are using a thick fabric, fold the hem only once.

14. Fold the main fabric in half and transfer the marry marks to the other edge, which will have the other profile sewn to it.

15. Starting from the bottom at the hem of the main fabric, place your pieces (the main fabric with one of the end profile pieces) together right side to right side, and sew them together ensuring the marry marks match up.

16. With one side profile of the headboard sewn, now is a good time to triple-check your measurements and stretch allowance, if used. Make any adjustments now before finishing.

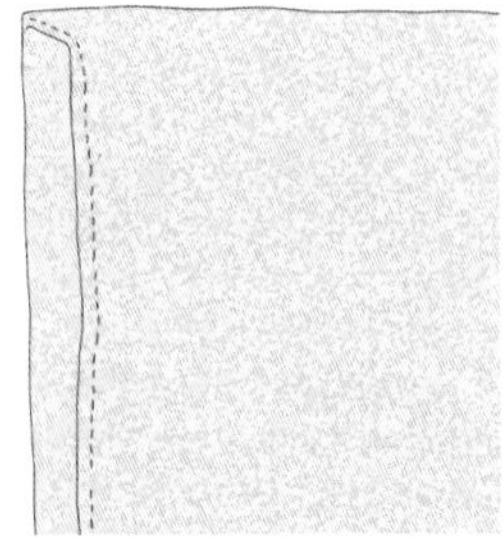

17. Sew the second end profile following steps 13–15, ensuring symmetry and proper fit. Again this is a really good time to triple-check that everything fits perfectly. Now that you have sewn both profiles to the main panel, hem the bottom edge all the way around starting and finishing at the back. Turn the hem twice if that is what you have planned or once for a thick fabric.

Final adjustments

18. I recommend adding pairs of ties to the bottom of the main section so that you can tie the front and back sections together, ensuring that the slipcover doesn't move around. You could use some ribbon or create some ties from matching fabric. Follow steps 6–8 in the Box seat cushion/with ties for a dining chair project on pages 56 and 58 for instructions on how to make six ties, approximately 30cm (12 inches) long.

19. Add a pair of ties to each of the sides and a pair in the middle. Once you have sewn these on you can final fit your headboard and tie off the ties.

Window seat on a wooden base

Creating a window seat cushion on a wooden base offers a sleek and tight fabric covering. This method is for achieving a shallow seat with 5cm (2 inch) foam, which is easier for beginners ... and for those with limited fabric! Here's how to make one for your space.

Tools and materials

Paper, calico or remnant fabric for patterning
Pencil
30cm (12 inch) ruler
Scissors (both paper and fabric)
12mm (½ inch) thick plywood or MDF
Jigsaw or hand saw (with dust mask and eye protection)
Rasp tool
Foam: 5cm (2 inch) firm seating-grade
Foam saw, craft knife with retractable blade or sharp bread knife
Upholstery contact adhesive
Polyester wadding (55g/2oz) or Woolguard
Top fabric of choice
Staple gun and staples
Bottom cloth

Creating a pattern

1. Lay a piece of paper, calico or remnant fabric on the seating area and weigh this down.

2. Using a pencil, lightly trace the seating area outline. If the corners are curved be sure to mark this on to your pattern.

3. Transfer the pattern to a flat surface and connect the traced lines using a pencil and ruler. Straighten any uneven lines but retain the seating area's shape.

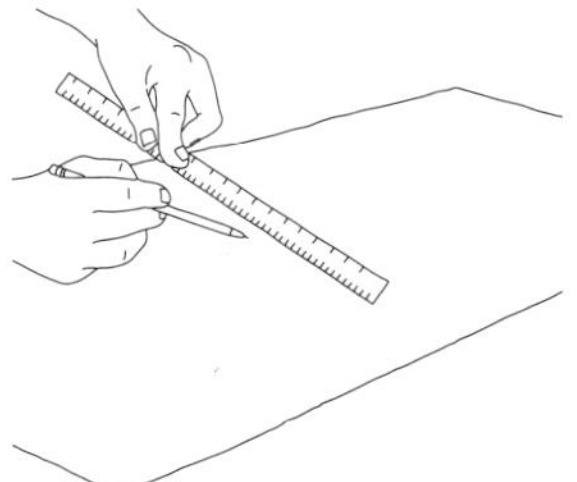

4. Cut your pattern out and place it on the seating area, adjusting the pattern shape if required. Reduce the pattern size by 3–4mm (⅛–³⁄₁₆ inch) all around – this is because the foam will wrap around the sides and pad out the shape. Cut the pattern shape out.

Cutting the wood

5. Lay the pattern on 12mm (½ inch) MDF or plywood and trace the outline on to the wood in pencil.

6. Cut on the line using a jigsaw or hand saw. Make sure you use a dust mask and goggles for this. A jigsaw is ideal, but a hand saw can also work. Alternatively, have the wood retailer cut the board to size.

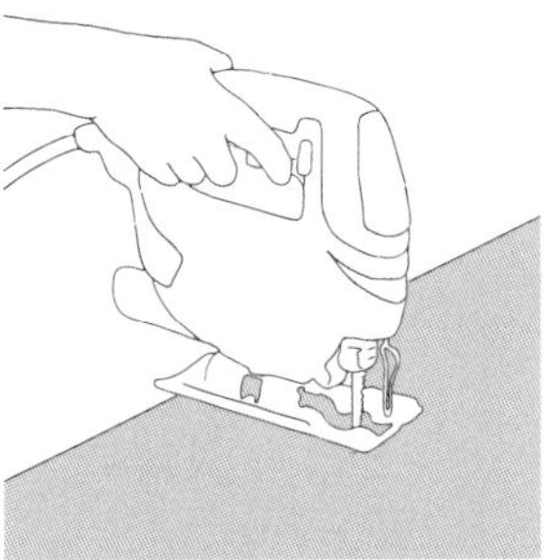

7. Rasp back the edges of the wood to create a slight bevel (arris). This is to stop sharp edges cutting through the foam and fabric.

Foam preparation

8. Lay the wooden panel on a piece of 5cm (2 inch) foam, mark and cut the foam 2cm (¾ inch) larger than the wooden base.

9. Chamfer the edge of the foam on all sides by marking 3.5cm (1⅓ inch) back from the edges. Cut at an angle from the marked line to the bottom edge to create a gentle slope. See also step 6 of the Drop-in seat base for an occasional chair/modern technique project on page 65.

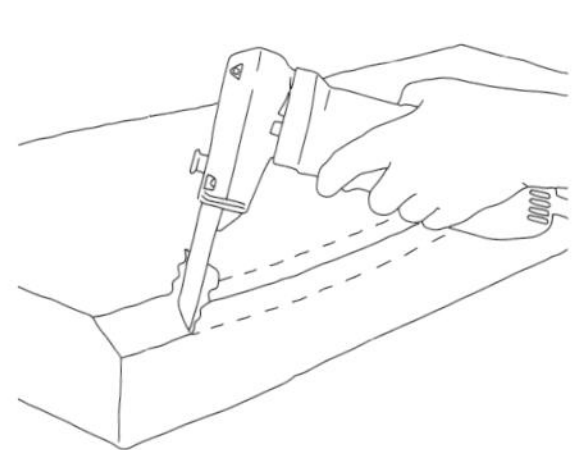

10. Lay the foam face down and spray upholstery contact adhesive on the back. Spray adhesive on the top of the board too.

11. Once the glue is tacky, centre and stick the wood to the foam.

12. Spray the chamfered foam edge - you may be going over the first layer of spray glue. Wait for the glue to be tacky so that it sticks well to the board, then roll the edge of the foam down to finish at the bottom edge of the wooden board.

13. When you arrive at the corners, stick the foam down as far as you can, then cut off the excess on the corners with a pair of scissors - cut it 5mm (3⁄16 inch) away from the corner of the wood. This will help fill out the fabric on the corners.

Wadding and fabric covering

14. Cover the foam with polyester wadding or a layer of Woolguard depending on whether your top fabric is FR treated. A very light layer of glue will help to keep this in place.

15. Cut the top fabric 7.5–12.5cm (3–5 inches) larger than the board all around.

16. Lay your fabric on the board, and using a staple gun, start fixing temporary staples into the middle of each edge of the board, alternating between sides to build tension.

17. Work the temporary staples towards the corners, smoothing the fabric out as you work.

Final fixing and corners

18. Once you're satisfied with the tension across the entire seat, begin fully securing the fabric with final fix staples on the back of the board. Start at the middle and work your way out towards the corners, positioning the staples evenly.

19. When you reach the corners, pull the fabric on the side sections up to the corner and staple it down on the back of the board. As you work, you'll notice the fabric may shift due to the foam dipping. Follow the dip and smooth out the fabric with the same tension as the rest of the sides. Fold the side fabric over and back over the top edge of the corner. Fix it into place with staples. At the corner, the fabric will naturally fold over itself – encourage this fold and staple it down. Trim excess bulk up to the staples.

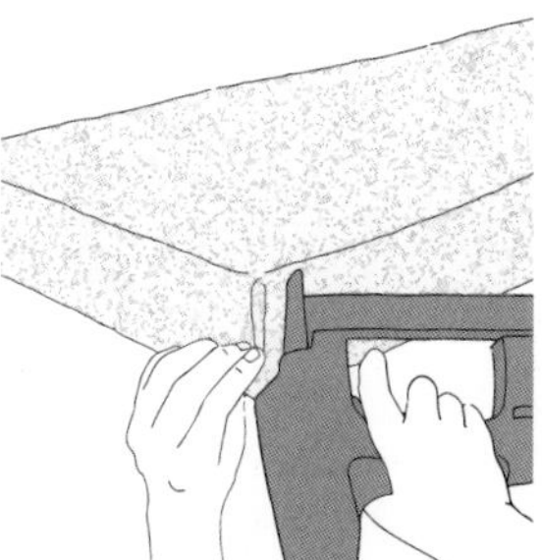

20. Test a box-style pleat (see page 36 in Essential Techniques: Box Pleats) on the corner to determine how much bulk needs to be cut out. Start by making a small V-shape cut to see how it fits, then adjust as required by cutting more if necessary.

21. After cutting the bulk, fold the top section of fabric over and staple it on to the back of the board. Repeat this process on all four corners. You may need to flatten any remaining bulk on the corners to achieve a smooth finish. Use your tack hammer for this.

22. Add a bottom cloth to cover all of the staples and staple this into place following steps 20–23 of the Drop-in seat base for an occasional chair/modern technique project on page 67.

23. Place the completed box seat into the seating area. Your project is now ready for use.

Window seat box cushion

If you prefer a more plumptious window seat cushion, the box cushion method is ideal. This version builds on the technique for a Window seat on a wooden base (see page 128), providing a thicker, softer seat.

This process closely mirrors the steps from the Box seat cushion/ hand sewn closed with piping/no zip project on page 52. If you have previously made a box cushion, you will find that the skills and techniques you used are directly applicable to this window seat version.

Tools and materials
Paper, calico or remnant fabric for patterning
Pencil
30cm (12 inch) ruler
Scissors (both paper and fabric)
Foam: minimum thickness 7.5cm (3 inches) firm seating-grade
Foam saw, craft knife with retractable blade or sharp bread knife
Polyester wadding (55g/2oz)
Stockinette
Upholstery contact adhesive
Top fabric of choice
Metre ruler
Set square or roofing square
Marking implements
Matching sewing thread
Sewing machine
Hand-sewing needle

PRO TIP The minimum thickness for a window seat cushion should be 7.5cm (3 inches) whether it is foam-filled or feather-filled. To determine the maximum thickness, consider the overall height of the window seat once the cushion is in place. You want to avoid making it too high and uncomfortable to sit on. Experiment by sitting on offcuts of foam to decide on the ideal height for your cushion.

Making the pattern

1. Follow steps 1–4 of the Window seat on a wooden base project on page 128 for creating the pattern.

Foam preparation

2. Lay the pattern on to your chosen thickness of foam, weighing or pinning this down so that it doesn't move.

3. Mark an additional 1cm (⅜ inch) all around the pattern edge using a sharp pencil and then join the marks with a ruler. Remove the pattern from the foam.

4. Using a foam saw or sharp knife and a steady hand, cut the foam along the marked line.

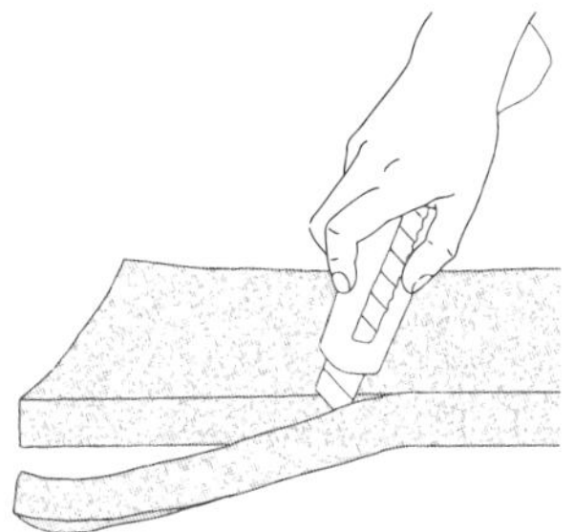

5. Wrap your foam in polyester wadding and a layer of stockinette, avoiding overlaps as these will be visible beneath the top fabric. If you prefer not to use the wadding, just add the layer of stockinette to the foam. Glue the stockinette to the back edge and sides, not the front as this bulk might be visible under the cover.

Fabric preparation

6. Once you have decided on your top fabric, test its stretchiness in both width (weft) and length (warp) directions.

PRO TIP For stretchy fabric, I recommend reducing the size of your fabric panels to account for the stretch. I tend to hold or clamp down a section of the fabric that is approximately the width of my pattern and, with a ruler at the other end to measure the stretch, I pull the fabric ever so slightly to see how much the fabric stretches.

Perfect lighting
Piet Oudolf
Landscapes in Landscapes
EUROPEAN GARDEN DESIGN
GARDENING WITH COLOUR

I then make a judgement call and deduct this measurement (or most of the measurement) from my fabric before adding the seam allowance to it and cutting.

7. Lay the fabric face down on a flat surface. Position the pattern on the fabric face down. If you are using a patterned fabric this is the stage to play around with isolating different parts of the fabric with the pattern piece until you are happy with the position.

PRO TIP Depending on the size of the window seat cushion you are making, you may need to join the fabric. If you have to join the fabric, make sure that you join the borders in the same place as well.

8. Transfer the pattern shape on to your fabric using a pencil and connect the marks together using a long ruler.

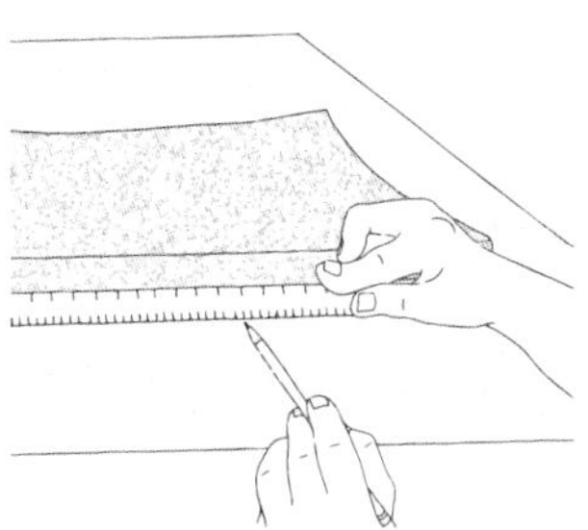

9. Add a seam allowance of approximately 1.2–1.5cm (½–⅝ inch) on all sides of the fabric.

Cutting the fabric for the top and bottom cushion panels

10. Cut the fabric according to the pattern and use the first cut piece as a template for the other side (the bottom of the cushion).

11. Lay the first piece of fabric right side down on to your fabric (which is right side up), mark around it and cut out the second piece.

12. Add marry marks in the middle of the longest edges and other strategic points to assist during sewing (see page 47).

PRO TIP Depending on the fabric, I sometimes only add a 5mm (3⁄16 inch) seam allowance/ cut line all the way around instead of a full 1.2–1.5cm (½–⅝ inch). You may want to consider this if you are using a fabric that is stretchy in both directions.

Cutting the border panels

13. Next you will need to create the panel(s) for your box cushion border. To do this, measure the front, sides and back of the foam using a soft tape measure. Ideally, you would make one continuous border to run along the front, both sides and the back of the cushion. Obviously, if you don't have enough continuous fabric to do this you can make several separate pieces for the border panels. Mark around the foam on to the reverse side of the fabric. Remember to add marry marks (see page 47).

14. Measure the top and bottom edges of your border panel(s) 2.5cm (1 inch) thinner than the foam's depth for a snug fit and then add a seam allowance of around 12–15mm (½–⅝ inch) to give the final cutting width. Add an extra 6cm (2½ inch) at each end of the length of your panel(s). Cut out your panel(s) carefully using fabric scissors.

Sewing the cushion pieces together

15. Start sewing the border to the top piece of fabric. Ensure there are no joins on the front edge of the window seat; place joins on non-visible sides or corners.

16. As you approach a corner, stop sewing about 5–7cm (2–2¾ inches) from the edge corner and mark the end of the cushion fabric panel on the border. Cut along this line which is then ready to have the next border sewn to it. This cut line already includes your seam allowance. Don't forget to snip into the seam allowance at the corners to help the fabric sit around the corner properly, it also helps reduce the amount of bulk.

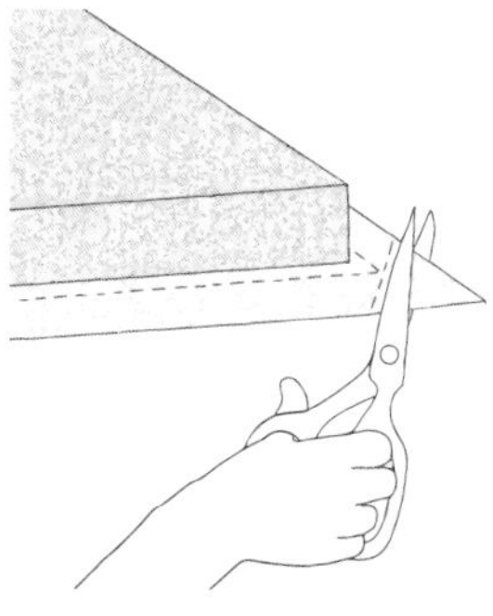

17. Continue this process, adding border pieces if applicable and referencing marry marks until the entire top or bottom is sewn. You add your next section of border by placing the new border on top, face to face and short edge to short edge, sewing them together along the stitching line, being sure to back tack at the beginning and end of the stitched line to keep the stitching secure. Continue to join the border strips all the way around and, when you get to the last side, join the two border ends together.

18. Now place the bottom piece of fabric right sides together with the border you have just sewn and sew the other side of the border to this piece. This time start sewing 5–7cm (2–2¾ inches) in from a corner. Sew all the way around, ensuring corners wrap nicely by snipping into the allowance. Once you arrive back at the same side you started, stop 5–7cm (2–2¾ inches) in from the corner again to leave an opening for inserting the cushion stuffing or infill.

Stuffing the cushion cover and final adjustments

19. Turn the cover right side out and push the corners out to ensure they have a crisp edge. Insert the foam inside the cover, making sure to dress the foam into the corners to fill them out.

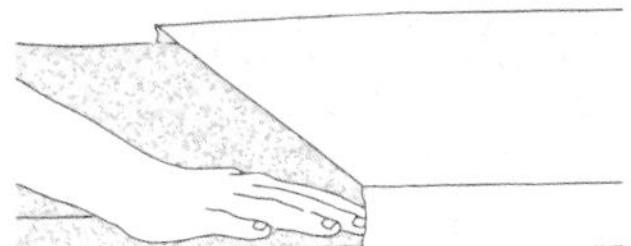

20. Before closing the opening, test the cushion in place to make sure it fits perfectly, and make any adjustments needed.

21. So that the cover looks neat and tidy when the foam insert is stuffed inside, make sure that the seam allowance bulk on the side of the cushion is laying on the side of the border and not the top of the cushion. You can check this is in place by using your hand on the inside of the cover and physically moving the allowance to the border side or when it is slip stitched closed (see step 22) roll the bulk in between your fingers and manipulate it to sit into place.

22. Use slip stitch (see How to slip stitch, page 35) to close the opening neatly.

Upholstered cube

An upholstered cube can serve as versatile furniture in your home – it's ideal as extra seating or a charming side table. In this guide, you'll learn to build and upholster a cube with a floral fabric and optional contrasting piping, though you can, of course, customize it with your choice of fabrics. The best way to make a box is by using MDF for the sides and face panels, with strengthening battens. Below I give a sizing guide and cutting list for a cube with a minimum size of 40cm squared (16 inches squared). If you prefer a larger design, adjust the dimensions accordingly.

Tools and materials

Metre ruler
Pencil
12mm (½ inch) or 18mm (¹¹⁄₁₆ inch) plywood or MDF
2.5cm (1 inch) wide batten lengths
18–25mm (¹¹⁄₁₆–1 inch) triangle corner supports
Jigsaw or hand saw (with dust mask and eye protection)
Set square or roofing square
Wood glue
Screwdriver and power drill
3mm (⅛ inch) drill bit
Size 4.0 wood screws (3 or 3.5cm/1¼ or 1½ inches)
Foam saw, craft knife with retractable blade or sharp bread knife
Foam: 12mm (½ inch) foam for sides and top; medium-density 2.5cm (1 inch) chip foam for the top
Upholstery contact adhesive
Polyester wadding (55g/2oz)
Top fabric of choice
Tailor's chalk
Sewing machine and matching sewing thread
Piping cord (optional)
Fabric scissors
Soft tape measure
Staple gun and staples
Bottom cloth
Magnetic upholstery hammer
2.5cm (1 inch) glides (also known as domes of silence)

NOTE The maximum weight load for this upholstered cube is 20kg (44lb). It is not designed to be used as a step stool or to support weight beyond this limit, such as standing on it to reach high shelves or bookcases.

Planning and preparation

1. Measure all the wood pieces and cut them out using a jigsaw or hand saw, using a set square to measure the sides. Follow the cutting list:

MDF or plywood panels:

- Top and bottom panels: Two 40 × 40cm (16 × 16 inch) panels
- Left and right panels: Two 40 × 37.6cm (16 × 14¾ inch) panels – label as A and C
- Back and front panels: Two 37.6 × 37.6cm (14¾ × 14¾ inch) panels – label as B and D

Batten lengths:

- 4 × 35cm (14 inches)

Triangle corner supports:

- 8 × 18mm (¹¹⁄₁₆ inch) or 15mm (⅝ inch) thick

For convenience, you may have the MDF and plywood panels cut to size by your wood retailer, as they often provide this service.

PRO TIP If you opt for a larger box, you will need to increase the screw size and the side/wall thickness. For larger designs, consider using 18mm (¹¹⁄₁₆ inch) or 14mm (⁹⁄₁₆ inch) thick MDF or plywood to ensure structural integrity.

Assembling the cube frame

2. Once all the component parts are cut, start assembly with sides B and D. Use a ruler and pencil to find and mark the centre of all four edges on B and D panels. Find the centre of all four battens.

3. Apply a small bead of wood glue on to the face of one of the battens. Place the edge of the B panel on top, aligning it with the centre marks. Use another batten to prop the B panel up, then screw the two sections together: mark three spots on the top of the B panel for screws, 1.2cm (½ inch) from the edge (halfway on to the batten), and drill pilot holes with a 3mm (⅛ inch) drill bit. Screw into these holes using wood screws. Repeat for the other edge of the B panel and then attach the D panel in the same way.

4. Find the centre of the A and C panels in the same way. Place the A panel against the B panel, ensuring

the width is 40cm (16 inches) and the height is 37.6cm (14¾ inches).

5. Mark pilot holes slightly off from the initial holes to avoid hitting existing screws. Drill and screw the A panel into place. Repeat for the C panel with the D panel.

6. Stand the two L-shaped sections on a flat surface and align them to create a square, four-sided framework. Glue, mark and drill pilot holes, and screw the sides together as before.

7. Stand the box on a flat surface with an open end facing up. Attach four triangle corner supports - these will fit into the spaces between the battens and the top edge of the frame. Mark pilot holes central to the thickness of the batten you are using. Glue and screw these sections into place. Flip the box over and repeat on the other open end with the remaining four corner supports.

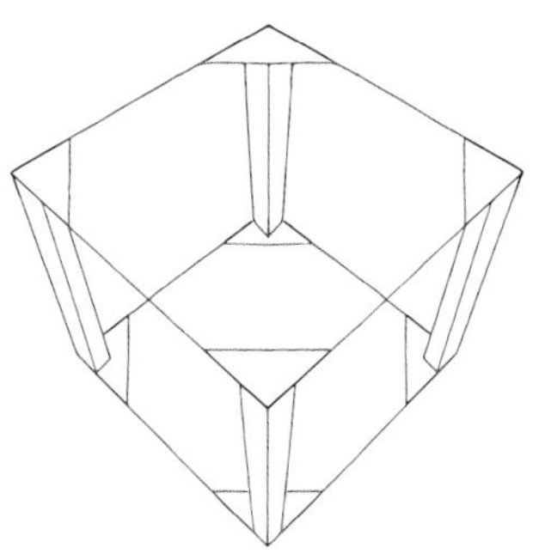

Attaching the top and bottom panels

8. Place the top panel on to the framework. The triangular sections will help align it squarely. If the top is slightly smaller, it is not an issue. Secure the top panel to the triangular sections with three fixings on each side: one in the corner and one at each of the triangle's far points. Mark pilot holes, drill and screw into place. Repeat this for the bottom panel for extra strength.

Preparing the foam and padding

9. For the top of the cube you will glue a layer of 12mm (½ inch) foam on to a layer of 2.5cm (1 inch) chip foam to create a comfortable seat. Use your ruler, set square or roofing square and pencil to measure and mark out pieces of the foam and chip foam that are 2.5cm (1 inch) larger than the top of the cube all around. Glue the foam to the chip foam before cutting.

10. Measure and cut 12mm (½ inch) foam panels to the correct size for the sides of the cube. Stick these panels to the sides with upholstery contact adhesive. Remember to account for the thickness of the foam on the sides you foam up first when pre-cutting your panels.

Covering with the wadding

11. Measure and cut polyester wadding to cover the entire foam. Apply it in one piece or in sections, trimming the overhang as you go.

Creating and attaching the fabric cover

12. Assess the stretch of your top fabric before measuring the fabric for the side and top panels (see Pro Tip, page 130) and account for this in your measurements. Oversize the top-to-bottom measurement by 5cm (2 inches) for seam allowance (and to give you some fabric to pull on when stapling off the bottom).

13. Lay the fabric face down, and mark the side and top panels based on the desired size. Add 1.2cm (½ inch) seam allowance and cut along this line.

14. If you would like your cube to have piping, follow the steps on page 37 of Essential Techniques: Piping. Cut fabric strips wide enough to encase the piping cord plus seam allowance.

15. Sew the sides together, right sides facing, then join the remaining sides. Sew the piping to the top panel, following steps 3–6 of the Scatter cushion/machine sewn with piping/no zip on pages 160 and 163.

16. Attach the sides to the top panel by pinning one corner, sewing around and easing fabric into the corners. Snip into the seam allowance around the corners to allow the fabric to ease around as you sew.

Fitting the cover

17. Place the top of the cover on to the cube first, rolling down the sides gradually. Ensure that the seam allowance along the top edge is facing down to the sides for a neat finish.

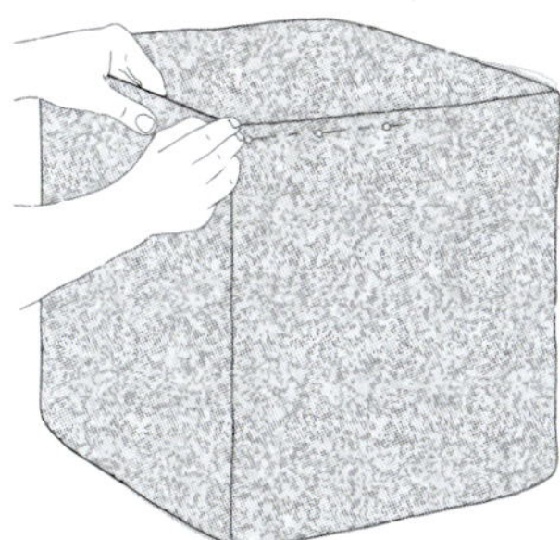

18. Temporary staple the corners and sides on the base, adjusting for tension and level. Once you are satisfied, replace temporary staples with final fix staples, leaving the corners till last.

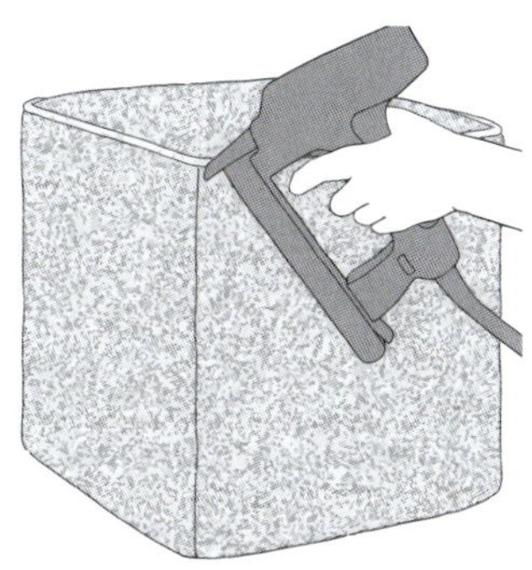

19. For thin fabric, fold the corners neatly and staple. For thick fabric, mark and cut triangular excess fabric, and fold into place, ensuring a clean finish.

Cutting out and fixing the bottom cloth

20. Follow steps 20–23 of the Drop-in seat base for an occasional chair/modern technique project on page 67 to attach the bottom cloth to the underside of the cube.

21. Finally, use a hammer to hit in the glides on each corner, leaving a 5mm (³⁄₁₆ inch) space between the sides and the glides.

Your upholstered cube is now complete and ready to add a touch of style and flexibility to your space. Enjoy the versatility and charm of your new piece of furniture!

Upholstered coffee table

An upholstered coffee table may not be the first thing that comes to mind when thinking about ways to dress your interior, but they can add another layer of interest to your space. When choosing fabric, it's essential to select a practical material that is easy to clean and durable, especially if the table will be in a high-traffic area. If you are making this to dress an area, then you have a wider range of fabric options.

The suggested design can be adjusted to your preference; the upholstering technique will remain the same. You can choose a Queen Anne-style leg for a traditional look or a square tapered leg for a more modern feel. Additionally, low upholstered coffee tables with deep upholstered tops and chunky bun feet offer a unique, robust option. Depending on where you plan to put this piece, you may want to consider adjusting the size or height of the legs to suit your individual needs and design requirements.

Tools and materials

- Wooden frame (ready-made or made to order)
- Wax or paint, to treat the legs
- Foam: firm-grade 7.5cm (3 inch) for the top; 6mm (¼ inch) scrim foam for the sides
- Pencil, chinagraph pencil or tailor's chalk
- Silicone spray (optional)
- Foam saw, craft knife with retractable blade or sharp bread knife
- Upholstery contact adhesive
- Low-tack masking tape (optional)
- Polyester wadding (55g/2oz) or Woolguard
- Soft tape measure
- Top fabric of choice
- Fabric scissors
- Staple gun and staples
- Dressmaking pins
- Sewing machine
- Matching sewing thread
- 7.5cm (3 inch) curved needle
- 4 dome-headed studs
- Regulator
- Stud hammer with a nylon tip
- Bottom cloth

PRO TIP Be mindful that the width of the coffee table does not exceed the width of your fabric. This beginner's version uses a single piece of fabric without borders or joins. Remember that the fabric will be tacked off underneath the frame by 5–8cm (2–3¼ inches), so allow for this in your measurements. Standard-width fabric is 130–137cm (51–54 inches) wide, and you can find double-width upholstery fabrics up to 300cm (118 inches) wide.

Frame preparation

1. I strongly advise that you either purchase a ready-made wooden frame or have one made. Instead of webbing the top of the frame, I recommend having the top covered with a piece of plywood that is reinforced underneath. A deep top rail provides a sturdy base for your upholstery, ensuring the corners sit neatly and securely once dressed.

2. Before starting, treat the legs with wax or paint and finish according to your design aesthetic.

Creating the foam top

3. Using 7.5cm (3 inch) firm-grade foam, first lay the foam on a flat surface. Position the wooden frame on top of the foam, with the flat surface of the frame in contact with the foam. Use a pencil or chinagraph pencil to mark around the frame on to the foam. After marking, cut the foam no more than 3–5mm (⅛–³⁄₁₆ inch) outside the marked lines. Take care not to oversize any more than this as the foam will be visible when the fabric is fitted.

PRO TIP Use a foam saw or a sharp bread knife to cut the foam square. Spraying silicone on to the blade will help it glide through the foam more smoothly. (Some suppliers accept foam scraps to repurpose into chip foam, so consider returning your leftovers.)

4. Use upholstery contact adhesive to glue the foam into place by first spraying the top of the foam with a generous layer and then spraying the top of the frame. Position the frame on to the foam using any

reference marks you have made, then apply pressure to bond the surfaces.

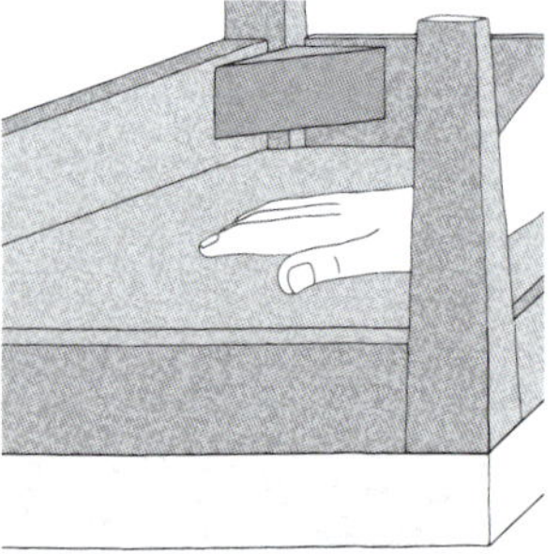

PRO TIP You could have the foam cut to size by your foam supplier. Be sure to oversize the foam by 3-5mm (⅛-³⁄₁₆ inch) all around following the same guidelines as if you were cutting it yourself.

Creating the foam sides

5. The simplest way to pad the sides is to cut four strips of 6mm (¼ inch) foam that are oversized in height by 3cm (1¼ inches) and oversized in length by 6-8cm (2⅓-3¼ inches). Mark the panels on to the foam using a pencil or chinagraph pencil, then use a retractable blade to carefully cut along the borders as squarely as possible. Cutting the edges square allows you to use these cut edges as the top edge, rather than having to re-cut a straight square edge again later.

6. Apply upholstery contact adhesive to both the side of the frame and the 6mm (¼ inch) foam. Attach the foam to one side of the frame, positioning it 4-5mm (³⁄₁₆ inch) down from the top edge of the foam and centring it on the width to ensure an even overhang on each side.

7. Use a retractable blade or sharp knife to trim the overhang on the sides so that it aligns flush with the vertical edge of the frame and the foam top. Repeat this trimming process on the other end, then glue and trim the excess foam on the remaining sides.

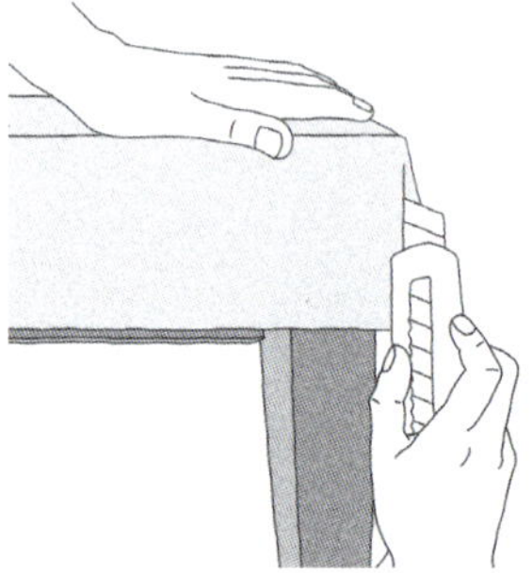

8. Spray a light layer of upholstery contact adhesive along the top lip where the 6mm (¼ inch) foam sits below the foam's edge. Using the lengths of your index fingers, gently pinch the foam edges together to create a gentle curve. If you haven't yet mastered the art of the spray glue, you could use low-tack masking tape to mask either side of the area you are gluing before applying the adhesive.

PRO TIP Some upholsterers recommend gluing the cut foam sides directly to the edge without pinching the edges closed. This approach can work if your cut edges are perfectly square. However, rounding off the edges helps to conceal the foam beneath the top cover, resulting in a smoother finish.

9. Turn the frame over and glue the bottom overhang of the 6mm (¼ inch) foam underneath the frame. This will provide a clean, soft finish to the bottom edge.

Adding the wadding

10. If your fabric is FR treated, apply a layer of polyester wadding. (If your fabric is not FR treated, use a layer of Woolguard instead.) Measure the amount needed with a soft tape measure, ensuring it covers all of the foam including the return underneath, allowing 3-6cm (1¼-2⅓ inches) more. Depending on the size of your table and the width of your piece of wadding, you may need to apply two or more strips of wadding. Once you have cut what you need, lightly spray a layer of upholstery contact adhesive on to the foam; there is no need to spray the wadding itself. Avoid overlaps as these will be visible beneath the top fabric.

11. Lay your wadding smoothly over the foam making sure not to pucker any sections. When you get

to the corners, flatten the wadding all the way to the edge and trim off the triangle-shaped excess 3–5mm (⅛–³⁄₁₆ inch) away from the foam to give you a small amount to pad the corner with. Repeat this process for all corners.

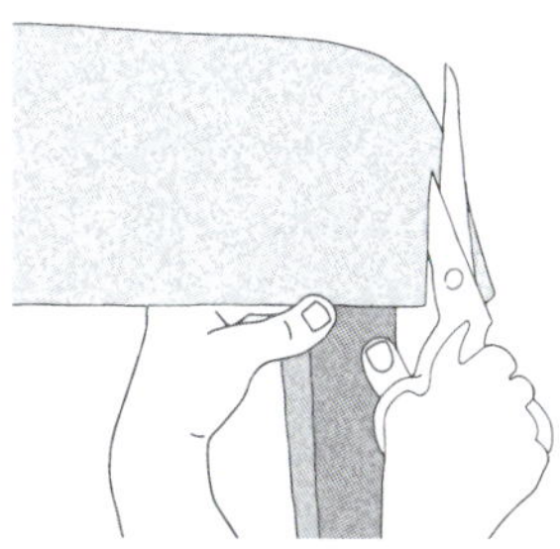

Adding the top fabric

12. Triple-check your top fabric measurements, allowing for an additional 5–8cm (2–3¼ inches) for tacking underneath the frame. Cut the fabric and mark the middle on each side (see page 47).

13. Mark the centre points on the underside of your frame. Lay your fabric on to the padded top, aligning the marry marks. Begin temporarily fixing the fabric into place by stapling it in three places along one side, 3cm (1¼ inches) apart. Move to the opposite side, pulling the fabric taut and temporarily stapling it into place while building tension. Repeat this process on the other side, using the fabric weave as a guide to ensure even tension. As you approach the corners, you may notice the fabric pulls down slightly more, which is normal.

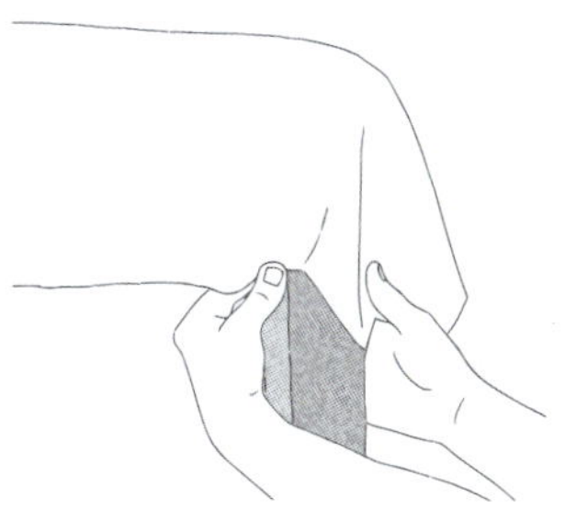

14. Repeat this technique on the remaining sides up to the legs.

PRO TIP Now is the best time to triple-check whether you need to make any adjustments.

15. To finish the table you will box pleat the corners and slip stitch the fold closed. To give a neat finish, I suggest cutting away the 6mm (¼ inch) scrim foam from around the legs by 1cm (⅜ inch) so that the fabric, when pleated, sits flush.

16. To help give you a perfectly horizontal line when pulling the fabric down, you could wrap a piece of low-tack masking tape around the top of each leg where it meets the frame. As a beginner, it's very easy to accidentally pull the fabric down too far without this reference.

17. To box pleat the corners follow the instructions on page 36 in Essential Techniques: Box Pleats. However, for this project, you won't staple the fabric around the legs; instead the fabric is folded under itself to give a neat finish. Start by deciding on the left and right sides, and the front and back, as you will be pleating in a particular sequence (see Pro Tip, below); the sides will wrap around to the front and back, while the front and back corners will be folded over the wrapped sides (see photograph opposite).

PRO TIP When box pleating corners on a piece like this you will do so in a specific sequence. First, decide on which side is the front. The fabric from the side will be pulled around to the front of the frame and secured in place and the front corner fabric will fold over this neatly. You will mirror this on the other front corner so that, when viewing the front, you can't 'see

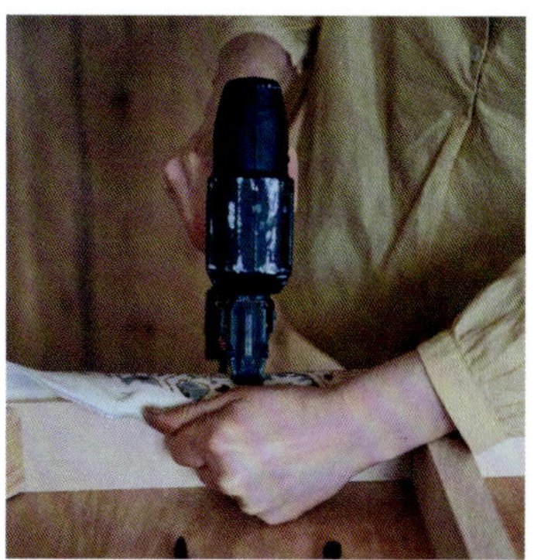

into' the pleats; you can just see the flat folded edge of the fabric. Mirror this for the back edge.

18. For the next stages, refer to the step photos on the right. Because of the thickness of the foam on the top of the frame you won't be pulling the fabric around the side as 'tight as possible' as this could create a dent in the corner. Instead, start by pulling tension into the fabric from the side and around the corner; pull the fabric down slightly to keep the top of the corner tight to the foam and aim to achieve a straight pulled line in the fabric edge. If this creates slack, pull more tension into the area around the leg section of the frame. Temporary tack the fabric on to the front of the frame (see photo 1), positioning the staples 2–3cm (¾–1¼ inches) in from the corner. Staple as far up and down as the frame will allow. Check the tension and position of the fabric and adjust if necessary.

19. Pull a small amount of tension into the side and use a pin to locate where the inside leg meets the bottom of the frame. Using your preferred marking tool, mark a 45-degree line from the pin to the outer edge on the fabric (see photo 2). Cut along this line and fold the excess of the other side fabric under itself. Test if it sits behind the leg neatly without puckering (see photo 3). Temporary tack into place on the underside of the frame.

20. Mark a cut line 1.2–2.5cm (½–1 inch) below where the side fabric will fold under to create a neat finish on the lower edge (see photo 4). Cut along this line and up the side where the fabric is temporary tacked. Use a regulator to neatly fold the fabric under and around the leg, removing

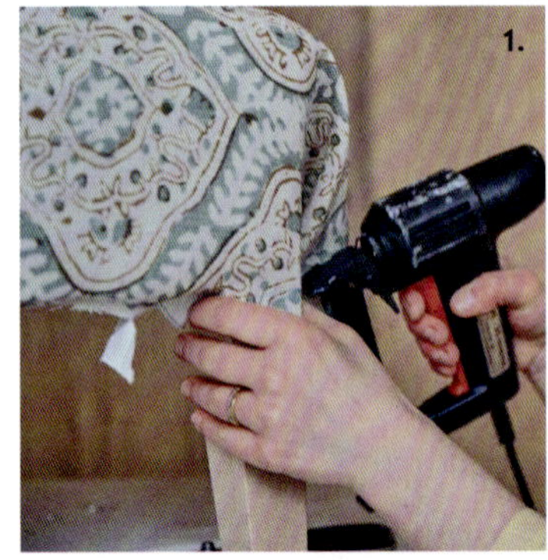

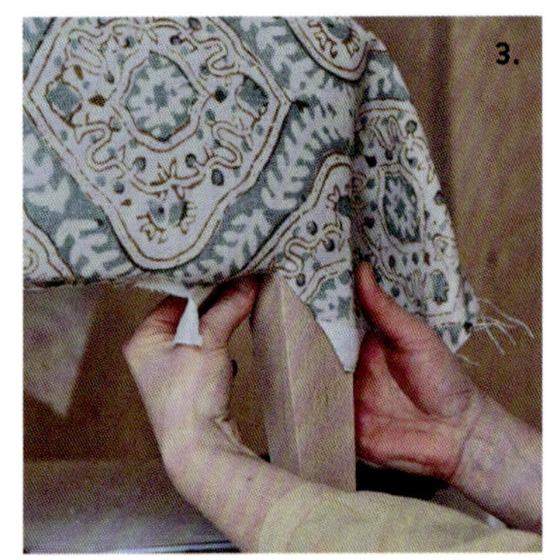

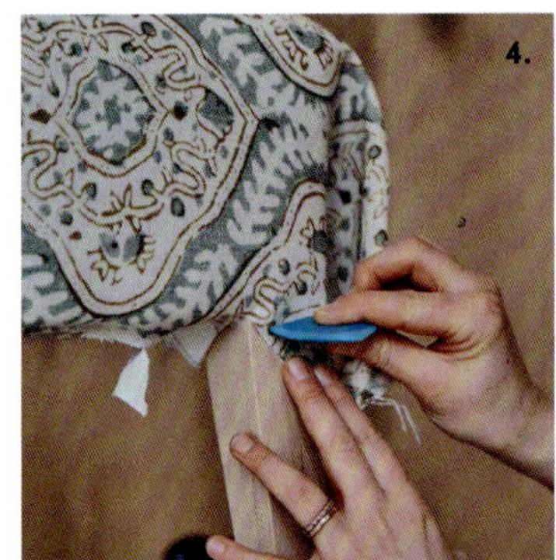

BOX-PLEATING THE CORNERS

any temporary staples that are in your way. Replace all temporary staples with final fixings, neatening the fold if required. Ensure that the folded edge is in line with the bottom of the wooden frame, or matches your masking tape line.

21. Fold the fabric on the other side into itself to create a vertical pleat; test that you have folded in enough by holding the pleat 2–3mm (⅛ inch) back from the edge of the frame (see photo 5). If there is slack fabric behind the fold, turn in more fabric. Temporary tack the corner closed and cut a 45-degree angle into the fabric around the leg, as in step 19.

22. Mark a cut line 1.2–2.5cm (½–1 inch) below where the side fabric will fold under. Cut along this line, removing the temporary staples. Use a regulator or skewer to fold the fabric under and around the leg neatly. Keep the tip of the regulator in the folded corner with the fabric pleat in position. Temporary tack the bottom corner in place (see photo 6).

23. Using a 7.5cm (3 inch) curved needle and doubled cotton thread that matches or complements your fabric, slip stitch the sides of the box pleat closed (see How to slip stitch, page 35).

24. Replace the temporary fixing on the corner with a complementary dome-headed stud, using a nylon-tipped stud hammer. Repeat steps 17–24 for the three remaining legs.

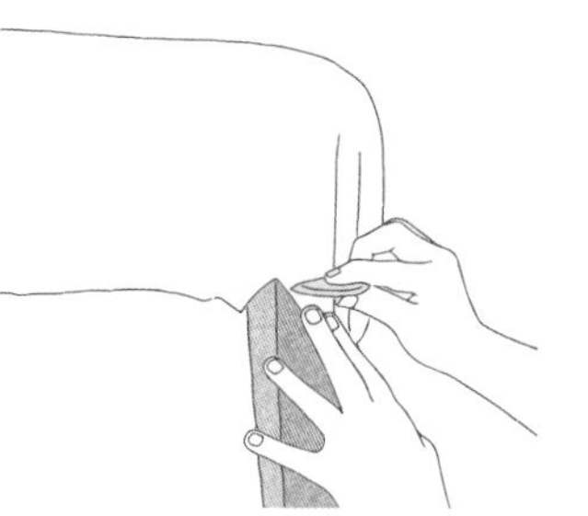

Adding the bottom cloth

25. For the bottom cloth, measure the underside of the upholstered coffee table, allowing 3–5cm (1¼–2 inches) extra all around. Cut the bottom cloth to size and lay this on to the underside of the frame.

26. Start on one side by folding the edge of the bottom cloth under and securing it with three staples spaced 1.5–2cm (⅝–¾ inch) apart. Repeat on the opposite side, then continue on the remaining sides.

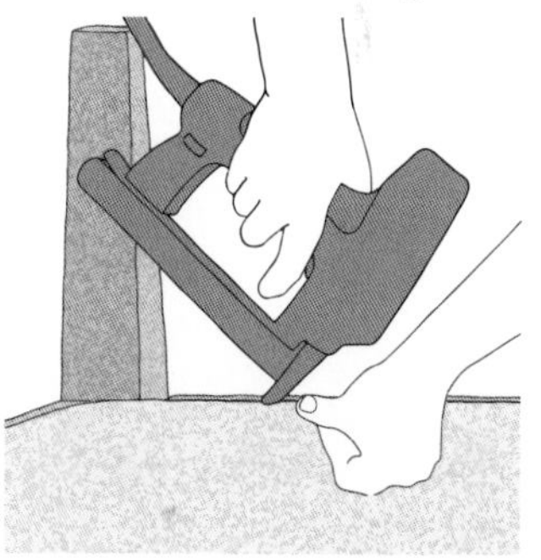

27. Work your way towards the corners, leaving a 5cm (2 inch) space away from the legs.

28. Fold the bottom cloth back on to itself and cut at a 45-degree angle towards the leg leaving 5mm (³⁄₁₆ inch) space away from the leg.

29. Fold the excess under on both sides, cut out any excess or bulk, and staple into place.

30. Repeat steps 26–29 for the remaining three legs.

To style your upholstered coffee table, consider adding elegant trays with small plants or a curated stack of coffee table books. You might also include a glass terrarium on a larger tray, paired with coasters or additional books. This is your opportunity to make the table uniquely yours!

Upholstered footstool

Putting your feet up on a footstool while relaxing in a chair is one of the nicest feelings. This project guides you through making a small footstool, perfect for limited space and offering a slight elevation for your feet. This version is simpler and smaller than a large footstool with a hardwood frame and tall integrated legs.

Tools and materials

18mm or 24mm (11/16 or 15/16 inch) plywood or MDF
4 × wooden shaped feet with fixings, maximum 10 × 8cm (4 × 3½ inches) high
Metre ruler
Set square or roofing square
Pencil
Jigsaw or hand saw (with dust mask and eye protection)
Wood paint or varnish (optional)
Rasp tool or medium-grit sandpaper
5cm (2 inch) foam block
30cm (12 inch) ruler
Soft tape measure
Foam saw, craft knife with retractable blade or sharp bread knife
T-nuts for the thread of the feet or the fixings supplied with the feet (if supplied)
Power drill and drill bit (depending on the size of the thread on your feet)
Wax or paint, to treat the legs
Magnetic tack hammer
Upholstery contact adhesive
Polyester wadding (55g/2oz) or Woolguard
Top fabric of choice
Tailor's chalk
Fabric scissors
Staple gun and staples
Bottom cloth

Cutting and preparing the wooden base

1. Choose your footstool (see Pro Tip, below). Have your chosen feet to hand – don't purchase anything higher than 10cm (4 inches) or wider than 8cm (3½ inches).

PRO TIP Because this stool is made from a sheet of plywood or MDF, there is a limit to its width and depth. I suggest one of two sizes: 30 × 38cm (12 × 15 inches) or 38 × 45cm (15 × 18 inches). If you make the stool too large, the wood may bow when used or if sat on. I don't recommend using this stool as a step.

2. Either have the wooden board cut by your wood retailer or cut it yourself. To cut it yourself, use a metre ruler and a set square to mark the dimensions of the stool with a pencil. Use a jigsaw or hand saw to cut the wood out and wear a dust mask and goggles.

3. Use a rasp tool or medium-grit sandpaper to smooth the edges of the wood and also to take off any sharp corners.

Preparing the feet

4. Treat the feet with wax or paint and finish according to your design aesthetic. Let them dry completely before attaching to your footstool.

Fitting the T-nuts

5. To find the correct drill point for each T-nut, measure the width of a foot and add 1cm (⅜ inch) to the measurement. Draw a square with this measurement on each of the four corners of the wooden board, as illustrated below. Connect the opposite corners of each square with diagonal lines – you will attach the feet at the points where the lines intersect. Using a drill and a drill bit the same size as or 1mm (1/16 inch) bigger than your T-nuts, drill a hole at each intersecting point. Hammer a t-nut into each hole until it is flush to the wood and the teeth bite in. To prevent the T-nut from untwisting itself from the wooden base board, carefully place two to four staples over the winged part of the T-nut.

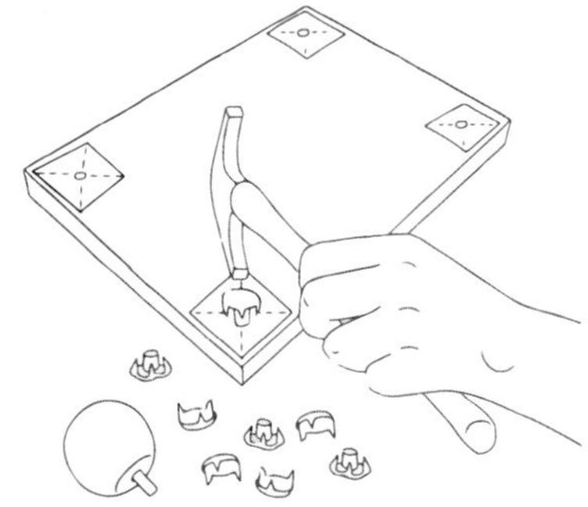

PRO TIP Purchase feet with a pre-attached thread and supplied fixings. This allows for easy replacement in the future. If you don't opt for the T-nut fitting, which allows you to screw the feet in at the end, you could screw down into the feet from the top of the board, BUT this does mean that you have to work on the project with the feet already attached and you won't be able to fix a bottom cloth in place.

Cutting the foam

6. Cut a piece of 5cm (2 inch) foam that is 3–4mm (⅛–3⁄16 inch) larger than your wooden board. Lay the board on the foam, measure out from the edge of the board 3–4mm (⅛–3⁄16 inch) with your ruler, and connect the marks. Cut with a foam saw or sharp blade.

Cutting the chamfer

7. Place the foam on a flat surface and, on the side that's facing you, measure back 5–7cm (2–2¾ inches) from the edge towards the inside, then on the upright side mark 5mm (3⁄16 inch) up, from the bottom edge, on the side of the foam. Do this on all four sides (see also step 6 of the Drop-in seat base for an occasional chair/modern technique project on page 65).

8. Cut away the marked chamfer on all sides with a foam saw or sharp knife.

Gluing the foam

9. Use upholstery contact adhesive to glue the board to the foam ensuring you are gluing the foam to the correct side (the side that you hammered the T-nuts into). Spray the glue on to the board and the foam and then position the board centrally on the foam.

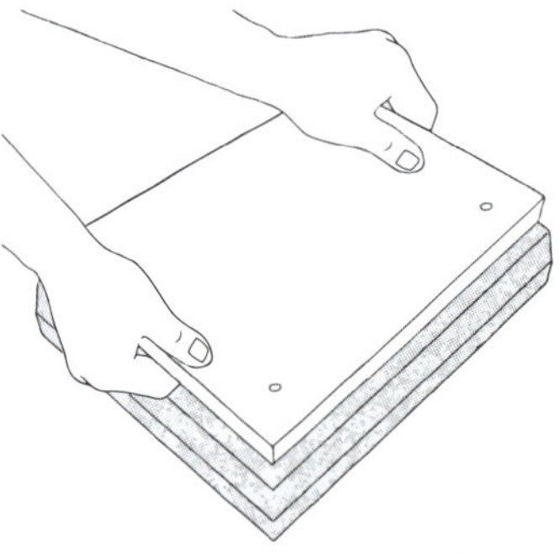

10. Re-spray the chamfer and the board with the board upside down so that you get a good coverage on the foam. Ensure the board is adequately sprayed with the glue also.

11. Wait for the glue to become tacky before sticking the foam down, positioning it towards the bottom edge of the depth of the board. Use your thumb to guide the foam on to the board, ensuring it sticks well.

12. You will find that the foam forms a point on the corner. Use a pair of scissors to cut away the excess in a vertical line 2–3mm (1⁄16–⅛ inch) away from the corner. This will give you enough padding on the corner to help fill out the fabric.

Adding padding

13. The next step is to add a layer of padding over the foam. Use a soft tape measure to measure a piece of polyester wadding or Woolguard, depending on whether your top fabric is FR-treated or not. Oversize this by 1cm (⅜ inch) only.

14. If you are using Woolguard, glue this on to the foam using upholstery contact adhesive (only spray the foam and not the Woolguard). If you are using polyester wadding you don't need to use glue because it will stay in place more easily than Woolguard while you work.

15. Cut away the bulk on the corners in the same way you did for the foam.

Adding the top fabric

16. Measure up and over the board and foam and wadding layer from one side to the opposite side to find the length, and then again for the other way to find the width. Add a safety margin allowance of 5-8cm (2-3¼ inches) to both measurements. Transfer these measurements on to the reverse side of your top fabric. For patterned fabric, be mindful to position the pattern where you would like it to sit on the stool. If using plain fabric, just cut it as economically as possible.

PRO TIP Always mark on the back of the fabric just in case you make a mistake and always triple-check your measurements before cutting.

17. Cut the fabric piece out. Fold the fabric in half and mark the middle folds on both sides with a pencil or tailor's chalk. Repeat on the other sides to help with positioning.

18. Turn the wooden board bottom up and find the middle of all four sides and mark discreetly with a pencil. You will use these marry marks (see page 47) to help you position the fabric on the board.

19. Lay the fabric on to the foam and gently smooth it into place. Flip the stool over and gently pull the sides of the fabric into position to marry up with the middle marks on the wooden base board. Building a small amount of tension into the fabric, secure with temporary staples 2-3cm (¾-1¼ inches) in from the edges at the centre of each of the four sides.

20. Working on all four opposite sides at the same time, work towards the corners in 3-4cm (1¼-1½ inch) increments, leaving 5-6cm (2-2½-inch) gaps from the corners. Ensure you are pulling the fabric out towards the corners as well as pulling tension round and down. You will find that the fabric will curve down when it's being pulled around the corners as it takes the shape of the foam. Up until this point, use the weave of the fabric to guide you in creating even tension.

Finishing the footstool

21. Triple-check you have even tension and that the position of the fabric is correct on all four sides, make any adjustments where necessary. Now you can final fix the staples on the main body of the footstool. The corners will be addressed in the next step.

22. To finish the corners, make neat pleats and snip out any excess fabric to avoid bulk. Secure with staples, ensuring the fabric is smooth and taut.

23. Measure and cut a piece of bottom cloth to cover the underside of the footstool. This piece should be slightly larger than the bottom surface as you will be folding the raw edge under to create a smart finish.

24. Secure the bottom cloth with staples, starting at the centre of each side and working towards the corners. Make sure it is smooth and well-fitted. Follow steps 20-23 of the Drop-in seat base for an occasional chair/modern technique project on page 67. Cut out small sections of bottom cloth where the fixings are for the feet.

25. Finally, screw the feet into the T-nuts. Ensure they are securely fastened.

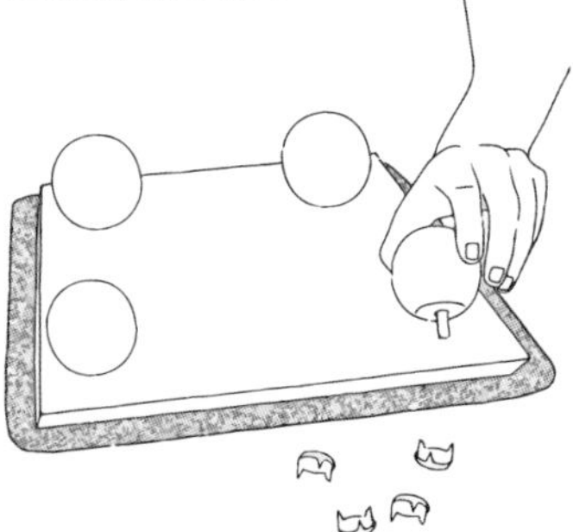

3.
Soft furnishings

Scatter cushion / hand sewn

Scatter cushions really are a fabulous accessory to adorn your home with, adding a pop of colour, texture and depth to any room. They can also make a sofa or chair more inviting. Making scatter cushions by hand is a great first step into your 'making' journey. The techniques are simple, and the results are quite quick compared to more complex projects like curtains.

Tools and materials

Soft tape measure
Notepad
Pencil
Fabric of choice
Ruler
Set square or roofing square
Pencil or tailor's chalk
Fabric scissors
Matching sewing thread
Hand-sewing needle
Dressmaking pins
Bulldog clips
Cushion filling of choice
(see Pro Tip, page 153)

Measuring and cutting the fabric

1. If you already have a scatter cushion you like, measure it from corner to corner. Let's use a 50cm (20 inch) square cushion as an example.

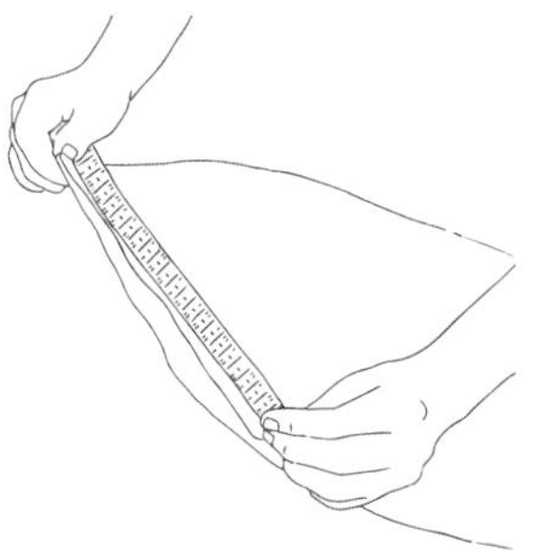

2. Using your notepad and pencil you can now begin to draw a square and start planning your steps. Planning is a vital part of any successful project.

3. Choose a plain or semi-plain medium-weight cotton or linen (or a fabric with a mix of those). Avoid velvet for hand sewing.

PRO TIP If you are feeling bold enough to use a patterned fabric, make sure to mark the back of the fabric to indicate which edge is the bottom. This ensures that the pattern will be aligned correctly on both sides when you start to sew. These markings will also help you know where to start sewing. We'll cover the starting point in detail later.

4. For a 50cm (20 inch) cushion we need to add a seam allowance of 1.2cm (½ inch) all the way around. This will make the final cut size of the fabric squares 52.5cm (21 inches). Use a ruler and set square to achieve straight lines and square corners, and a tailor's chalk or pencil to add marks to the fabric.

5. Cut two 52.5cm (21 inch) squares from your fabric of choice – one for the front and one for the back of the cushion.

Sewing the cushion

6. Thread a long, strong needle with doubled cotton thread no longer than 50cm (20 inches). Knot the end. Cotton threads can knot and twist in on themselves, so keeping the thread length short can avoid this happening.

7. Pin the fabric pieces together, right sides facing. Avoid the edges as this is where we will be running our line of stitching.

8. Start sewing 2cm (¾ inch) in from a corner (not on a corner) – all will become clear when we get to the end of this stitching section – and 1.2cm (½ inch) from the edge (this is your seam allowance). Secure the thread by looping it through the initial stitch.

9. Use a running stitch, with a stitch length between 6mm (¼ inch) and 1.2cm (½ inch). Stitch as far as the thread will take you and, when you start running out of thread, stitch in the same place three or four times to lock the stitching. Use the same technique to start with a new length of thread as you did in step 8.

10. Sew around all three sides and stop 2cm (¾ inch) in from the fourth side's corners. Secure your thread and get ready for the home straight!

11. If your fabric is thick, trim the bulk from the corners by cutting diagonally across the corner, about 3mm (⅛ inch) away from the stitches. Be careful not to cut too close to the stitches to avoid creating holes.

Turning and stuffing your cushion

12. Turn the cushion cover right-side out through the gap.

PRO TIP Choosing the right infill is a bit of an art form and depends on your fabric. If you are using a thick fabric I'd recommend a fuller cushion because the fabric can collapse under its own weight. A thin fabric may allow feathers to poke through so if that might be an annoyance then I would suggest going for a fibre-filled cushion. I like a nice plumptious cushion, so if I'm using a feather infill, I use one 10cm (4 inches) larger than the cover size. If I'm using a hollow fibre scatter cushion infill, then I tend to choose an infill 5–7cm (2–2¾ inches) larger than the cover finish size. This really is about preference, so it's worth experimenting.

---

13. Insert the infill into the cushion cover, ensuring corners are filled.

Sewing your cushion closed

14. Bull dog clip, or pin, the opening edges together making sure that you have your seam allowance of 1.2cm (½ inch) evenly folded inside along the entire length.

15. Use a slip stitch (see How to slip stitch, page 35) to close the opening.

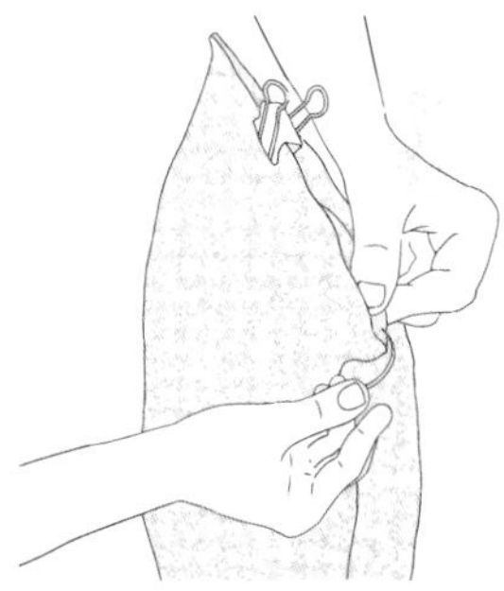

16. Repeat the slip stitch about 10 more times then gently pull the thread to create some tension, but not too tight. The stitching should be nearly invisible, giving a clean, seamless look. Continue this method until you reach the end, removing pins or bulldog clips as you go.

17. Extend your stitches about 5–8cm (2–3¼ inches) past the initial stitching line, then double back using smaller slip stitches. If you have enough thread on your needle, go back again to make it totally secure.

And there you have it, your very own homemade plumptious scatter cushion!

Scatter cushion / machine sewn

Scatter cushions are a fantastic way to add colour, texture and comfort to any room. Here I show you how to make one using a sewing machine, which is quicker and more efficient than hand sewing. If you've already made a hand-sewn cushion, you'll find this method a breeze, and it will allow you to experiment with different fabrics and sizes more easily.

Tools and materials

Soft tape measure
Notepad
Pencil
Fabric of choice
Ruler
Set square or roofing square
Pencil or tailor's chalk
Fabric scissors
Dressmaking pins
Matching sewing thread
Sewing machine
Cushion filling of choice (see Pro Tip, page 153)
Hand-sewing needle

PRO TIP Once you have mastered the basics, feel free to experiment with different fabrics, sizes and patterns to create a variety of scatter cushions.

Measuring and cutting the fabric

1. Follow steps 1–5 of the Scatter cushion/Hand sewn project on page 150. Pin the two fabric pieces together with the right sides facing.

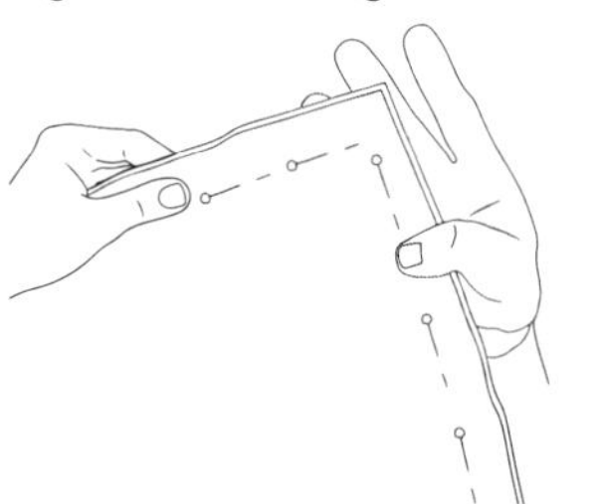

Starting the machine stitching

2. Using a sewing machine, begin sewing approximately 5cm (2 inches) along from the edge of one side. This will leave a gap for inserting the cushion filling later.

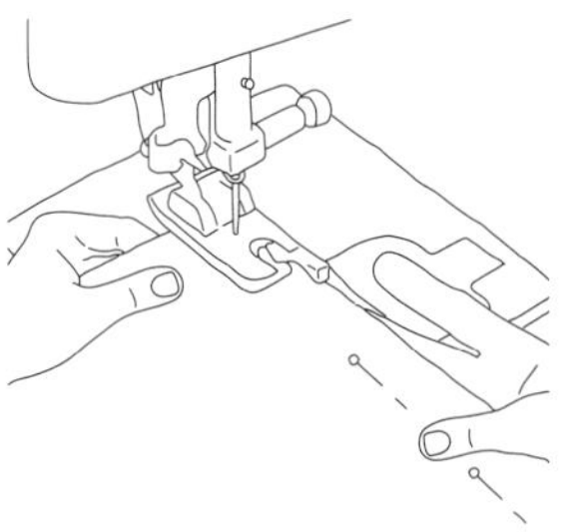

3. Ensure your stitch length is around 3mm (⅛ inch). Too long, and the stitches will be too visible when the cushion is turned out and stuffed; too short, and the fabric may pucker under the machine foot.

4. Sew along the edges, stopping 1.2cm (½ inch) from each corner to pivot and continue along the next side. Stop stitching 5cm (2 inches) past the last corner, leaving an opening for the cushion filling.

Trimming the corners

5. If your fabric is thick, trim the bulk from the corners by cutting diagonally across the corner, about 3mm (⅛ inch) away from the stitches. Be careful not to cut too close to the stitches to avoid creating holes.

Turning and stuffing the cushion cover

6. Turn the cushion cover right-side out through the opening.

7. Insert the cushion filling, making sure to push it into the corners for a full, plump appearance.

Closing the opening

8. Fold in the edges of the opening inwards along the seam allowance and pin them together.

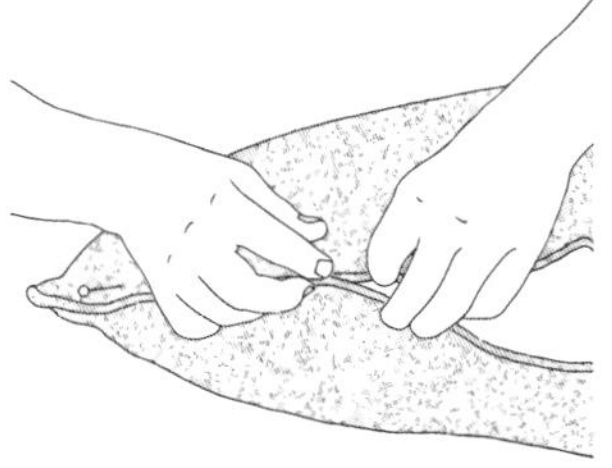

9. Use a needle and thread to slip stitch the opening closed (see How to slip stitch, page 35, and follow steps 14–17 of the Scatter cushion/Hand sewn project on page 153), ensuring the stitches are tight and invisible.

Scatter cushion / machine sewn with zip

If you're familiar with sewing projects and using a sewing machine, you might already have experience of incorporating zips into fabric. If so, you're well-equipped to tackle adding a zip to your scatter cushions. Including a zip means you won't need to sew the opening closed, making it easy to replace the cushion inner or remove the cover for washing. I like to match the colour of the zip to the colour of the fabric.

Tools and materials

Closed-end zip
Soft tape measure
Notepad
Pencil
Fabric of choice
Ruler
Set square or roofing square
Pencil or tailor's chalk
Fabric scissors
Matching sewing thread
Sewing machine with zip foot
Dressmaking pins
Cushion filling/inner pad (this should be 2–4cm/¾–1½ inches bigger than your cushion size depending on how plump you want your cushion to be – see Pro Tip, page 153)

PRO TIP For this project, we'll be using a 'closed-end' zip rather than a 'continuous' zip. Closed-end zips come in fixed sizes with the slider already attached, making them more straightforward for beginners.

Choosing the zip

1. Select a zip colour that matches or complements your fabric. The zip length should be around 5cm (2 inches) shorter than the overall finished size of the cushion, although you can go up to 7cm (2¾ inches) shorter. Avoid using a zip that is too short, as it will make inserting the cushion difficult.

Measuring and cutting the fabric

2. Follow steps 1–5 of the Scatter cushion/Hand sewn project on page 150.

Attaching the zip

3. Change the foot on your sewing machine to a zip foot. Measure the length of the zip and mark the middle point on the zip and both faces of the scatter cushion fabric. Open the zip up using the slider and position one side of the zip on the fabric – the right side of the zip on the right side of the fabric – aligning the middle marks and pinning it in place centrally along the lower edge.

4. Ensure the zip stitching line, which should be 2–3mm (1⁄16–⅛ inch) in from the zip 'teeth', sits on your seam allowance and is not higher or lower, so that you keep within the planned sewing distance in from the edge of the fabric.

5. Position the foot of the sewing machine at one end of the zip length, roughly 1cm (⅜ inch) in from the ends. Sew along the zip, keeping 2–3mm (1⁄16–⅛ inch) away from the teeth, and back tack at the beginning and end to make sure the stitching doesn't open up.

PRO TIP If the slider is in the way at any point when sewing the zip into place, lower the needle into the fabric, lift the sewing machine foot up and move the slider out of the way. This may open or close the two sides of the zip together. Once the slider is out of the way, continue to sew.

6. Repeat this process on the other side of the zip, ensuring you start and stop at the same points as you did on the first side.

7. Once the zip is sewn into place, take the fabric away from the sewing machine and assess it from the right side. Close the zip up using the slider. You are checking to make sure the zip has been sewn in on the correct line and that you have not sewn into the teeth of the zip. If you have, unpick that section and re-stitch in the correct place.

Pinning and sewing the sides

8. Hold the cushion faces together. If you feel more comfortable doing so, you can pin them together

3–5cm (1¼–2 inches) in from the edge to avoid interfering with the machine foot.

9. Starting from the left-hand side as you look at the zip, position the sewing machine foot as close to the start of the zip as possible on the stitching line and move the fabric ends of the zip out of the way of the needle. You will notice that the fabric does not sit flat there because of the zip bulk, so try to work with it as best you can.

Back tack at the start and then sew towards the first corner. Stopping your seam allowance in from the corner, leave the needle in the fabric, which will allow you to lift the foot and pivot the cushion fabric around so you can sew along the next side of the cushion along the seam allowance line. Repeat this process on the remaining three corners.

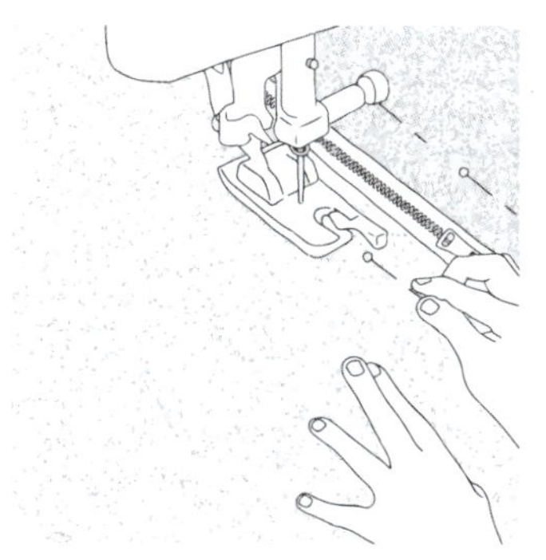

10. When you arrive at the other side of the zip, repeat the same process as at the start, back tacking as close to the zip bulk as possible.

Trimming the corners

11. If your fabric is thick, trim the bulk from the corners by cutting diagonally across the corner, about 3mm (⅛ inch) away from the stitches. Be careful not to cut too close to the stitches to avoid creating holes.

Turning and stuffing the cushion cover

12. Turn the cushion cover right side out by opening the zip from the back. Use your nail or a pin to do this if it proves tricky.

13. Poke out the corners of the cushion cover to make them square, then insert the cushion filling, ensuring it is pushed into the corners for a full, plump appearance. Close the zip to finish and enjoy the ease of zipping and unzipping your cushion!

PRO TIP If you are adding a zip to a piped cushion, start by sewing the zip to the piped side first. Sew as close to the piping as possible, taking your time, as it's much easier to accidentally catch the teeth of the zip when sewing it next to piping.

Scatter cushion / machine sewn with piping / no zip

Piping adds a decorative edge to your cushion, allowing for creative freedom in fabric choices. You could choose to 'self-pipe', which means making the piping in the same fabric as the cushion, or you could choose a contrasting colour and texture. There are various styles of edging that you can choose to embellish your cushions with, including flanged cords, frilled edges made with fabric or tasseled edges.

Tools and materials

Soft tape measure
Notepad
Pencil
Fabric of choice
Ruler
Set square or roofing square
Pencil or tailor's chalk
Fabric scissors
Dressmaking pins
Fabric for piping (if not self-piping)
Piping cord
Matching sewing thread
Sewing machine
Cushion filling/inner pad (this should be 2–4cm/¾–1½ inches bigger than your cushion size depending on how plump you want your cushion to be – see Pro Tip, page 153)
Hand-sewing needle

Preparation

1. Follow steps 1–5 of the Scatter cushion/Hand sewn project on page 150.

Making the piping

2. Follow the steps for making piping on page 37 Essential Techniques: Piping. Cut fabric strips wide enough to encase the piping cord plus seam allowance.

Attaching and joining the piping

3. You could pin and tack the piping into position if you want to but this isn't 100 per cent necessary. I like to start and stop piping in areas on cushions that are not visible and so, for a scatter cushion, this is the edge where the opening is.

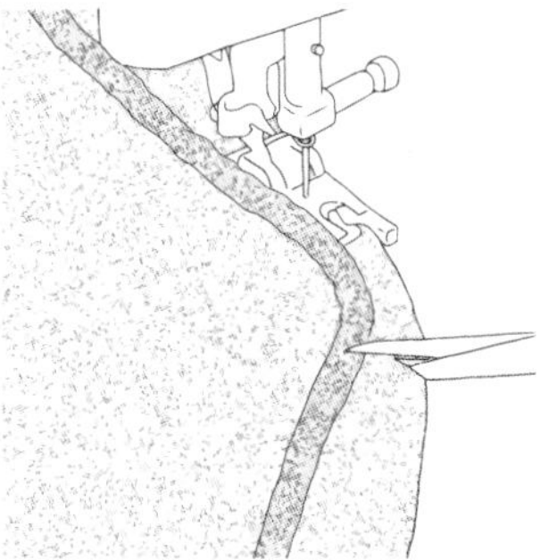

PRO TIP Sew the piping on to one of the cushion faces with the raw edge of the piping aligned to the raw edge of the fabric, and the rounded bulk of the piping facing inwards.

4. Starting from approximately the centre bottom of the cushion, and leaving a 'tail' of piping approximately 5cm (2 inches) so that you can work with it when you need to join the two ends, sew the piping on to the face all the way around, making sure you snip into the flange on the corners so that the piping easily sits around the corners. Continue sewing until you reach the starting point.

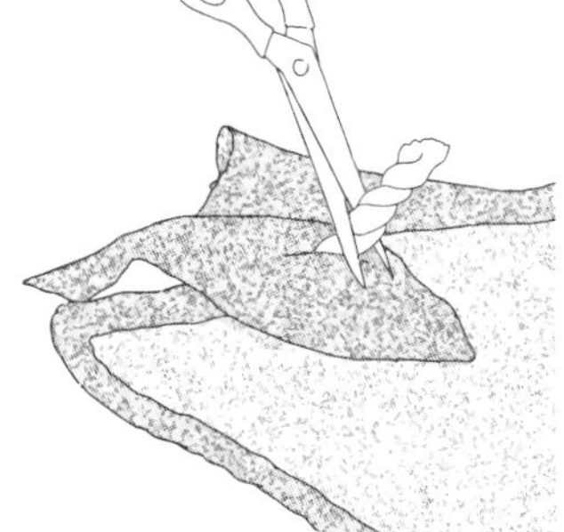

5. To join the piping I like to make a small reference mark on the cover within the seam allowance depth so that it won't be seen. Align one end of the piping with this mark, which will be the stitching line, transfer the mark to the piping. Add a seam allowance by cutting past the stitching line mark. Repeat this with the other end.

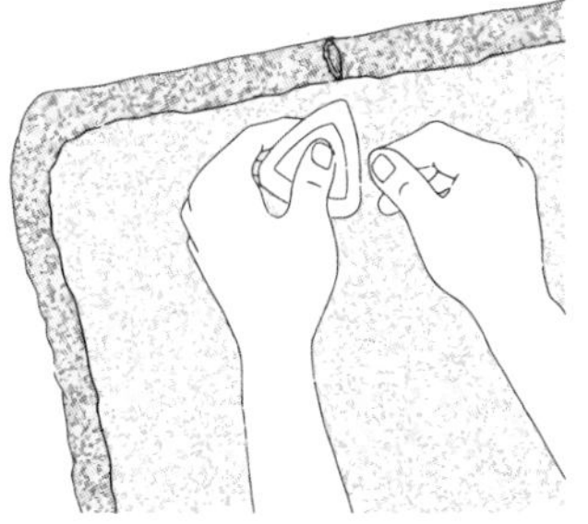

6. Sew the piping ends together, press the seams open to reduce bulk, and encase the piping cord ends by folding the piping fabric over and stitching closed. If you have too much piping cord you can always snip some away before stitching.

Sewing the cushion faces

7. Place the second cushion square right sides together with the one you have piped.

8. Ensure the stitch length on your machine is around 3mm (⅛ inch). The thickness of the fabric you have used for your piping will determine how long your stitches have to be. For example, if you have a thicker fabric you may need a longer stitch.

9. Sew the cushion faces together, navigating around the piping and corners without sewing over the piping bulk.

10. Stop stitching 5cm (2 inches) past the last corner, leaving an opening for the cushion filling.

11. If your fabric is thick, trim the bulk from the corners by cutting diagonally across the corner, about 3mm (⅛ inch) away from the stitches. Be careful not to cut too close to the stitches to avoid creating holes.

Turning, stuffing and closing your cushion cover

12. Turn the cushion cover right side out through the opening. Insert the cushion filling, making sure to push it into the corners for a full, plump appearance.

13. Fold the edges of the opening inward along the seam allowance, pin together, and slip stitch the seam closed (see How to slip stitch, page 35, and follow steps 14–17 of the Scatter cushion/Hand sewn project on page 153), ensuring to cover the stitch line on the piping.

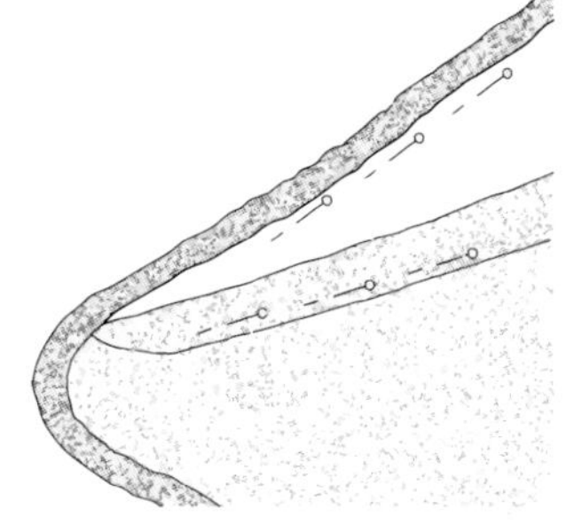

PRO TIP After turning the cushion cover right side out but before stuffing, I like to run the sewing machine around the piped edge once more. Depending on the fabric and the sewing machine foot, this helps to push the stitching closer to the piping cord, ensuring no stitch lines are visible from when the piping was initially sewn.

Box scatter cushion / no piping

Here's a straightforward method for making box scatter cushions that ensures consistent results and a polished finish.

Box scatter cushions offer a touch of luxury and sophistication, and combining them with traditional scatter cushions can add both interest and depth to your space. These cushions can be crafted in various shapes, including rectangular and square, and can be used as both decorative elements and functional seat bases. When making box cushions for seat bases, there will be a few additional considerations (see Window Seat Box Cushion project on page 130).

Tools and materials

Soft tape measure
Notepad
Pencil
Fabric of choice
Ruler
Set square or roofing square
Pencil or tailor's chalk
Fabric scissors
Matching sewing thread
Sewing machine
Cushion filling/inner pad (this should be 2–4cm/¾–1½ inches bigger than your cushion size depending on how plump you want your cushion to be – see Pro Tip, page 153)

Preparing the fabric and cutting the borders

1. Follow steps 1–5 of the Scatter cushion/Hand sewn project on page 150.

PRO TIP You may be able to use a standard-style of cushion infill without a border but, if you'd prefer, you could make your own bordered infill in the same way as you have just done with the top fabric.

2. Decide on the width of the border and cut the border pieces to this size, including seam allowances on the top and bottom. For guidance, I suggest a minimum border size of 4–5cm (1½–2 inches) for a box scatter cushion. The depth of the border on the cushion shown opposite is 6cm (2⅓ inches).

PRO TIP Depending on the size of your cushion, you might need to join fabric pieces at the corners or along the bottom where your opening will be, if your fabric is not wide enough. For plain fabrics, you may be able to cut the fabric up the roll, allowing for fewer joins. This approach isn't suitable for all fabrics but it's an option you may want to consider.

Attaching the borders

3. If your cushion is larger than 40cm (16 inches), consider adding central 'marry marks' on each edge of the cushion (see page 47). Place your first main cushion section (top or bottom piece) and a border piece right sides facing and pin the two fabric pieces together. Start sewing 5–7cm (2–2¾ inches) from the edge, sewing your border to the cushion, maintaining your seam allowance distance from the edge.

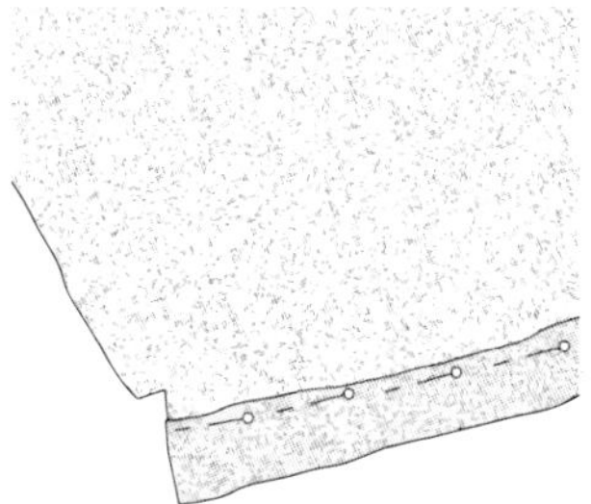

4. When you get close to the next corner, stop about 5–7cm (2–2¾ inches) from the edge. Mark where the cushion fabric ends on the border and cut the border to this point, including your seam allowance. Don't forget to press the seam open and snip into the allowance on your corner to make sure the fabric sits around the corner smoothly.

5. Attach the next border piece to the border you have just cut back to size and continue sewing the border to the main fabric, repeating the previous steps. Work your way around the cushion until you return to the starting point, closing up the last corner and not forgetting to transfer your marry marks to the opposite side of the border ready to sew the border to the second face.

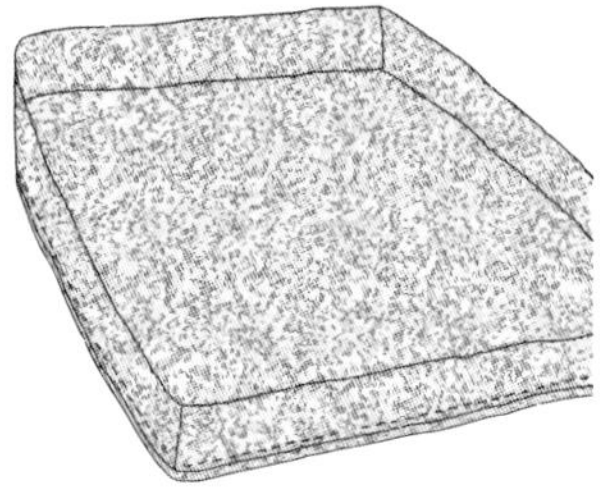

Attaching the second face

6. Place the other fabric piece right sides together with the bordered section you have just sewn, pinning the border to this next piece if you find it helpful to do so. Sew the other side of the border (the unsewn edge) to this main cushion piece, starting 5–7cm (2–2¾ inches) from the edge. This gap will create an opening for inserting the cushion fill.

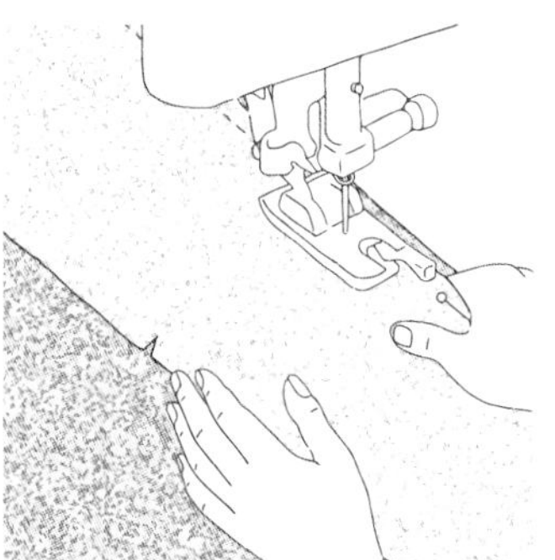

7. Continue sewing around the cushion, repeating step 4 to press open the seam and snipping into the allowance so that the border wraps around the corner smoothly. Stop 5–7cm (2–2¾ inches) past the last corner, leaving an opening for the cushion insert.

Finishing the cushion

8. Turn the cushion cover right side out and insert your cushion infill. Slip stitch the opening (see How to slip stitch, page 35) to close the opening neatly.

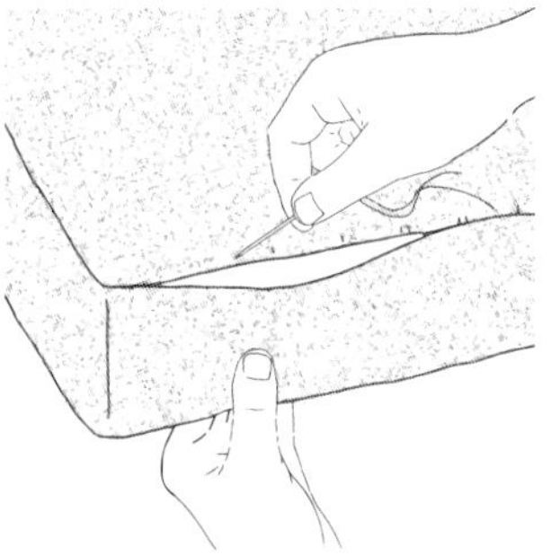

Box scatter cushion / with piping

Adding a piped border embellishment allows you to incorporate a complementary or contrasting fabric, and you can even choose a different texture of fabric to further enhance the overall look of your cushion. This project builds on the previous two box scatter cushion projects.

Tools and materials

Soft tape measure
Notepad
Pencil or tailor's chalk
Fabric of choice
Fabric for piping (if not self-piping)
Piping cord
Fabric scissors
Matching sewing thread
Sewing machine
Dressmaking pins
Cushion filling/inner pad (this should be 2–4cm/¾–1½ inches bigger than your cushion size depending on how plump you want your cushion to be – see Pro Tip, page 153)

Preparing the fabric and cutting the borders

1. Follow steps 1–5 of the Scatter cushion/Hand sewn project on page 150. I suggest a minimum border size of 4–5cm (1½–2 inches). The border on the box scatter cushion shown in the photograph overleaf is 6cm (2½ inches). Additionally, I recommend finishing the cushion 2.5–5cm (1–2 inches) smaller than the insert size, depending on the firmness of the cushion infill.

2. Decide on the width of the border and cut the border pieces to this height, including seam allowances on the top and bottom. This project is written as if you were sewing four separate borders with joins on each corner, so oversize the border lengths so that when you sew them in, you can cut them down to size as you go. I tend to opt for a 1.2cm (½ inch) seam allowance; you could increase this to 1.5cm (⅝ inch), but I would suggest no bigger.

PRO TIP Some people prefer to measure and join their borders first before sewing them on to the main panel. However, I recommend sewing, marking and joining as you go. This technique, which I have learned from the most skilled seamstresses over the years, always results in a perfect finish. It is much easier to work this way if you are pattern-matching, too.

Preparing the piping

3. Make enough piping for both sides of the border, ensuring you have extra for closing the piping at the join. Measure one edge length of one of the face pieces of your cushion cover. Multiply this by eight. This is the minimum length of piping you will need. Decide on the seam allowance (see step 2) then make an oversized length of piping (I would be generous here as you can always cut excess piping away, whereas it's more difficult to add more piping!). Follow the steps in Essential Techniques: Piping on page 37.

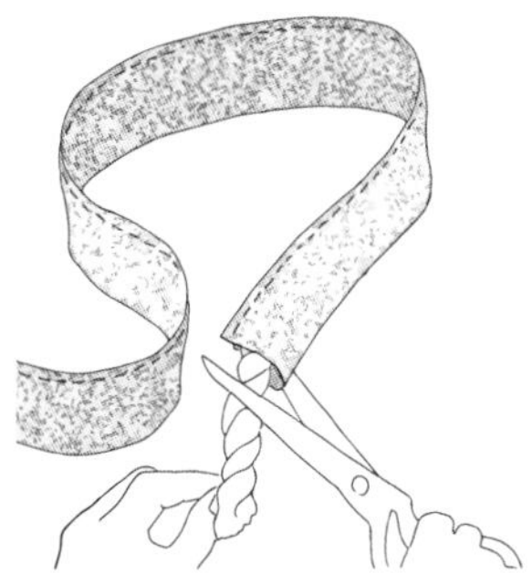

Attaching the piping

4. Starting from approximately the centre bottom of the cushion, pin the piping to one of the face pieces with right sides together. Leave a 5cm (2 inch) 'tail' of piping at the start. This will give you enough length to work with when joining the ends.

5. Sew the piping on to the face all the way around, making sure you press the seam open and snip into the flange at the corners so the piping sits neatly around the corners. Bring it back to the bottom centre where you started.

6. To join the piping, follow steps 5 and 6 of the Scatter cushion/ machine sewn with piping/no zip project on page 163.

7. Repeat the piping process for the second panel face of the fabric.

PRO TIP For certain fabrics, such as velvet, it can be effective to sew the piping with the face of the fabric down and the piping underneath. This helps prevent gathering and can result in a better finish.

Attaching the borders

8. Place your first main section of fabric with piping attached and the border right sides facing, pinning them together. This will sandwich the piping between the main face panel and the border. Ensure the edge of the border aligns with the edge of the main fabric and piping. Starting 5-7cm (2-2¾ inches) along from a corner, sew the border fabric to the cushion, maintaining your seam allowance distance from the edge.

9. When you get close to the next corner, stop stitching 5-7cm (2-2¾ inches) in from that corner. Use your hands to lay the remaining border along the edge of the cushion to the next corner, marking the end of the cushion fabric (including the seam allowance) on the border, and then cut it down. Join the next section of border to this cut-to-size piece and repeat the process. Don't forget to cut into the allowance a few times, about 1-2cm (⅜-¾ inch) on either side of the join, to ensure the fabric sits around the corner nicely. Also, press open the allowance on the join to reduce the bulk when sewing around the corner.

10. Continue attaching the borders until you have worked all the way around to the first border. Repeat the process and close up the last of the corners.

Sewing the second face fabric

11. Now place the other face of the cushion with piping right sides together with the top of the other side of the border, pinning the border to this next piece if you find it helpful to do so. The next step is to sew this together. Again start 5-7cm (2-2¾ inches) along from the corner edge, creating an opening through which to insert the cushion infill.

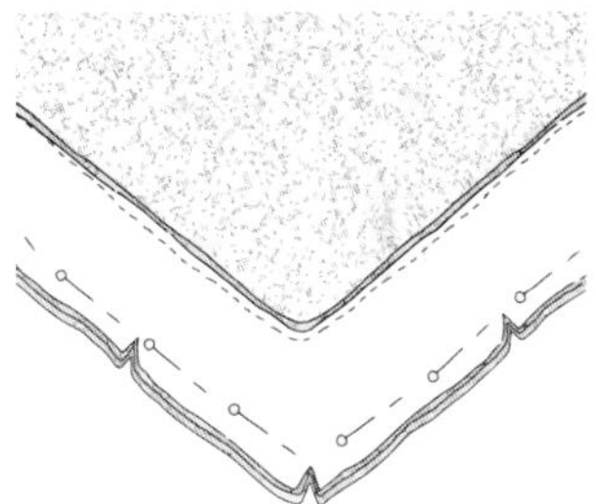

12. Sew all the way around, repeating the steps of snipping into the allowance and opening up the corners. Stop sewing 5-7cm (2-2¾ inches) past the last corner to leave an opening.

Finishing the cushion

13. Turn the cushion cover right side out. Insert the cushion infill (see the Pro Tips on page 164), making sure to shape the corners and dress them by pulling on the piping to sit square.

14. Use slip stitch (see How to slip stitch, page 35) to close the opening neatly.

Box scatter cushion / with braid border

Take your box scatter cushion up a notch by using a wide-width braid as a border instead of fabric (as used in the Box Scatter Cushion projects on pages 164 and 167). This method adds elegance and sophistication to your cushion, enhancing both its appearance and texture.

Tools and materials

Braid of choice for the border
Fabric of choice
Fabric scissors
Pencil or tailor's chalk
Ruler
Dressmaking pins
Matching sewing thread
Sewing machine
Cushion filling/inner pad (this should be 2–4cm/¾–1½ inches bigger than your cushion size depending on how plump you want your cushion to be – see Pro Tip, page 153)

Choosing your braid

1. Select a braid that complements your face fabric and interior decor in terms of design, colour and texture. Ensure it has a sufficient edge for a seam allowance.

PRO TIP Braids are typically ordered by the metre (yard), so you can avoid joins at the corners, having only one join at either the bottom corner or the centre bottom.

Preparing the fabric

2. Prepare your face fabrics by following steps 1–5 of the Scatter cushion/Hand sewn project on page 150, ensuring they are cut to size. I always cut my scatter cushion covers to finish between 2.5–5cm (1–2 inches) smaller than the cushion insert, depending on how full the insert is.

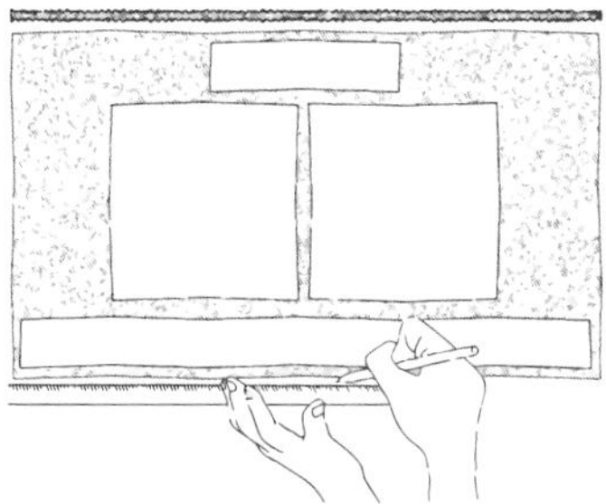

Cutting and attaching the braid

3. Measure one edge length of one of the face pieces. Multiply this by four and this is the minimum length of braid you will need. Decide on the seam allowance, then cut an oversized length of braid for your border (I would be generous here as you can always cut excess braid away, whereas it's more difficult to add more border braid!). Decide whether you will join the braid at the centre bottom or at a corner of the facing piece.

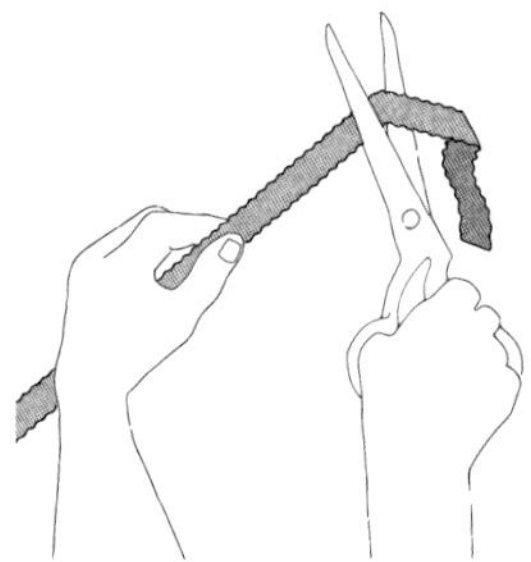

4. If you have decided to join the braid in the middle bottom, then find the centre point of that edge of the panel. You can either make a marry mark (see page 47) with a pencil or snip slightly into the seam allowance as a guide. As you would if you were starting from a corner, start pinning the two pieces of the fabric panel (the braid to the face piece) right sides together 5–7cm (2–2¾ inches) in from the marry mark so that you have enough length available for handling when sewing the two ends of the braid together. Sew the braid on to the cushion in the same manner as a fabric border by following steps 3–5 of the Box scatter cushion/ No piping project on pages 164 and 166. The braid may be flexible enough to wrap around corners without needing to snip the edges.

5. Once you have sewn one edge of the braid all the way around the cushion face, and joined the braid at the last section, you can attach the other side of the cushion to the border.

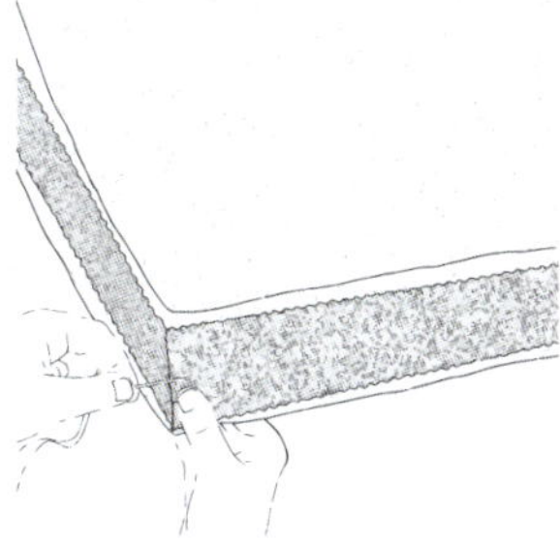

Attaching the second face fabric

6. Follow steps 6–8 of the Box scatter cushion/No piping project on page 166.

PRO TIP You may be able to use a standard-style of cushion infill without a border but, if you'd prefer, you could make your own bordered infill in the same way as you have just done with the top fabric.

---

7. Remember to push your cushion inner into the box corners to fill them out properly.

Bolster cushion / with sewn-in ends

A bolster cushion is a long, narrow pillow or cushion stuffed with fibre, feathers, or both. Occasionally, they might come with foam inners. They frequently feature a zip or are sewn closed using a slip stitch and are not a uniform size or shape.

A bolster is typically situated at the top of the bed, serving as a head or lower back support, as well as an arm support on furniture like sofas. They can span the depth of the seat on a sofa or sit in front of pillows on a bed. Bolsters can add a touch of decadence to your decor, combining both utility and aesthetics.

There are two ways to finish the ends of a bolster: with gathered ends (see page 175) or with sewn-in ends as shown here.

Tools and materials

Soft tape measure
Bolster insert (see Pro Tip, page 153)
Pencil or tailor's chalk
Fabric of choice
Fabric scissors
Dressmaking pins
Matching sewing thread
Sewing machine
Curved or straight hand-sewing needle

PRO TIP For beginners, I recommend a plain fabric, like cotton or linen. If you are feeling a little more confident, velvet works well for a bolster – the pile of the velvet adds a bit more of a challenge but it is definitely achievable.

Measure your insert

1. Measure the length and the diameter of the bolster insert. For a plump look, make the cover at least 2.5cm (1 inch) shorter in length than the insert. Adjust the size according to your preference for firmness.

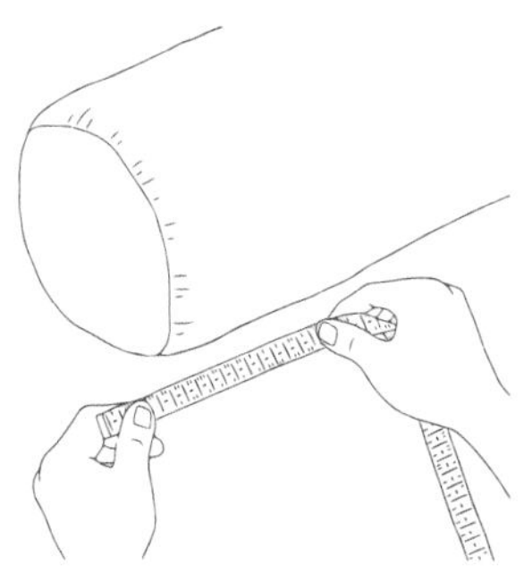

Calculating and cutting out the fabric pieces

2. Use tailor's chalk or a similar marking tool to mark the exact measurements on the reverse side of your fabric. Mark out three pieces: the main central tube panel and two circular end pieces. Add a 1.5cm (⅝ inch) seam allowance to all three pieces, then cut them out. Remember to adjust the length of the central tube panel so it is 2.5cm (1 inch) shorter if you're aiming for a plump cushion.

PRO TIP If you want to be really precise, use Pi to calculate the circumference of the end panels. For example, if the diameter of the cushion insert is 10cm (4 inches), the circumference is 10cm × 3.14 = 31.4cm (4 × 3.14 = 12.56 inches) (round to 31.5cm/12.5 inches for ease). The circumference measurement should be the same as the width measurement of the central tube panel.

Sewing the main section

3. Fold the main section in half lengthways, right sides together, to create a tube. Pin and then sew along the seam allowance, leaving enough of an opening to push the bolster insert into the cushion cover once the round ends have also been attached. I suggest leaving an opening the same length as the diameter of your insert to ensure you can easily fit it in.

4. I like to add 'marry marks' (see page 47) at this stage. Mark the halfway and quarter points on both the main body and the round ends to ensure alignment when sewing.

5. Snip into the seam allowance of the main fabric end edges so that when you attach the circular end pieces, the fabric sits better on the curve.

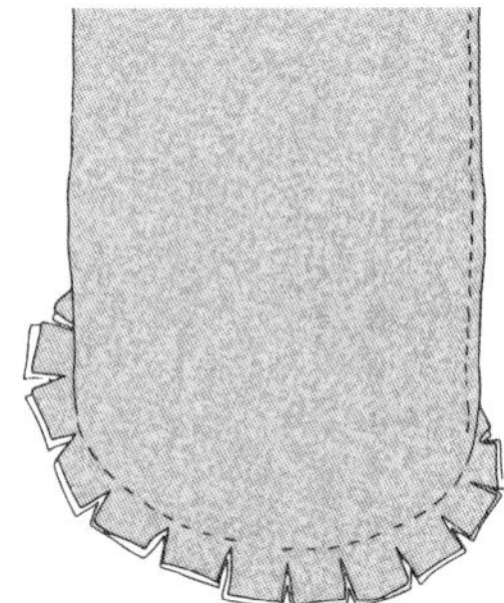

Attaching the round end pieces

6. Pin the round ends in place using your marry marks to properly align the fabric pieces. Tack the two pieces together (this is optional). Alternatively, you might want to go straight to the machine stitching stage. Machine sew around the circle, ensuring each marry mark matches as you go.

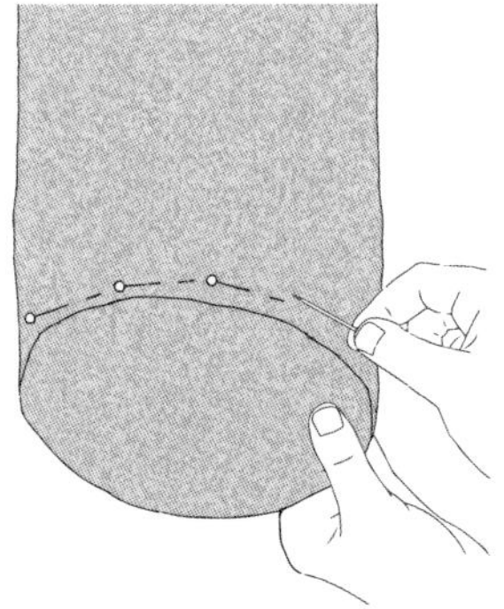

7. Repeat this on the other side, pinning and sewing the second round end piece into place.

Turning and hand-stitching the cushion cover

8. Now turn your cover right side out, insert the bolster insert and fold in the fabric on the opening to form a hem.

9. Pin the two sides to one another, leaving enough room to be able to slip stitch this together. Use a curved or straight needle to slip stitch the gap closed (see How to slip stitch, page 35).

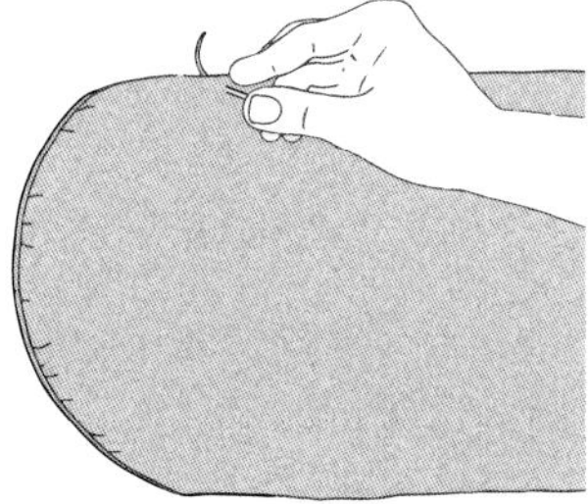

Et voilà! You have a plumptious and fabulous bolster cushion. May it be the first of many!

Bolster cushion / with gathered ends

A bolster cushion is a versatile and decorative element that can add elegance and comfort to your home decor. The gathered-end style creates a sophisticated look, perfect for both functional and ornamental purposes. Follow these instructions to create a bolster cushion with beautifully gathered ends.

Tools and materials

Soft tape measure
Bolster insert (see Pro Tip, page 153)
Pencil or tailor's chalk
Fabric of choice
Fabric scissors
Dressmaking pins
Matching sewing thread
Sewing machine
Hand-sewing needle
Covered button or rosette

PRO TIP If you want to be really precise, use Pi to calculate the circumference to give you a precise measurement for the width of the centre section. For example, if the diameter of the bolster insert is 10cm (4 inches), the circumference is 10cm × 3.14 = 31.4cm (4 × 3.14 = 12.56 inches) (round to 31.5cm/ 12.5 inches for ease).

Measuring and cutting the fabric

1. For the central tube panel, measure the length and circumference of the bolster insert (see Pro Tip, left, for calculating the exact circumference). You will attach separate panels to create the gathered ends, using the circumference of the bolster insert for the length and half the diameter (the radius) for the width.

2. Mark the measurements on the wrong side of the fabric. Mark out three pieces: the central tube panel and two rectangular end pieces. Adjust the dimensions according to your preference for cushion firmness; for a plump look, reduce the length by at least 2.5cm (1 inch). Add a 1.5cm (⅝ inch) seam allowance to all three pieces, then cut them out.

Sewing the cover

3. Pin one end panel to one end of the central panel, with right sides facing. Sew together, taking a 1.5cm (⅝ inch) seam allowance and securing the thread at the beginning and end. Press the seams open. Repeat to attach the second panel to the opposite end of the central section.

4. Fold the completed, extended panel in half lengthways, right sides together, to create a tube with the rectangular sections at the open ends. Pin and sew along the seam allowance, securing the thread at the beginning and end.

Closing up the cushion ends

5. Turn the cover right side out. On one end, turn under a hem to match the seam allowance. With doubled thread in a hand-sewing needle, make long gathering stitches around the end, approximately 5mm (3/16 inch) in from the folded edge.

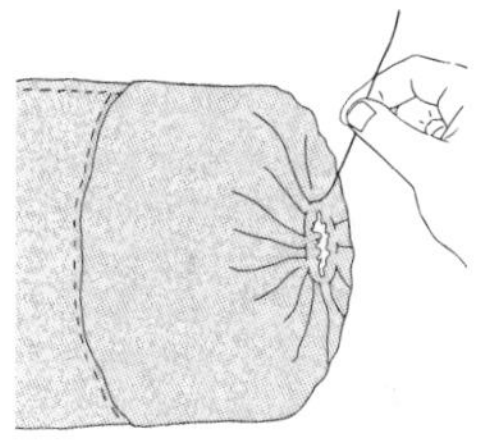

6. Pull the gathering thread as tight as you can, feeding the gather into the centre. Adjust any folds that are not sitting correctly; each stitch should create a fold that sits neatly against the next. Fasten off tightly.

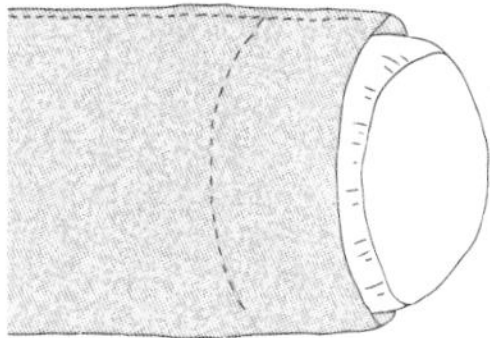

7. Insert the bolster cushion, then gauge if you need to reduce the length to ensure a snug fit. This is the perfect time to make any adjustments.

8. Repeat steps 5 and 6 to gather and close up the other end. Add a decorative touch, such as a covered button or rosette, to cover and finish off the gathered section.

Bolster cushion / with gathered ends and piping

You can add some real flare and styling to a bolster cushion by adding piping to its gathered end. This detail adds another layer of texture and you could opt for a different fabric if you wanted to.

Tools and materials
Soft tape measure
Bolster insert (see Pro Tip, page 153)
Pencil or tailor's chalk
Fabric of choice
Fabric for piping (if not self-piping)
Fabric scissors
Dressmaking pins
Matching sewing thread
Sewing machine
Piping cord
Hand-sewing needle
Covered button or rosette

Measuring and cutting the fabric

1. Follow steps 1 and 2 of the Bolster cushion/with gathered ends project on page 175.

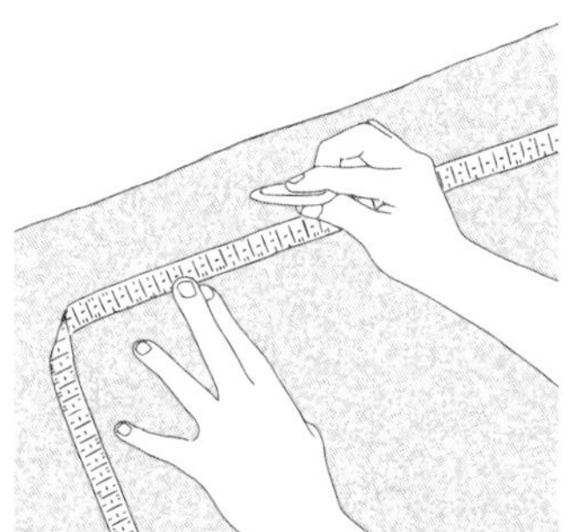

2. Fold the main central section you created in step 1 in half lengthways, right sides together, to create a tube. Pin and then sew this together along the seam allowance.

Making the piping

3. Make enough piping to go around each of the round end panels, with an added seam allowance of at least 5cm (2 inches) following the instructions in Essential Techniques: Piping on page 37. You can use the same fabric as the cushion cover or a contrasting/complementary fabric, depending on your design scheme.

Attaching the piping to the main section

4. Now it's time to add your piping. Start at the same position as the central hem of the main section. This ensures that the join is not visible once the bolster is complete, as the seam should be positioned facing down. Be sure to leave a little 5cm (2 inch) tail of piping at the start.

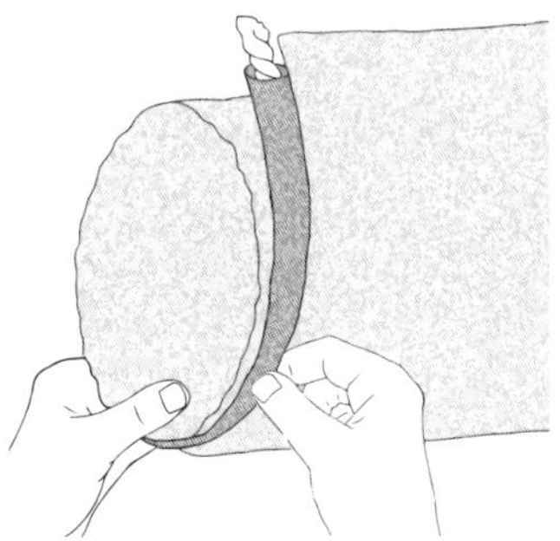

5. Make sure you pin the piping to the right side of the central tube fabric.

6. Sew the piping on to the face all the way around, making sure you snip into the flange if necessary so the piping sits neatly. Snip into the seam allowance of the main fabric end edges so that, when you attach the circular end pieces, the fabric sits better on the curve.

7. Sew the piping ends together, opening up the seams to reduce bulk, and encase the piping cord ends by folding the piping fabric over and stitching closed. If you have too much piping cord, snip some away before stitching.

Creating the ends to be gathered

8. Take the two end pieces of fabric you made in step 2. These sections should be long enough to cover the ends once gathered and include a seam allowance on both edges – one for sewing to the main fabric and one for turning in and gathering the end. Each end piece needs to be made into a tube as you did with the central tube piece in step 3. It is imperative that the circumference of each end piece when sewn matches that of the central tube.

9. Pin and sew each end piece to the central tube of fabric with the piping already attached.

Gathering the end pieces and finishing the cushion cover

10. Turn the cover right side out. On one end, turn under a hem in line with your seam allowance. Doubling up thread for your hand stitching, start making large gathering stitches around the edge, approximately 5mm (3/16 inch) in from the folded edge.

11. Pull this thread as tight as you can, feeding the gather into the centre if needed. Adjust and dress any folds that are not sitting correctly. Each stitch should create a fold that sits neatly against the next fold. Fasten the thread tightly.

12. Insert the bolster insert into the cushion cover.

13. With the bolster insert in place, gauge whether you need to reduce the length of the fabric to ensure a snug fit. The cover should hug the insert for a plump feel.

14. Repeat step 11 to close up the other end. Fasten off the thread and add a decorative touch, such as a covered button or rosette, to finish off the gathered section.

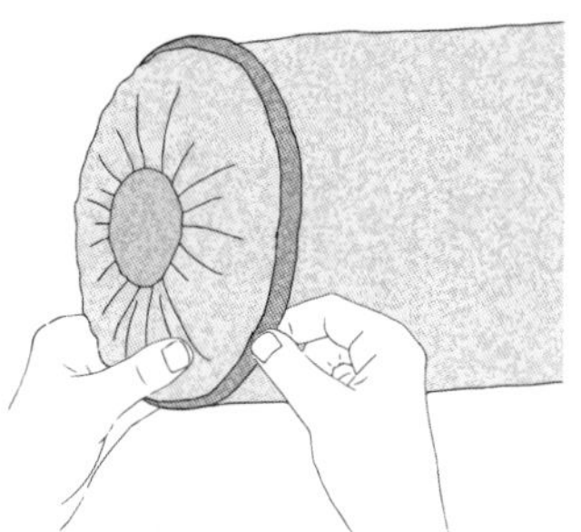

Bed throw

Adding a bed throw not only enhances the decorative element of your room interior but also provides an extra layer of warmth during winter. This guide covers two versions: a purely decorative throw and a full bed throw that encompasses your pillows for added warmth. The latter is a traditional style that I adore! This guide is perfect for beginners, using simple techniques for maximum style.

Tools and materials

Soft tape measure
Double-width reversible fabric of choice
Ruler
Set square or roofing square
Pencil or tailor's chalk
Fabric scissors
Iron
Dressmaking pins
Matching sewing thread
Sewing machine

PRO TIP A double-width reversible fabric works best for making a bed throw. If you are using a standard-width reversible fabric, you can join multiple widths together. Decide whether you prefer a central join or side joins. For joined fabrics, use French seams to hide raw edges (see page 38).

Decide on the style

1. Determine whether you would like the throw to be decorative and sit across a portion of the bed (A) or big enough to cover the entire bed, including the pillows (B).

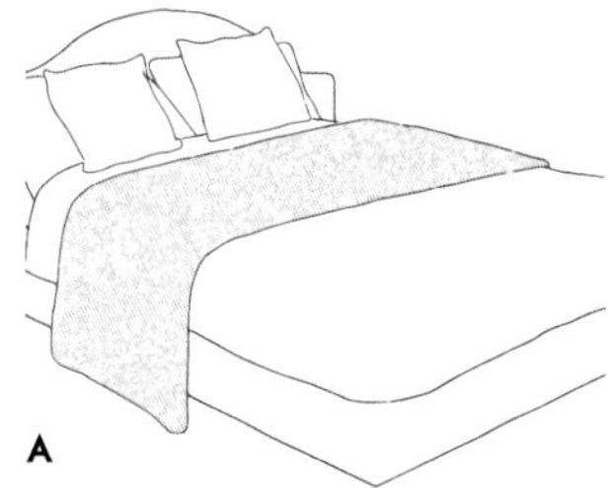

A

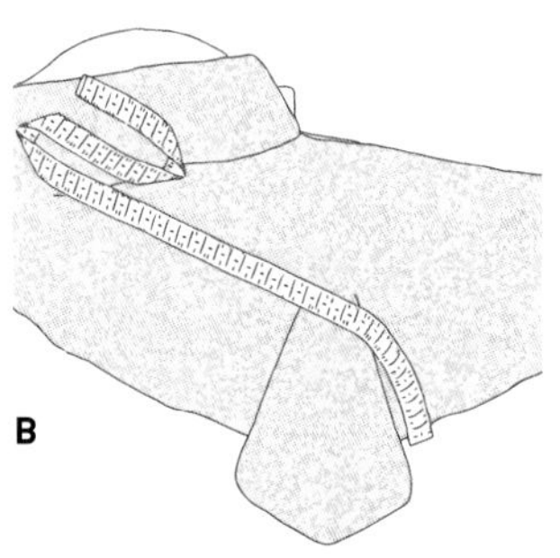

B

PRO TIP If you let the bed throw finish to the floor on all three sides, the two bottom corners of the throw will cascade on to the floor. This can be a design choice, but if it's not the look you want, consider making the throw finish halfway down the sides of the bed or less.

Prepare the fabric

2. Use a soft tape measure to measure the finished length and width of fabric required. The throw can finish either halfway down the sides of the bed or all the way to the floor. Refer to the illustration below for where to measure if encompassing pillows. Unless you are using a double-width fabric you will have to add joins to your bed throw. The traditional way to do this is to add an additional narrow panel of fabric on either side of the full-width middle section. For me this is less jarring on the eye than other approaches.

3. Use a ruler and set square to achieve straight lines and square corners, and a tailor's chalk or pencil to add marks to the fabric. Add 6cm (2⅓ inches) to the edges (this will fold in to create a 3cm/1¼ inch hem), then cut it out.

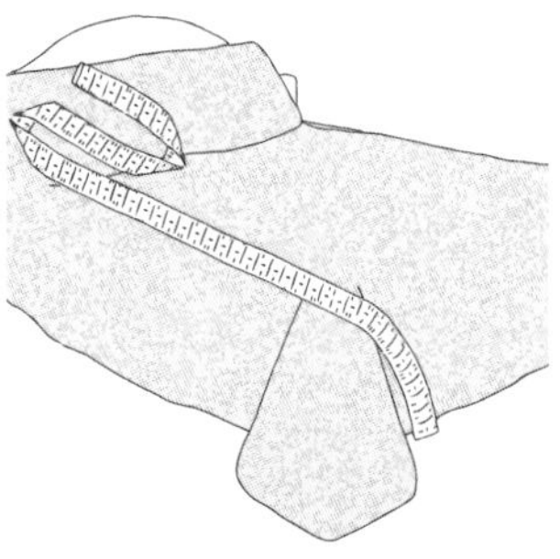

4. Join your three panels using the French seam technique (see French seams, page 38) to give a neat result with no raw edges visible on the underside of the bed throw. Fold and press the first 3cm (1¼ inches) on all four sides, then fold and press the second 3cm (1¼ inches), pinning the hem in place as you work along the edges.

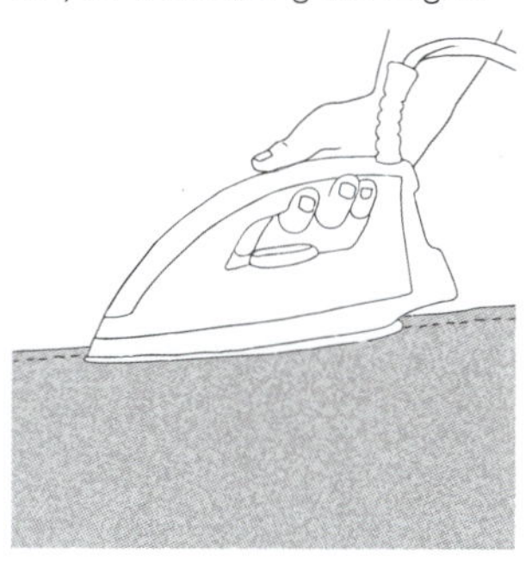

PRO TIP For fabrics that create a lot of bulk at the corners when folded, cut the bulk out by cutting across the bias on the first fold. For thicker fabrics, experiment with raising the sewing machine foot height/pressure before sewing the hem. This helps prevent the pressure of the foot from pushing the top fold of the fabric.

Sewing the hem

5. Using a longer stitch, sew down the hem, removing the pins as you work along the edge.

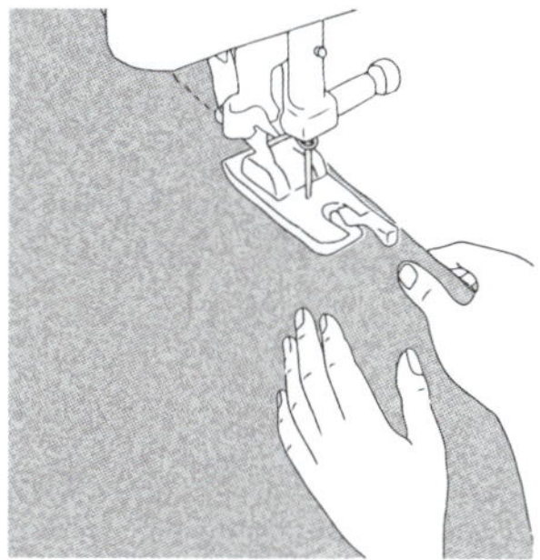

6. When you reach a corner, you can either stitch all the way to the edge and start the next line from the beginning of the next edge or turn the bed throw around when your needle reaches the same stitch line position as on the first edge.

7. Once you have sewn all four edges your bed throw is ready to dress your bed!

Drum lampshade

Creating your own drum lampshade can be a rewarding and creative project. Whether you're refreshing an old lamp or crafting one from scratch, this guide will take you through all the steps to achieve a professional finish. We'll focus on using a thinner woven fabric for ease and better results. Lampshade-making kits are available online or you can purchase the individual elements if you prefer.

Tools and materials

Fabric of choice
Iron
Lampshade rings (plain ring and utility ring with gimbal and fitting)
Self-adhesive PVC lining with a finished side
Soft tape measure
Metre ruler
Pencil
Scissors (both paper and fabric)
Craft knife with retractable blade
Dressmaking weights (optional)
30cm (12 inch) ruler
High-tack double-sided tape
Regulator or an old store card

Choosing your fabric

1. Select a thin, woven fabric for best results. Cotton or linen are ideal. Avoid heavy, textured or stretchy fabrics. Iron your fabric to ensure it is completely crease free. Any creases will show up and ruin the look of the final lampshade.

Determining the height of your lampshade

2. If you have purchased a lampshade-making kit follow the instructions that come with this. If not, then follow the steps that are outlined below. You can either start from scratch or reuse rings from an old lampshade, ensuring they are clean from any previous adhesive.

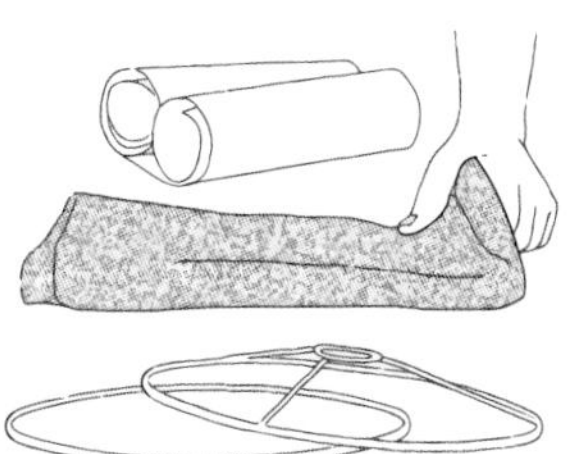

Measuring and cutting the self-adhesive PVC lining

3. Start by deciding the height of your drum lampshade, then measure the circumference of your lampshade using a soft tape measure around one of the metal lampshade rings. Cut the self-adhesive PVC lining to the finished height and 4cm (1½ inches) longer than the circumference of your lampshade. Transfer this measurement to your lining using a metre ruler and pencil, and cut it with scissors or a retractable blade.

Cutting the fabric

4. Lay your fabric of choice right side down on a large work surface. Position the self-adhesive lining on top of your fabric. Using a ruler and pencil, measure and mark 10cm (4 inches) larger than the lining on your fabric. Connect these marks using a ruler and cut out the fabric. If you are using a patterned fabric pay attention to pattern positioning.

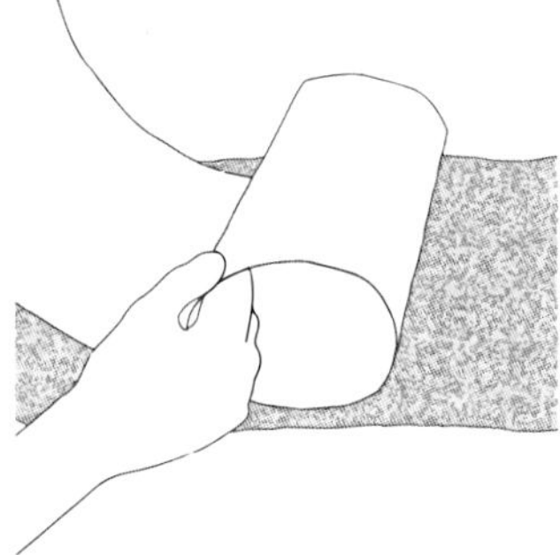

PRO TIP Use leftover fabric from other projects to match your lampshade to existing decor.

Sticking the lining to the fabric

5. Place the fabric face down on a flat surface and position the self-adhesive lining on top, with the adhesive side facing down.

Ensure the lining is properly aligned on the fabric. If your fabric is patterned, pay close attention to positioning the lining in the right place. You could even use masking tape to hold the fabric in place. Check there are no loose fibres sandwiched between the lining and the fabric as these will show up on the finished lampshade.

PRO TIP Weigh the lining down while its sitting on top of your fabric, this helps to prevent it from moving while you adhere the two layers together. Dressmaking/sewing weights are great for this.

6. Starting at one end, lift the lining up carefully and peel the backing paper 4–5cm (1½–2 inches) away to expose the sticky side of the lining. Use your hand to press this down on to the fabric, making sure it's sticking in the correct position on the fabric. Remove any weights as you do this, if used. It is crucial that you use your hand to smooth the lining on to the fabric slowly and carefully, removing any air bubbles and creases. Always check the right side of the lining/fabric for any ripples or puckers before moving on to peeling and sticking the next section. Adjust if necessary by unpeeling and re-sticking problem areas.

7. Slowly peel the backing paper away in 5–8cm (2–3¼ inch) increments, pressing the lining on to the fabric to avoid puckering. Keeping one hand on the end you have just stuck down, use the other hand to peel the backing off and to apply pressure to encourage the two layers to stick together. Work along the whole length of the lining, repeating this process until you reach the other end.

8. Turn the lining/fabric over to check for any ripples or puckers. Unpeel and re-stick any problem areas. Once satisfied, apply pressure across the entire panel to ensure even adhesion.

Trimming the fabric

9. Now mark a 2.5–3cm (1–1¼ inch) allowance greater than the edge of the lining on three sides of the fabric, leaving one end flush with the lining. Cut along these lines.

10. Apply high-tack double-sided tape along the short end of the panel with the 2.5–3cm (1–1¼ inch) fabric overhang. Peel the backing and fold the fabric over the tape, trimming excess fabric. Add another layer of tape to this end, but DO NOT remove the backing of the tape at this stage.

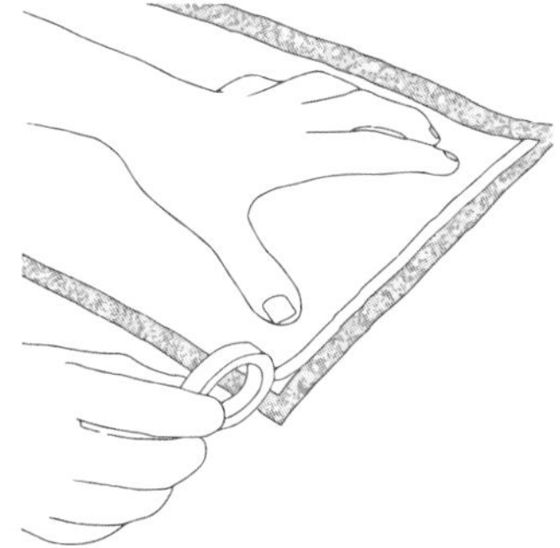

Attaching the double-sided tape to the rings

11. Take the two metal lampshade rings and run high-tack double-sided tape around the edge of each ring, being careful not to overlap the tape where you started. Press the tape down all around the wire without any flaps.

Attaching the rings to the lining/fabric panel

12. Position your panel fabric side down on a large work surface. Make sure you can easily access the short end of the panel that does not have the folded over and taped fabric end.

PRO TIP Ensure you have the rings oriented correctly, especially with patterned fabric. For lampstands and table lamps, the utility ring goes at the bottom; for ceiling lights, it goes at the top.

13. Before you remove any tape, position the rings on the top and bottom edges of the lining and double check you have them the right way around in relation to the fabric you are using. And always remember that the gimbal fitting on the utility ring MUST face inwards.

14. Once satisfied, find the point where the double-sided tape starts on each ring and gently peel back about 5cm (2 inches) of tape. Start at the end of the panel where the fabric has been cut flush to the lining. Take a ring in each hand and position them along the top and bottom edge of the lining. Roll both rings simultaneously along the panel edges, removing the tape backing in equal increments and carefully ensuring proper alignment.

PRO TIP Ideally position the utility ring with the arm/strut placed 5–8cm (2–3¼ inches) from the panel's starting edge. Ideally you don't want to join the panel in the same place as the arm.

15. You may need to re-stick the area where you started, roll back, and reposition a section you have just rolled on to the lining. Take your time to ensure the rings are correctly positioned. As you continue rolling, it will become easier and the rings will become more stable as the shade takes shape and eventually becomes self-supporting.

Securing the ends of the panel

16. As you approach the end of the lining panel, remove the backing from the tape on the short edge of the panel and press to join. On your work surface, lay the lampshade down and roll the rings across the join. Use your hand to apply gentle pressure to the join, which will encourage the tape to stick.

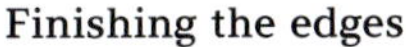

Finishing the edges

17. With your shade on its side, starting at the join, use your fingers to roll the fabric around the rounded edge of the plain ring first, which will encourage the fabric edge facing into the lampshade to fit snugly around the ring. Do the same on the utility hoop. Make a small incision in the fabric with scissors at the point where each of the three gimbal arms/struts meets the ring.

18. Use the regulator or an old store card to tuck the excess fabric underneath itself on each of the rings, ensuring a tight wrap.

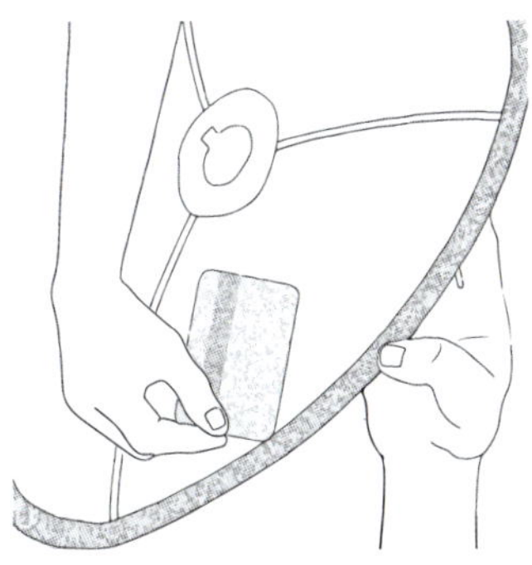

19. You may find that you have to run your tool of choice back around the inside edge again to neaten up any areas or re-stick into place if necessary. The fabric should be wrapped tightly around each ring. Your lampshade is now ready to fit!

LINW

Table runner and placemats

The humble table runner and placemats are often overlooked but can add personality, style and another layer of charm to your dining experiences. Table runners are narrow pieces of cloth that extend along either the length or width of your dining table and can be crafted from a variety of materials such as organza, linen, casement, crochet and more. Some runners feature tapered edges and playful tassels that hang over the ends of the table, giving an extra decorative touch. Fabric placemats usually sit under wooden, wicker or firmer stiff placemats. Whether for Christmas, birthdays, special occasions or everyday dining, creating your own design aesthetic is a fun and rewarding process. Once you have mastered the basics, you can experiment with adding lace, trims, braids and other embellishments.

Tools and materials

Soft tape measure
Fabric of choice
Pencil or tailor's chalk
Ruler
Set square or roofing square
Iron
Matching sewing thread
Sewing machine
Fabric scissors
Lace, braid or fringing (optional)
Hand-sewing needle and translucent thread for adding embellishments (optional)
Dressmaking pins

Choosing your style of runner

Decide whether you want your runner to lay lengthways along the table or across the table widthways.

Making a lengthways runner

1. Decide where you want the runner to stop and measure this length. There are three options available to you:

- Stopping at the end of the table.
- Cascading over the end of the table.

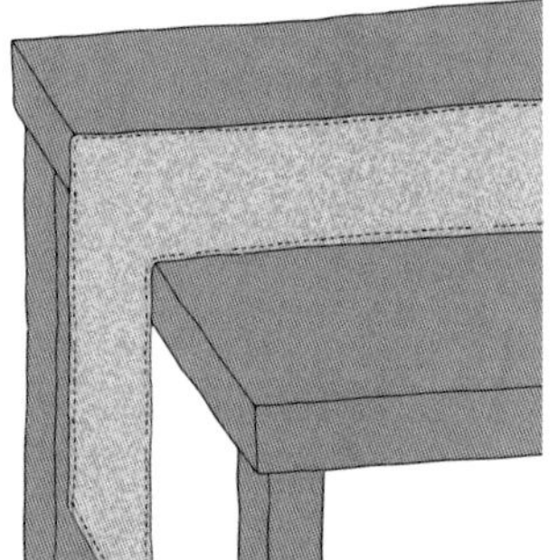

- Cascading over the end of the table and close to the floor.

2. Measure the maximum width the runner can be, ensuring you are happy with the finished size of the runner and it's positioning.

3. Choose a fabric that suits your colour scheme. Plain fabrics can enhance other elements of your tablescape, like crockery or candles.

4. Lay your fabric out on to a flat surface right side down. Transfer your length and width measurements on to the fabric using a pencil or tailor's chalk. Use a ruler and set square to achieve straight lines and square corners.

5. Add a folded hem allowance to the finished size you require all the way around the runner. For a finished width of 30cm (12 inches), add 2.5cm (1 inch).

6. Press the hem into place on all four sides to the finished size required. To do this, fold the edge in 1.2cm (½ inch), press, fold the edge over again, hiding the raw edge, and press firmly.

6thApril 2013

PRO TIP If your fabric creates bulk on the corners when folded, cut the bulk out by cutting across the bias on the first fold.

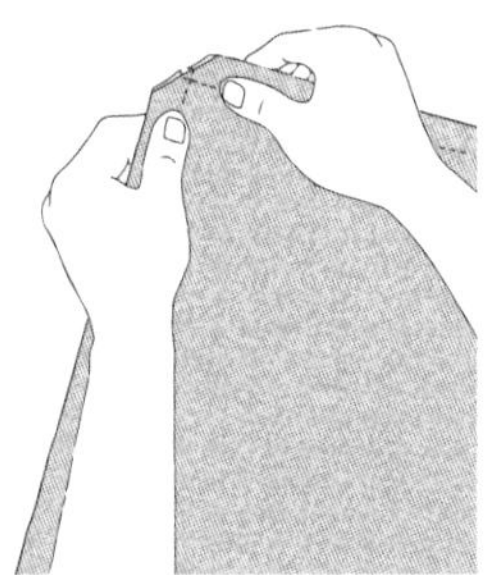

7. Use a long stitch length to sew down the hems on the edges of the fold.

Making a widthways table runner

1. You have two options here: You can lay the table runners widthways across the table either on every other place setting or on every setting. Choose an option and then measure the minimum and maximum width that the runners need to finish at to ensure they do not touch when placed on the table.

2. Decide where you want the runner to stop and measure this length. There are several options available, however, keep in mind that you may only want this runner to cascade a short way over the edge of the table to avoid discomfort for your guests:

- Stopping at the table edge.
- Cascading over the edge of the table.
- Cascading over the edge of the table and close to the floor.

3. Follow steps 3–7 of the lengthways runner instructions on pages 186 and 188.

Making placemats

1. Before you start, ensure that placemats and table runners will not interfere with each other. Your table may not be deep enough to accommodate both.

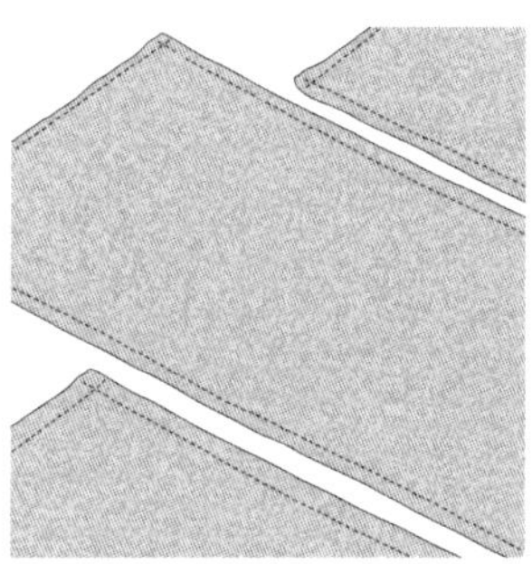

2. Calculate the size and shape of your placemats (you could make rectangular or square ones), and the number you would like to make. Transfer these measurements to your chosen fabric then follow steps 5–6 of the lengthways runner instructions on page 186.

Choosing your embellishments

1. You may want to add embellishments to your table runners and placemats. The creative freedom is yours. Options include:

- Lace
- Fringing
- Braid

Attaching lace or fringing

2. For lace and fringing, I suggest choosing a design with decorative shapes or curves at the bottom and a straight section at the top. This straight section can be hand-sewn on to the underside edge of the hem using a hand-sewing needle and translucent thread.

3. Turn the cut end of the lace edging under itself and pin it to the middle front of the placemat on the underside.

4. Using a running stitch, sew the lace to the hemmed edge without piercing through to the face of the placemat.

5. When you reach a corner, snip into the flat edge to help it sit around the corner, then pin and sew it in place.

6. Continue sewing around the placemat, finishing by tucking the edge under and sewing it to meet the beginning.

Attaching braid

7. If you opt to use braid, you can position it 3–4cm (1¼–1½ inches) in from the shorter edges

8. Pin the braid in place, folding under the start and end to hide the raw edge.

9. Using a straight or zig-zag stitch, run a line of stitching down both sides of the braid.

10. Repeat this process on the opposite side.

Decorative braid for curtains

Adding decorative braid, also known as passementerie, to your curtains can breathe new life into them. Passementerie is an art form that dates back to the 17th century, reached its peak during the baroque and rococo periods, where tassels, fringes, braids and cords were meticulously crafted from valuable materials like silk, gold and silver thread.

These beautiful finishings can enhance both contemporary and traditional curtain designs, adding a touch of elegance, style and personality to your room. These seemingly small details, often overlooked, can elevate your interior and give your space a refined, designer touch.

Here I will walk you through the steps to retrospectively add braid to the leading edge of existing curtains. You can also incorporate this detail if you are making curtains from scratch.

Tools and materials

Set of existing curtains
Iron
Braid of choice
Clamp (optional)
Dressmaking pins
30cm (12 inch) ruler
Hand-sewing needle
Translucent thread

PRO TIP Use a translucent thread and double it up.

Preparing your curtains

1. Remove the curtains you plan to work on from the curtain track or pole. Press any areas of the leading edge (the edge of the curtain that meets in the centre of the window) of the curtains if there are creases.

Choosing the braid

2. Consider the following when selecting your braid:

- **Width** Ensure there is enough space for the braid to be stitched into place in-between the leading edge and the first pinch pleat at the top of the curtain (the header).
- **Colour** The braid should complement or contrast with the curtain fabric as desired.
- **Design** The braid should fit in with your existing interior.
- **Measurement** Calculate the amount of braid you will need correctly. Measure the drop of your curtain plus at least an extra 10cm (4 inches) at each end for turning under.

Positioning the braid

3. Lay the leading edge of the curtain along the long edge of a table. I like to clamp the curtain to the table, helping keep it in place while I work and ensuring everything stays as straight as possible.

4. Decide on the distance in from the edge of the curtain where you want the braid to sit. Make sure you have positioned the braid so that you have an equal overhang at the top and the bottom.

Securing the braid to the curtain

5. Pin the braid to the curtain. You may have to adjust the pins as you progress, as the curtain and braid can shift.

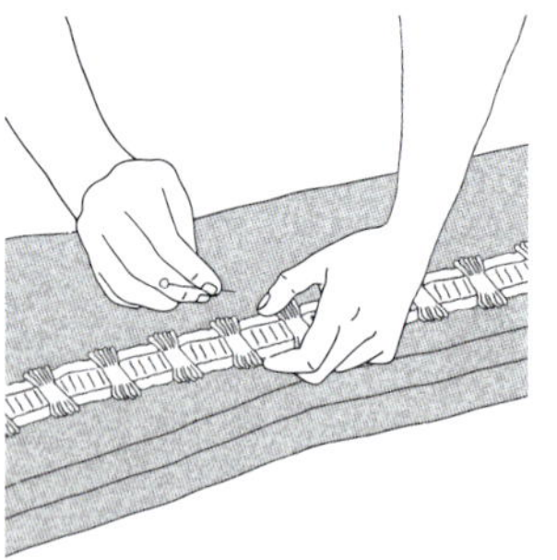

6. To finish the braid at each end, you have two choices. You can either turn the braid under at the top and bottom and sew the ends down, or you can open up the lining at the top, tuck the braid into the lining and sew it closed. For the bottom hem, you could take the braid and return it up inside the lining and sew the lining closed over the braid to conceal the end.

7. Once you have decided on the finish you prefer and pinned everything accordingly you can begin sewing, either from the top or the bottom of your curtains.

8. Start sewing either down the centre of the braid if it is thin (maximum 12mm/½ inch wide), or down either side of the braid (for a wider braid). If you are sewing down both sides of the braid, it is easier to sew down one side first and then down the other side. You can sew the braid on using a small running stitch with a maximum stitch length of 1cm (⅜ inch). For thick woven braids with deep pile designs, use the pile to your advantage; the stitches will disappear into the bulk of the design.

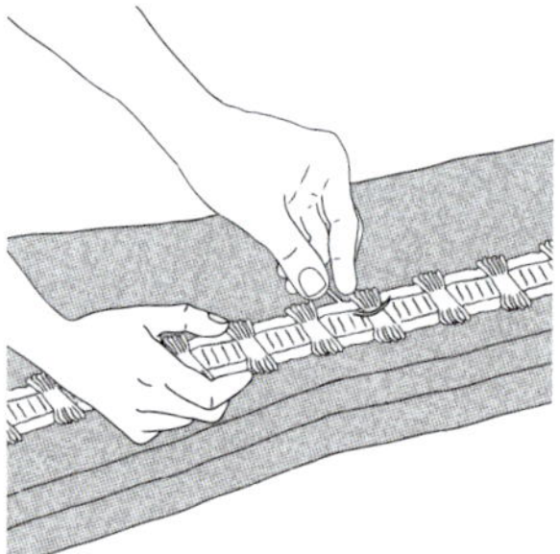

9. Once you have finished off the ends the curtains can be rehung and admired.

MACKEREL

Safety

Ensuring your safety during upholstery projects is crucial. By following these safety guidelines, you will protect yourself from potential hazards and enjoy a safer and more productive working environment:

Personal Protective Equipment (PPE)

Dust mask – Ensure the straps are placed correctly over your head and that the metal nose strip is pinched to form a seal over your nose. I prefer masks with a metal strip for a more secure fit. Alternatively, you might choose a heavier-duty dust mask with a moulded, flexible plastic shape that seals around your nose and mouth. These masks typically feature an internal valve for easier breathing and a harness-style strap that goes around the entire head.

Fumes/vapour mask – Make sure the straps are tight enough over your head to create an airtight seal, ensuring that the air you breathe in is filtered through the mask. This is crucial when using sprays or working with adhesives to avoid inhaling harmful fumes. When stripping paint or varnish from any piece of wooden furniture, always wear a mask. It is a good habit to adopt. For some upholstery projects, you may need to cut shapes from a plywood sheet, so it is essential to wear a mask to prevent inhaling any small particles. Keep a mask on when you are cleaning up too, as dust can fly around when being swept or vacuumed.

Protective eyewear – Always wear protective eyewear when stripping any existing upholstery from furniture (known as stripping out). Likewise, be sure to wear eye protective glasses or goggles when cutting wood.

Lifting safely

When moving any pieces of furniture that you are upholstering, such as a chair or headboard, always seek help if needed. If you do have to lift something by yourself, remember to bend your knees rather than your back, and keep your core strong and engaged. For more information on lifting safely and manual handling, refer to official websites such as www.hse.gov.uk and www.osha.gov.

Using aerosol sprays

Choose aerosols that are non-chlorinated and only use them in a well-ventilated space. Always wear a vapour mask, which is specifically designed for protection against fumes, especially when using upholstery contact adhesives.

Working safely

To avoid injury when stripping a chair, or any other piece of furniture, always work away from yourself. Never work towards yourself in case any staples or tacks fly out, or your hand slips while using a tack lifter.

Using blades

Likewise, always cut away from yourself when using a blade. Remember, the sharper the blade the safer it is, so never be tempted to use a blunt blade.

Using fire-retardant materials

Even when a piece of furniture is exempt due to its age, it is advisable to use a fire-retardant (FR) barrier cloth when reupholstering. If a fabric cannot be treated, I always use FR Woolguard or FR calico. FR Woolguard is naturally fire retardant due to its inherent properties, whereas FR calico is chemically treated. Familiarize yourself with the most up-to-date regulations issued by the Furniture Industry Research Association (FIRA) in the UK or the National Upholstery Association in the US, which can be found at www.fira.co.uk and www.nationalupholsteryassociation.org.

By following these safety guidelines, you will stay safe while working on your upholstery projects, allowing you to focus on creating beautiful and timeless furniture pieces.

Glossary of terms

Arris: In woodworking and carpentry, an arris is the sharp edge formed at the intersection of two surfaces. This term is commonly used in upholstery to describe the clean, defined edge where two pieces of fabric meet, typically along the edges of a cushion or seat. Properly creating and maintaining an arris is essential for achieving a professional, polished look in upholstered furniture.

Back stitching or Back tacking: A method of sewing using overlapping stitches to secure the beginning and end of a seam.

Back-tacking strip: A narrow cardboard or paper strip used to create consistently straight edges on chair backs or arms. The fabric is laid on the piece with the wrong side facing upwards, the tacking strip is laid along the edge of the fabric and stapled in place, then the fabric is folded back and pulled tight over the tacking strip, which ensures a crisp line, so the right side of the fabric is now visible. This is a modern upholstery technique.

Bias: The diagonal direction of the fabric, which provides stretch. *See* Cutting on the bias.

Blind stitching: A hand-sewing technique where stitches are made without penetrating the surface layer, making them invisible from the front.

Bottom cloth: Used to cover the underside of chairs, concealing the webbing and internal components and giving the underside a neater appearance.

Braid: Decorative trim used to embellish soft furnishings, often made from silk, gold, or silver threads.

Bridle tie: A type of stitch used in traditional upholstery to secure the stuffing in place. It is typically used for securing horsehair or other traditional stuffing materials within a stitched pad.

Chamfer: To cut an edge to create a sloping, angled edge rather than a blunt, square edge. This technique is often used to create a more refined and aesthetically pleasing finish on wooden components or a comfortable and rounded edge on foam seat cushions or padding.

Cutting on the bias: Cutting fabric at a 45-degree angle to the grain, used for making bias tape or achieving a more fluid drape. *See* Bias.

Double hem: A hem that is folded twice before stitching to hide the raw edge of the fabric. Using a double seam allowance, fold and press the edge in half then fold again, press and stitch close to the fold.

Dress a corner: Using a regulator or skewer to manipulate foam or padding so it sits fully into a corner, filling it out properly. A term also used to refer to making a fold or box pleat fold neat and crisp by using a regulator or skewer to manipulate the fabric into a straighter or neater line.

Face fabric: The primary fabric used for the visible parts of upholstered furniture.

French seam: A seam that is sewn twice – first on the wrong side with a narrow seam allowance, then the piece is turned right side out and sewn again from the right side to enclose the raw edges and create a raised edge.

Gathering: Drawing fabric together in folds or puckers by sewing a running stitch and then pulling the thread tight.

Hem: The edge of a piece of fabric that is turned under and sewn to prevent unravelling.

Leading edge: The vertical edge of a curtain that meets the other curtain when closed.

Marry marks: Marks that are strategically planned and drawn within the seam allowances at the edges of the fabric. When the pieces are sewn together, matching these marks ensures that the fabric is aligned correctly and not stretched or distorted. Marry marks are often made at the centre of a panel and border to be sewn together to make sure the pieces match up perfectly. As they are made within the seam allowance, these marks are not visible when the piece is complete. For example, when sewing a box cushion where you have a top, bottom and border, you will pre-mark the top and bottom panels with mirrored marry marks. As you sew the border to these panels, you transfer and align the marks to ensure the cushion is sewn together perfectly square. For curves you may have three marks – one at the beginning of the curve, one in the centre and one on the other side.

Oversize: Adding extra dimensions to materials before cutting out to allow for adjustments.

Passementerie: Passementerie refers to decorative trimming or edging used in textiles and interior design. Often made from luxurious materials like silk, gold and silver threads. Originating from the French term for 'trimmings', passementerie reached its peak of popularity during the baroque and rococo eras. Today, it is used to add elegance and intricate detail to curtains, furniture, cushions and clothing, enhancing the aesthetic appeal and sophistication of the design.

Patterning up: The process of creating patterns from paper or existing pieces of fabric or from measurements to cut new fabric pieces for upholstery. This ensures that the new fabric fits correctly and follows the contours of the furniture.

Permanent tack(s): Tacks used to permanently fix fabric or other materials in place. These tacks are not intended to be removed and are used in the final stages of upholstery to secure the fabric.

Pilot holes: Small, pre-drilled holes that serve as guides for driving screws or nails into a material.

Pinch pleat: A type of curtain heading with pleats sewn into the top for a tailored look.

Piping: A trim or edging formed by sewing a strip of fabric over a cord, used for decoration or to reinforce seams.

Profile: The profile of a piece of furniture refers to its outline or silhouette when viewed from the side or from a particular angle. It highlights the shape, contours and any distinctive features of the piece. For example, the profile of a headboard includes its height, the curve or straightness of its top edge, any decorative elements like cut-outs, scrolls or carvings, and how these features integrate with the overall design of the bed.

Regulator: A long, slender tool used in upholstery to adjust stuffing and padding, ensuring an even distribution and smooth surface.

Scrim hessian: Loose-weave hessian used primarily with traditional upholstery techniques.

Seam allowance: The area between the edge of the fabric and the stitching line.

Selvedge: The finished edge of a fabric that prevents it from fraying, often used as a guide for cutting and sewing.

Show wood: Any exposed wood frame or legs/arms of upholstered furniture that is intentionally left uncovered.

Slip stitch: A hand-sewn stitch used to join two panels of fabric together. The needle is taken from the first folded fabric edge to the second, run along the second folded fabric edge according to the desired stitch length, then brought back through the first edge. The finished stitch is invisible from the right side and is also known as a ladder stitch because the stitches resemble the rungs of a ladder when opened out.

Staple off: The technique of securing fabric, webbing or other materials in place using staples. This term is often used interchangeably with 'tack off' in modern upholstery techniques.

Stitched pad: A cushioned pad that is traditionally made with layers of hessian and padding materials, such as horsehair and/or coir fibre. Stitches are formed from twine using a double-pointed or curved needle to create a series of knots and stitched lines that form shapes and a firm edge. These pads are valued for their long-lasting quality and classic, handcrafted look.

Stockinette: Applied over the top of cushions to make them better suited to covers. Its elastic nature allows it to stretch smoothly over the foam cushion and its unique machine-stitched design creates friction on the inside while promoting smoothness on the outside.

Strip out: To remove all the existing upholstery from a piece of furniture to be re-covered. This includes removing old fabric, padding, tacks and staples.

Stuffing ties: Stuffing ties are fabric or thread ties used to secure the stuffing or filling inside a cushion, pillow or upholstered item. These ties help maintain the shape and even distribution of the stuffing, preventing it from shifting or bunching up over time.

Tacking: Temporary stitching to hold fabric in place before permanent sewing.

Tack lines or tack drag: Where you can see an indent on the fabric where it's fixed down.

Tack off: *See* Staple off.

Tack-off rail: Also known as a tack strip, is a structural component in upholstered furniture. It is a narrow strip of wood, metal or cardboard that runs along the edges of the frame, providing a secure surface to attach the upholstery fabric. The tack-off rail is used to anchor the fabric in place by tacking, stapling or securing it with nails, creating a neat and firm edge.

Temporary tack(s): Tacks used to temporarily hold fabric or other materials in place. These tacks are intended to be removed and are used during the initial stages of upholstering to position the fabric correctly before making permanent fixings.

Tensioning: The process of pulling fabric tight to ensure a smooth, wrinkle-free finish on upholstered furniture.

Webbing: Strong, woven fabric strips used to create a support structure for upholstered seats and backs. Webbing is stretched across the frame of the furniture and secured in place to provide a sturdy base for the padding and fabric.

Welting: *See* Piping.

UK vs. US UPHOLSTERY TERMS

When it comes to upholstery, the UK and the US often have different terms for the same materials, techniques or tools. Here are some notable distinctions:

1. Calico

UK: Calico refers to a plain-woven fabric made from unbleached and often partially processed cotton.
US: This fabric is known as muslin.

2. Hessian

UK: Hessian is a coarse cloth made from jute or hemp, frequently used in upholstery.
US: The equivalent term is burlap.

3. Wadding

UK: Wadding denotes a soft, thick material used for padding and insulation in upholstery.
US: This is referred to as batting, serving the same purpose.

4. Tacks

UK: Upholstery tacks are small, sharp nails used to secure fabric.
US: While the term tacks is used, upholstery nails or decorative nails may be more commonly heard.

5. Piping

UK: Piping is a decorative edge created by sewing fabric around a cord.
US: The same term is used for this decorative element.

ADDITIONAL NOTES

Measurements

The UK uses the metric system (centimetres, metres), whereas the US employs the imperial system (inches, feet).

Terminology

In both regions, specific jargon and brand names may also influence the terms used for certain items.

Understanding these differences can help prevent misunderstandings when discussing or purchasing upholstery materials and tools between the UK and US.

Suppliers

Seek out your local upholstery sundries supplier who can help you source the materials and sundries you require. Building a relationship with your local supplier or maker is always a good foot forward. Ask your local upholsterers or soft furnishers if they would be happy to sell you the materials and sundries you require. Failing, that there are some great online retailers you could purchase from.

BLENDWORTH

Blendworth, founded in 1921, is an independent design-led interiors company with roots in early 20th-century Regent Street, London. Now based in Hampshire, it blends heritage with innovation, creating unique collections inspired by its extensive archive and the surrounding countryside. Its design philosophy focuses on originality and distinctive colour, crafting enchanting seasonal collections.
https://blendworth.co.uk

BUTE

Bute was established in 1947 by the 5th Marquess of Bute to provide employment for service members returning from WWII. Located in the Firth of Clyde, Bute's mill draws inspiration from the diverse Scottish landscapes around it, ranging from heather-covered moorland to sweeping beaches. The company is committed to innovation in textiles and has strong community ties.
www.butefabricsltd.com

F.C. HANCOX FOAM

Established in 1960, this family-run business is renowned for its extensive experience in supplying foam and upholstery materials. Based on the south coast of the UK, it is one of the longest-standing suppliers in the industry, offering a wide range of high-quality products for all foam and upholstery needs.
www.fchancoxfoam.co.uk

FERMOIE

Fermoie is a natural extension of Farrow & Ball's expertise in colour and light. Founded by Tom Helme and Martin Ephson, it specializes in highly pigmented paints and fine textiles. Known for its unique design and printing techniques, Fermoie's fabrics feature layers of colour on textured weaves, creating an ephemeral and intriguing quality that interacts beautifully with light.
https://fermoie.com

GLOVER BROTHERS

Suppliers to the upholstery and soft furnishing trades, Glover Bros. was established in London in 1899 and is now based in the West Country.
https://www.gloverbros.co.uk

HOUSE OF SONNAZ

House of Sonnaz specializes in interior design, home and lifestyle products. Utilizing innovative materials and collaborating with artisans and craftspeople, we create rich, storied items and craft beautiful, bespoke interiors to create fabulous homes.
www.houseofsonnaz.com

IAN MANKIN

Founded in 1983, Ian Mankin is celebrated for its stylish interpretations of natural and organic fabrics. Known for its timeless colour palette, it offers a range of British-woven fabrics and furnishings, including signature stripes, checks and plains. The company is lauded for its dedication to quality and design excellence.
https://ianmankin.co.uk

LEWIS & WOOD

Lewis & Wood started as a London basement operation and is known for its high-quality, considered fabric and wallpaper designs. Founded by Stephen Lewis and Creative Director Magdalen Jebb, the company produces a select number of designs each year, emphasizing individuality and craftsmanship. Lewis & Wood's distinctive output is cherished by decorators for its bold yet sophisticated style.
www.lewisandwood.co.uk

LINWOOD

Linwood was founded in 1994 and remains a family-run business based in Hampshire. Named after a picturesque village in the New Forest where its directors grew up, it draws inspiration from diverse sources. Its creative studio showcases finds such as Japanese kimonos, Byzantine textiles and Buddhist temple paintings. Linwood's design process involves hand-sketching and painting with watercolours and gouache to perfect each design. The company collaborates with mills in Britain, Europe and beyond, creating fabrics and wallpapers renowned for their rich, saturated hues.
https://linwoodfabric.com

MARTINS UPHOLSTERY SUPPLIES LTD

This family-run business supplies and distributes upholstery and curtain products, from adhesives to zips and everything in between, throughout the UK.
https://martinsupholstery.co.uk

MOON

Founded in 1837, Moon is a British textile designer/manufacturer and one of the rare remaining vertical woollen mills within the UK. It manufactures and sells its cloth directly to its customers from a single site, which allows it to control each stage of the production process to exacting standards.
www.moons.co.uk

SAMUEL & SONS

Samuel & Sons is a coveted source for the finest quality trimmings, such as tassels, borders, braids, gimp and fringes. Interior designers and architects around the world rely on the quality and selection stocked. Innovation, variety and availability are key to Samuel & Sons' success. The introduction of exclusive collections featuring diverse materials such as silk, wool, grass and wood has led to its selection of over 10,000 trims being eagerly sought after by designers and architects for both residential and hospitality interiors.
https://samuelandsons.com

SCHUMACHER

Synonymous with style, taste and innovation since its founding in 1889, this family-owned company continuously introduces new collections, maintaining its heritage while staying at the cutting edge of design. With showrooms in New York, London, Paris and Milan, Schumacher is known for its exceptional fabrics, wallcoverings and trims, blending an appreciation for beauty with an unwavering commitment to quality.
https://schumacher.co.uk

STOWAWAY LONDON

Established in 2015 by Sophie Ruth and Sam Ridges and specializing in curated, design-led objects, Stowaway London focuses on style, authenticity, quality and form. It sources unique pieces from across the UK and Europe. In addition to its online shop, Stowaway London offers sourcing, hire and seat-weaving services.
https://stowawaylondon.com

WOODVILLE STRETTON (POOLE) LTD

Woodville Stretton has been operating as a body shop at the same location since the mid-1930s. It specializes in spraying a wide range of items, including cars, artwork and furniture. Known for its expertise in custom finishes, it is dedicated to providing exceptional service and undertakes both conventional and unique projects.
www.woodville-stretton.co.uk

SPOTNAILS LTD

Founded in 1954, Spotnails is a long-established independent distributor of premium tools and fastenings, including staple guns, compressors and more.
www.spotnail.co.uk

Resources

There are many courses available if you would like to extend your upholstery skills further.

THE BRITISH SCHOOL OF UPHOLSTERED FURNITURE

Jacksons Lodge
Bosmore Lane
Fawley Bottom
Buckinghamshire RG9 6JJ
www. britishschoolof upholsteredfurniture.co.uk
schoolofupholsteredfurniture @gmail.com
07803 096380

UPHOLSTERY SKILLS CENTRE

Asheton Farm
Tysea Hill
Stapleford Abbotts
Essex RM4 1JU
www.upholsteryskills.co.uk
admin@upholsteryskills.co.uk
07826 191054

LONDON DESIGN & ENGINEERING UNIVERSITY TECHNICAL COLLEGE

15 University Way
London E16 2RD
www.ldeutc.co.uk
admin@ldeutc.co.uk
020 3019 7333

THE ASSOCIATION OF MASTER UPHOLSTERERS & SOFT FURNISHERS (AMUSF)

5th Floor
167–169 Great Portland Street
London W1W 5PF
www.amusf.org
enquiries@amusf.org
07926 128899

List of fabrics

Page 1, Ashfield II, Ashfield by Linwood/ 031 Shamrock

Page 3, Left: Omega III, Omega by Linwood/140 Winter Moss; piped in Verde by Linwood/019 Banana
Right: Honey Tweed CF740 by Bute Fabrics/3417

Page 6, Manipur Midnight by Designers Guild/FDG2832/23

Page 7, From top to bottom:
1. Omega II, Omega by Linwood/ 091 Sky
2. Omega III, Omega by Linwood/ 182 Caribbean
3. Freya by Linwood/014 Mineral
4. Omega II, Omega by Linwood/ 077 Satsuma
5. Omega III, Omega by Linwood/ 129 Watermelon
6. Claribel La Moulade Coral/Pink by Nina Campbell/NCF4280-01
7. Omega II, Omega by Linwood/ 099 Adriatic
8. Omega III, Omega by Linwood/ 118 Pink Lace
9. Nantessa by Lewis & Wood/Rhone

Page 8, Ashfield II, Ashfield by Linwood/010 Marigold

Page 14, Coriandoli by Dedar/ 003 Coquelicot

Page 37, Ticking Stripe 1 by Ian Mankin/Sky

Page 39, Aspen by Larsen, L9187-02/Gull

Page 43, Tango Weaves, Bolero by Linwood/005 Parakeet

Page 50, Coriandoli by Dedar/ 002 Tournesol

Page 53, Box seat cushion / hand sewn closed with piping / no zip
Top: Fontana by Fermoie/FONT-002
Middle: Wave by Fermoie/WAVE-001
Bottom: Ticking by Fermoie/TICK-002

Page 57, Box seat cushion / with ties for a dining chair
Top: Ticking by Fermoie/TICK-002
Middle: Wave by Fermoie/WAVE-001
Bottom: Fontana by Fermoie/ FONT-002

Page 61, Shaped cushion / with ties for a dining chair
Goose Green N-022 by Fermoie/N-022

Page 63, Drop-in seat base for an occasional chair / modern technique
Tango Weaves, Bolero by Linwood/005 Parakeet

Page 69, Drop-in seat base for an occasional chair / traditional technique
Chair: Omega II, Omega by Linwood/093 Pacific
Lampshade: Verde by Linwood/ 019 Banana
Upholstered coffee table: Bibi, Kala by Linwood/010 Aloe

Pages 75 and 76, Rectangular fixed back dining chair
Omega II, Omega by Linwood/ 093 Pacific

Page 79, Fixed seat base for a dining chair / modern technique
Omega III, Omega by Linwood/ 182 Caribbean

Page 87, Carver chair
Chair: Tango Weaves, Bolero by Linwood/001 Yellow
Lampshade: Ashfield II, Ashfield by Linwood/010 Marigold

Page 95, Straight back dining chair / all covered recover
Chair: Sienna by Linwood/019 Blue Stone
Scatter cushion: Small Prints II, Helter Skelter by Linwood/012 Valley

Page 103 Straight back dining chair / chair slipcover
p.103 Chair: Verde by Linwood/ 019 Banana
p.105 Table runner: Verde by Linwood/019 Banana

Page 111, Room divider
p.111 Odyssey, Songbird by Linwood/001 Sand
p.112 Sienna by Linwood/024 Sapphire
p.115 Omega Prints, Japanese Garden by Linwood/001 Blossom

Page 117, Rectangular headboard for beginners
Headboard: Fable Weaves, Tanuki by Linwood/003 Candy
Scatter cushion: Trickledown, Natural by Schumacher/181552
Bed throw: Aspen by Larsen, L9187-02/Gull

Page 127, Headboard slipcover
Ashfield II, Ashfield by Linwood/ 010 Marigold

Page 135, Upholstered cube
Cube: Mauve Fabric by Blendworth/ LI1822
Piping: Omega by Linwood/025 Pink

Page 139, Upholstered coffee table
Upholstered coffee table: Bibi, Kala by Linwood/010 Aloe
Lampshade: Ashfield II, Ashfield by Linwood/010 Marigold
Shaped cushion: Goose Green N-022 by Fermoie/N-022

Page 145, Upholstered footstool
Dazzle Ship Velvet, Verdant by Schumacher/ 77244

Page 148, Coriandoli by Dedar/ 004 Malachite

Page 151, Scatter cushion / hand sewn
Back: Ticking Stripe 1 by Ian Mankin/Sky
Front: Benaki by Lewis & Wood/ Blue Umber

Page 155, Scatter cushion / machine sewn
Left: Benaki by Lewis & Wood/ Blue Umber
Right: No longer available

Page 157, Scatter cushion / machine sewn with zip
Left: Benaki by Lewis & Wood/ Blue Umber
Right: No longer available

Pages 158–9, Scatter cushions
From left to right:
1. Omega III, Omega by Linwood/ 140 Winter Moss; piped in Verde by Linwood/019 Banana
2. Small Prints II, Helter Skelter by Linwood/012 Valley
3. Verde by Linwood/019 Banana
4. (Bolster cushion) Trickledown, Natural by Schumacher/181552
5. Boucle, Travertine by Moon/ U1779/P09
6. Small Prints II, Helter Skelter by Linwood/013 Borneo; piped in Winston Cotton Braid Medium by Schumacher/Sky
7. Honey Tweed CF740 by Bute Fabrics/3417

Page 161, Scatter cushion / machine sewn with piping / no zip
Small Prints II, Helter Skelter by Linwood/012 Valley

Page 165, Box scatter cushion / no piping
Ticking Stripe 1 by Ian Mankin/Sky

Page 168, Box scatter cushion / with piping
Ticking Stripe 1 by Ian Mankin/Sky

Page 171, Box scatter cushion / with braid border
Left: Boucle, Travertine by Moon/ U1779/P09
Right: Small Prints II, Helter Skelter by Linwood/013 Borneo; piped in Winston Cotton Braid Medium by Schumacher/Sky

Page 173, Bolster cushion / with sewn-in ends
Bolster and scatter cushion: Trickledown, Natural by Schumacher/181552
Box seat cushion (left): Fontana by Fermoie/FONT-002
Box seat cushion (right): Ticking by Fermoie/TICK-002

Page 179, Bed throw
Bed throw: Aspen by Larsen, L9187-02/Gull
Headboard: Fable Weaves, Tanuki by Linwood/003 Candy

Page 180, Drum lampshade
Ashfield II, Ashfield by Linwood/ 010 Marigold

Pages 184–5, Drum lampshades
From top left to bottom right:
1. Voysey Park by Lewis & Wood/ Cluny
2. Deer Park by Lewis & Wood/Black
3. No longer available
4. No longer available
5. Verde by Linwood/019 Banana
6. (Hanging fabric) Ashfield II, Ashfield by Linwood/010 Marigold

Page 187, Table runner and placemats
Suffolk Check Large Fabric by Ian Mankin/ FA042-052 Pink

Page 190, Decorative braid for curtains
Braid: Samuel & Sons

Page 192, Dazzle Ship Velvet, Verdant by Schumacher/ 77244

Page 197, Small Prints II, Helter Skelter by Linwood/012 Valley

Page 207, Ticking Stripe 1 by Ian Mankin/Sky

Page 208, Bibi, Kala by Linwood/ 010 Aloe

OTHER ITEMS USED

Page 61, Shaped cushion / with ties for a dining chair
Chair: Stowaway London (www.stowawaylondon.com)

Page 63, Drop-in seat base for an occasional chair / modern technique
Frames painted by Woodville Stretton (Poole) Ltd (www.woodville-stretton.co.uk)

Page 87, Carver chair
Chair: 'Karen', House of Sonnaz (www.houseofsonnaz.com)

Page 135, Upholstered cube
Cube: 'Cube stool', House of Sonnaz (www.houseofsonnaz.com)

Page 139, Upholstered coffee table
Lamp shade base and chair: Stowaway London (www. stowawaylondon.com)

Page 151, Scatter cushion / hand sewn
Bench seat: Stowaway London (www.stowawaylondon.com)

Pages 158–9, Scatter cushions
Bench seat: Stowaway London (www.stowawaylondon.com)

Page 171, Box scatter cushion / with braid border
Bench seat: Stowaway London (www.stowawaylondon.com)

Index

Acknowledgements

It may be a cliché, but I never, ever thought that I would have the opportunity to write a book, or that I would even be *able* to... and yet here we are!

Without wanting this to become a thank you speech worthy of the Oscars, it would be remiss of me if I didn't thank the people who have supported me along the way: Octopus Publishing Group, for encouraging me to take a leap of faith; *The Repair Shop* team, for the unique opportunity it provided me; my clients, who trusted me and my team and continue to ask us back into their homes; and all my friends and colleagues who took time to advise and challenge me. You know who you are.

And the greatest thanks, of course, to my Mum, whose ability to make, sew, draw, design and breathe into life anything she sets her mind to continues to inspire me to this day.

Thank you.

INTRODUCTION
GOGOL THE PLAYWRIGHT
by
JANKO LAVRIN